LIMONOV

LIMONOV

Emmanuel Carrère

TRANSLATED FROM THE FRENCH BY

JOHN LAMBERT

FARRAR, STRAUS AND GIROUX

NEW YORK

Farrar, Straus and Giroux
18 West 18th Street, New York 10011

Copyright © 2011 by P.O.L éditeur
Translation copyright © 2014 by John Lambert
All rights reserved
Printed in the United States of America
Originally published in French in 2011 by P.O.L, France
English translation published in the United States by Farrar, Straus and Giroux
First American edition, 2014

Library of Congress Cataloging-in-Publication Data
Carrère, Emmanuel, 1957– author.
[Limonov. English]
Limonov / Emmanuel Carrère ; translated by John Lambert.
    pages   cm
ISBN 978-0-374-19201-3 (hardback) — ISBN 978-0-374-70921-1 (ebook)
    1. Limonov, Éduard—Fiction.   I. Lambert, John, 1960– translator.   II. Title.

PQ2663.A7678 L5613 2014
843'.914—dc23

                                                    2014004040

Designed by Abby Kagan

Farrar, Straus and Giroux books may be purchased for educational, business, or
promotional use. For information on bulk purchases, please contact the Macmillan
Corporate and Premium Sales Department at 1-800-221-7945, extension 5442,
or write to specialmarkets@macmillan.com.

www.fsgbooks.com
www.twitter.com/fsgbooks • www.facebook.com/fsgbooks

1   3   5   7   9   10   8   6   4   2

Whoever wants the Soviet Union back has no brain.
Whoever doesn't miss it has no heart.

—VLADIMIR PUTIN

CONTENTS

ಐಂ

Prologue: Moscow, October 2006, September 2007   1

  I. Ukraine, 1943–1967   21

  II. Moscow, 1967–1974   67

  III. New York, 1975–1980   91

  IV. Paris, 1980–1989   143

  V. Moscow, Kharkov, December 1989   177

  VI. Vukovar, Sarajevo, 1991–1992   199

  VII. Moscow, Paris, Republic of Serbian Krajina, 1990–1993   223

  VIII. Moscow, Altai, 1994–2001   259

  IX. Lefortovo, Saratov, Engels, 2001–2003   299

Epilogue: Moscow, December 2009   329

PROLOGUE

Moscow, October 2006,
September 2007

ॐ

I

UNTIL ANNA POLITKOVSKAYA was shot dead in her elevator on October 7, 2006, only those who had been closely watching the Chechen wars knew the name of this courageous journalist and declared opponent of Vladimir Putin's politics. At that moment, her sad, determined face became an icon of freedom of expression in the West. At the time I was traveling to Russia often, and had just filmed a documentary in a small Russian city, which is why as soon as the news broke a magazine suggested I get on the first plane to Moscow. My assignment wasn't to investigate Politkovskaya's murder, but rather to talk with the people who'd known and loved her. That's how I came to spend a week in the offices of *Novaya gazeta*, the newspaper where she'd been a star reporter, as well as in the offices of associations for the defense of human rights and committees made up of mothers of soldiers who'd been killed or wounded in Chechnya. These offices were tiny, poorly lit, and equipped with old computers. The activists who welcomed me were often old as well, and there were pathetically few of them. Everyone knew everyone in this very small circle, and it didn't take me long to get to know them all too. This tiny group constituted practically the entire democratic opposition in Russia.

My several Russian friends aside, I know a small circle in Moscow made up of French expatriates, journalists, and businessmen, and when I told them in the evening of my visits during the day they smiled, condescension mixing with sympathy: of course these virtuous democrats and civil rights activists were respectable people, they said, but the truth is that no one here gives a damn. They were fighting a war that was lost before it even began in a country where people care little about formal liberties, as long as everyone has the right to get rich.

Moreover, nothing amused or annoyed my expatriate friends as much, depending on their character, as the view widely held in France that Politkovskaya's murder had been ordered by the FSB—the political police known as the KGB in the days of the Soviet Union—and more or less by Putin himself.

"Now hold on just a second," said Pavel, a Franco-Russian academic turned businessman. "You're being ridiculous. You know what I read—in the *Nouvel Observateur*, I think? That it's pretty strange that, as if by chance, Politkovskaya was killed on Putin's birthday. *As if by chance!* Can you imagine how stupid you would have to be to write that 'as if by chance,' in black and white? Just imagine the scene: crisis meeting at the FSB. The boss says: 'Okay, guys, we're really going to have to rack our brains. It's going to be Vladimir Vladimirovich's birthday soon and we've got to come up with a gift that'll really make him happy. Any ideas?' Everyone hems and haws, then someone pipes up: 'What if we bring him the head of Anna Politkovskaya, that pain in the ass who's always criticizing him?' A murmur of approval runs through the room. 'Now there's an idea! Everybody get to work, you've got carte blanche.' I'm sorry," Pavel said, "but I don't buy it. Maybe in a Russian remake of *Monsieur Gangster*. But in real life? No. And you know what? The truth, which really shocked the bleeding hearts in the West, is what Putin said: that Anna Politkovskaya's assassination and all the stink it caused hurt the Kremlin far more than the articles she published while she was alive in a newspaper no one read."

I listened to Pavel and his friends, in the gorgeous apartments people like that rent for a fortune in the heart of Moscow, defending the powers that be by saying that first of all, things could be a thousand times worse, and second, the Russians make do with the situation as it is—why should we go around lecturing them? But I also listened to sad, worn-out women who told me day in, day out of nighttime kidnappers who whisked their victims away in cars with no plates, soldiers tortured not by the enemy but by their own superiors, and above all, justice denied. That's what came up again and again. If the police and army are corrupt, well, that's the way things are. If human life is cheap, that's the Russian tradition. But the arrogance and brutality of the authorities when simple citizens dared ask them for an explanation, the authorities' knowledge of their own impunity—that was what neither the mothers of the dead soldiers, nor those of the children massacred at the school in Beslan in the Caucasus, nor those of the victims of the Dubrovka Theater, could stand.

You remember: it was in October 2002. Every television in the world showed nothing else for three days. Chechen terrorists had taken the theater's entire audience hostage during the performance of a musical comedy called *Nord-Ost*. Foreclosing any possibility of negotiation, Russian special forces resolved the situation by gassing the hostages along with their hostage takers—demonstrating an inflexibility later celebrated by President Putin. The number of civilian casualties is still in question. Official estimates put the total at around 150, and their next of kin are considered accomplices when they ask if things might have been done somewhat differently and whether they—and their mourning—might be treated with a little more respect. Each year since the hostage-taking, these families have gathered for a commemoration ceremony which the police don't dare ban outright but nevertheless surveil like a seditious gathering—which in fact it's become.

I went. There were two or three hundred people, I'd say, on the square in front of the theater, and around them just as many OMON riot police, equipped with helmets, shields, and heavy clubs. It started to rain. Umbrellas opened above the candles; the candles, with their paper rings meant to shield fingers from the burning wax, brought to mind the Orthodox services I was taken to at Easter when I was little. Signs with the photos and names of the dead now replaced the icons. The people holding these candles and signs were orphans, widows and widowers, parents who'd lost a child—something for which, as in French, there is no word in Russian. No representative of the state had come, as the families' representative emphasized with cold anger in the few words he spoke—the only ones in the whole ceremony. No speeches, no slogans, no chanting. The people were content to stand there in silence with their candles in their hands, or to talk quietly in small groups among the ranks of OMON police, who'd sealed off the perimeter. Looking around, I recognized several faces. In addition to the mourning families, every last member of the small world of opposition figures I'd met over the last week was there, and I exchanged a few nods with them, gestures marked by a fitting sense of grief.

Right at the top of the steps, in front of the closed doors of the theater, a silhouette struck me as vaguely familiar, someone I couldn't quite identify. It was a man dressed in a black coat, holding a candle like the others, surrounded by several people with whom he spoke in a low voice. In the center of a circle, dominating the crowd, standing back and yet still attracting attention, he exuded importance; strangely, I was reminded of a gang leader attending the funeral of one of his own, attended by a close guard. I could just see parts of his profile, a little beard jutting from the raised collar of his coat. A woman beside me who'd seen him as well said to her neighbor: "Eduard's here, that's good." Despite the distance, he turned his head as if he'd heard. The flame from the candle sketched the features of his face.

I recognized Limonov.

2

HOW LONG HAD it been since I'd thought of him? I'd gotten to know him at the beginning of the eighties when he moved to Paris, crowned by the success of his scandalous novel *It's Me, Eddie*. In it he told the story of the superb and squalid life he'd led in New York after emigrating from the Soviet Union. Odd jobs, living from day to day in a sordid hotel or on the street, flings with both men and women, drunken benders, robberies and brawls: in its violence and rage, it was faintly reminiscent of the life of the urban drifter played by Robert De Niro in *Taxi Driver*; in its vigor, of the novels of Henry Miller— whose tough skin and cannibal's composure Limonov shared. The book wasn't half bad, and those who met its author weren't disappointed. In those days we were used to Soviet dissidents being bearded, grave, and poorly dressed, living in small apartments, filled with books and icons, where they would spend all night talking about how Orthodoxy would save the world. And here was this sexy, sly, funny guy, a cross between a sailor on leave and a rock star. We were in the midst of the punk era; his proclaimed hero was Johnny Rotten, the lead singer of the Sex Pistols; he didn't think twice about calling Solzhenitsyn an old fart. This new-wave dissidence was refreshing, and when he arrived, Limonov was the darling of the small literary world in Paris—where I was making my own timid debut. He wasn't a novelist—all he could write about was his life—but his life was captivating, and he told its story well in a simple, unadorned style and with all the energy of a Russian Jack London. After his chronicles of emigration he published memoirs about his childhood in the suburbs of Kharkov in Ukraine, his time as a juvenile delinquent, and his life as an avant-garde poet in Moscow under Brezhnev. He talked of this era and of the Soviet Union with a wry nostalgia, as if it had been a paradise for resourceful hooligans, and every so often, at the end of dinner, when everyone was drunk but him—he can really hold his liquor—he sang Stalin's praises, which we chalked up to his taste for provocation. You'd see him at a club like Le Palace wearing a Red Army officer's jacket. He wrote in *L'Idiot international*, the newspaper put out by Jean-Edern Hallier, which was rather dubious ideologically but brought together brilliant, anticonformist minds. He liked to argue and was incredibly successful with women. His unconventional behavior and adventurous past impressed us bourgeois youths. Limonov was our barbarian, our thug: we adored him.

Things began taking a turn for the bizarre with the collapse of communism. Everyone was delighted but he, and he didn't seem to be kidding around anymore when he said Gorbachev should face a firing squad. He started disappearing to the Balkans for long periods of time, where we discovered to our horror that he was fighting on the Serbian side—which was pretty much the same thing, in our eyes, as siding with the Nazis or with the genocidal Hutus. In a BBC documentary we saw him bombard besieged Sarajevo under the benevolent eye of Radovan Karadžić, the leader of the Bosnian Serbs and a known war criminal. After these exploits he returned to Russia, where he created a political group with a compelling name: the National Bolshevik Party. News reports sometimes showed young people with shaved heads, dressed in black, marching in the streets of Moscow giving a half-Nazi (raised arm), half-Communist (balled fist) salute while braying slogans like "Stalin! Beria! Gulag!" (implying: We want them back!). The flags they waved imitated that of the Third Reich, with the hammer and sickle in place of the swastika. And the fanatic in the baseball cap, gesticulating at the head of these columns with a megaphone in his fist, was the amusing, seductive boy who, several years earlier, we'd all been proud to call our friend. It was about as strange as discovering that an old school buddy had gone into organized crime or blown himself up in a terrorist attack. You think back to your time with him, sift through the memories, and try to imagine the chain of circumstances and blend of personal motivations that have led his life so completely away from your own. In 2001 we learned that Limonov had been arrested, tried, and imprisoned for rather obscure reasons—something to do with arms trafficking and an attempted coup in Kazakhstan. Needless to say, in Paris we weren't exactly elbowing one another out of the way to sign the petition calling for his release.

I had no idea he was out of prison and, perhaps more important, I was astonished to find him here. He looked less like a rocker than before, more intellectual, but he still had the same imperious, energetic aura you could feel even a hundred yards away. I considered joining a line of people who, clearly touched by his presence, were coming to say a respectful hello. But then I caught his glance for an instant and, since he didn't seem to recognize me and since I didn't know exactly what to say to him, I let the idea drop.

Troubled by this encounter, I went back to the hotel where a new surprise awaited me. While leafing through a collection of articles by Anna Politkovskaya, I discovered that two years earlier she'd covered the trial of forty National Bolshevik Party militants accused of having occupied and vandalized the offices of the presidential administration, shouting "Putin must go!" They'd been given lengthy prison sentences and Politkovskaya loudly took up their defense, calling them young, courageous people of integrity, practically the only ones who could inspire hope in the moral future of their country.

I could hardly believe it. To me it seemed like an open-and-shut case, no chance for appeal: Limonov was a hideous fascist leading a militia of skinheads. But here was a woman who since her death has been unanimously considered a saint, describing him and his followers as heroes in Russia's fight for democracy. Same tune, on the Internet, from Yelena Bonner. Yelena Bonner! The widow of Andrei Sakharov, the learned scientist, dissident, and moral authority, winner of the Nobel Peace Prize. She too was all in favor of the *nazbols*, as I discovered the Russians call members of the National Bolshevik Party. Maybe they should think about changing their party's name, Bonner said, which for some carries unpleasant connotations. Otherwise, marvelous people.

Several months later I learned that a political coalition called Drugaya Rossiya, The Other Russia, was forming under the leadership of Gary Kasparov, Mikhail Kasyanov, and Eduard Limonov—that is to say one of the greatest chess players of all time, a former prime minister under Putin, and an author whom by our criteria you shouldn't even be seen with: quite the troika. Something had obviously changed—perhaps not Limonov himself but the position he occupied in his country. Which is why when Patrick de Saint-Exupéry, whom I'd known as Moscow correspondent for *Le Figaro*, told me he was preparing to launch a news magazine and asked if I had a subject for the first issue, I responded without a second's hesitation: Limonov. Patrick looked at me with wide eyes. "Limonov's a petty thug."

"I'm not sure," I said. "It's worth checking out."

"All right then," Patrick said, not needing any further explanation, "go check it out."

It took me a while to track him down and get his cell phone number from Sasha Ivanov, a Moscow editor. And then once I'd got the num-

ber it took a while to dial it. I hesitated about what tone to adopt—not
only toward him but also for myself. Was I an old friend or a guarded
journalist? Should I speak Russian or French? Use formal or informal
language? I remember these hesitations but not, curiously, what I said
when he picked up—on my very first call and before the second ring.
I must have said my name. Without a moment's delay, he answered,
"Ah, Emmanuel. How're you doing?" Somewhat taken aback, I stam-
mered that I was doing fine: we didn't know each other that well and
hadn't seen each other for fifteen years; I expected to have to remind
him who I was. He went on without pausing, "You were at the
Dubrovka ceremony last year, weren't you?"

I was speechless. Separated from him by a hundred yards, I'd given
him a long look, but we'd only exchanged glances for a second and nothing in his face—not a slight hesitation, not a raise of his eyebrows—
had indicated that he'd recognized me. Later, once I'd gotten over my
astonishment, it struck me that our mutual friend, the editor Sasha
Ivanov, could have told him I was planning to call, but I'd said nothing to Sasha about having been at the Dubrovka Theater. It was a total
mystery. Later I understood that it wasn't a mystery; Limonov simply
has a prodigious memory and a no less prodigious capacity for self-
control. I said I wanted to do a long article on him and he seemed to
have no problem with my hanging around for a couple of weeks—
"Unless," he added, "they put me back in prison."

3

TWO YOUNG, BURLY guys with shaved heads, dressed in black jeans,
black jackets, and combat boots, come pick me up to bring me to their
leader. I half expect them to blindfold me, but no, we cross Moscow
in a black Volga with tinted windows. When we arrive, my guardian
angels just take a quick look around the courtyard, then the stairway,
then finally the landing that gives onto a dark little apartment, furnished like a squat, where two more skinheads are killing time smok-

ing cigarettes. One tells me that Eduard divides his time among three or four Moscow apartments, moving from one to the next as quickly as possible, keeping no fixed hours and never venturing anywhere without bodyguards—that is, party militants.

While waiting, I think to myself that my story is getting off to a good start: hideouts, clandestine movements, what could be more romantic? Only I have a hard time deciding between two versions of this romanticism—is it the romance of the terrorist cell or the resistance network? Carlos the Jackal or Jean Moulin?—though it's true that as long as the official version hasn't yet been written, the two are pretty similar. I also wonder what Limonov is expecting from my visit. Is he wary, put off by the few portraits Western journalists have done of him, or is he counting on me to rehabilitate him? I myself have no idea what to expect. It's rare, when you're preparing to meet and write about someone, to have so little clue as to where you stand.

I'm finally shown into a spartan office with drawn curtains; he's standing up in black jeans and a black sweater. A handshake, no smile. On his guard. In Paris we'd said *tu* to each other, but he used the formal *vous* on the phone and that's what we use now. Despite being out of practice, his French is better than my Russian, so he opts for my native tongue. In the old days he did push-ups and lifted weights for an hour a day, and he must have kept it up because at sixty-five he's still slim: flat stomach, adolescent's silhouette, the smooth, olive skin of a Mongol, only now he sports a gray mustache and goatee that make him look a little like the aged d'Artagnan in *Twenty Years After* and a lot like a Bolshevik commissar, in particular Trotsky—only Trotsky didn't go in for bodybuilding, at least as far as I know.

On the plane I reread one of his best books, *Diary of a Loser*, whose back cover sets the tone: "If Charles Manson or Lee Harvey Oswald had kept a journal, this is what it would have been like." I copied several passages into my notebook. This one, for example: "I dream of a violent insurrection. I'll never be Nabokov. I'll never run across meadows collecting butterflies on old, hairy, Anglophone legs. Give me a million and I'll spend it on weapons and stage an uprising in any country." This was the scenario he painted for himself at thirty as a penniless immigrant on the streets of New York, and thirty years later there you go, the film becomes reality. He's playing the role of his dreams: the professional revolutionary, the urban guerrilla, Lenin in his armored car.

I tell him that and he lets out a cold, dry little laugh, blowing the air through his nostrils. "It's true," he admits. "My life's gone pretty much according to plan." But he sets me straight: the time is no longer right for an armed uprising. He no longer dreams of a violent insurrection, but of something like the recent Orange Revolution in Ukraine. A pacifist, democratic revolution, which is what the Kremlin fears above all else and will stop at nothing to crush, he says. That's why he lives the life of a hunted man. Several years ago he was beaten with baseball bats, and only recently he narrowly escaped an assassination attempt. His name is at the top of the list of "enemies of Russia"—that is, of people to kill, put out by those in power to incite public hatred, complete with addresses and telephone numbers. Politkovskaya, taken down with an Izh pistol, was also on this list, as was the ex–FSB officer Litvinenko, poisoned with polonium after having denounced criminality among his former colleagues, as was the billionaire Khodorkovsky, who spent time in Siberia for having meddled in politics. And the next one is him, Limonov.

The next day he holds a press conference with Kasparov. In the room I recognize most of the militants I met researching my story on Politkovskaya, but there are also quite a few journalists, above all foreign. Some seem very excited—the group of Swedes, for example, who aren't just doing a short feature but a whole documentary, three months of shooting, on what they hope will be the irresistible rise of the Drugaya Rossiya movement. They give every indication of believing it lock, stock, and barrel, and are banking on selling their film for a fortune all over the world once Kasparov and Limonov have come to power.

With his powerful build, his warm smile, and a peculiarly Jewish-Armenian charm, the former chess champion is the more imposing of the two when they take the podium; Limonov, with his goatee and glasses, seems to be playing the cold-blooded strategist in the shadow of the natural leader. And it's Kasparov who goes on the offensive, explaining why the presidential elections that must take place the following year—2008—present a historic opportunity. Putin is coming to the end of his second term, the constitution prevents him from running for a third, and he's sealed himself off so securely that no officially endorsed candidate has yet emerged to fill the void. For the first time in Russian history, a democratic opposition has its chance. The media is gagged and so people don't know how fed up the Russians are with the oligarchs, the corruption, the limitless power of the FSB, but he, Kasparov, knows. He is eloquent, with a voice like a cello, and I start to think that maybe the Swedes are right. I want to believe I'm witnessing something extraordinary, like the beginning of Solidarność, when the guy beside me, a British journalist, snickers and says to me with a whiff of gin on his breath: "Bullshit. The Russians love Putin and they can't understand why a screwed-up constitution prevents them from electing such a good president for the third time in a row. But don't forget: what the constitution forbids is three *consecutive* terms. Not skipping a turn while a straw man keeps the seat warm, then coming back. You'll see."

This aside brings me back down to earth. In one fell swoop the truth lands back on the realists' side, with people like my perceptive friend Pavel, who know what's what and don't let themselves be taken in, and who say this whole business about a democratic opposition in Russia is like wanting to castle when you're playing checkers: simply not part of the rules, something that has never worked and never will. Kasparov, whom just a moment ago I was ready to consider a Russian Wałęsa, now seems entirely emptied of prestige. All his talk now strikes me as noisy, provincial rambling, and my neighbor and I develop the conspiratorial relationship of two slackers swapping dirty pictures at the back of the class. I show him a book of Limonov's I've just bought. Translated only in Serbia, it's called *Anatomy of a Hero* and has a section with over-the-top photos of the hero in question, Limonov himself, marching in camouflage fatigues alongside the

Serbian paramilitary leader Arkan, the French right-wing politician Jean-Marie Le Pen, the Russian populist Zhirinovsky, the mercenary Bob Denard, and a couple of other humanists. "Fucking fascist . . . ," the British journalist comments.

We look up at Limonov. Standing beside and somewhat behind Kasparov, he patiently listens to him complain about the persecutions carried out by the authorities; he doesn't seem to be waiting, as all politicians usually are, for the speaker to stop talking so they can take the floor themselves. He just sits there attentively, as straight and calm as a Zen monk in meditation. Kasparov's warm voice has receded to a peripheral droning: it's Limonov's inscrutable face I'm examining now. And the more I look at it, the more I realize I don't have the slightest idea what he thinks. Does he really believe in this Orange Revolution? Does it amuse him, the outlaw, the mad dog, to play the virtuous democrat among these longtime dissidents and human rights activists that he's been calling naive his whole life? Is he secretly enjoying being the wolf in sheep's clothing?

I find another passage from *Diary of a Loser* in my notebook: "I've sided with evil—with the small newspapers, with the Xeroxed leaflets, with the parties that stand no chance. I love political meetings with just a handful of people and the cacophony of inept musicians. And I hate symphony orchestras. If I ever came to power I'd slit the throats of all the violinists and cellists." I'd have liked to translate it for the British journalist, but it isn't necessary, he must be thinking the same thing at the same time because he leans over, this time not laughing at all, and says, "His friends had better watch out. If he does manage to take power the first thing he'll do is have them all shot."

This has no statistical value, but for what it's worth: while researching this piece I discussed Limonov with more than thirty people, strangers whose cars I've been in—because anyone and everyone moonlights as a taxi driver for a few extra rubles in Moscow—as well as friends you could safely call Russian yuppies: artists, journalists, and editors, who buy their furniture at IKEA and read the Russian edition of *Elle*. In other words, not fanatics. And yet not one said a word against him. No one so much as mentioned the word *fascism*. When I said, "Still, the flags, the slogans . . . ," they shrugged their shoulders; they treated me like something of a prude. It was as if I'd come to interview Michel Houellebecq, Lou Reed, and Daniel Cohn-Bendit all at the same time: two weeks with Limonov, what luck! Which doesn't mean for a second that these reasonable people would be ready to vote for him—no more than the French would vote for Houellebecq, I imagine, were they given the chance. But they like his fiery personality, they admire his talent and audacity. The newspapers know it too, and feature him incessantly. In short, he's a star.

I accompany him to the gala thrown by the radio station Echo of Moscow, one of the social highlights of the season. He's got his musclemen in tow, but he also brings his new wife, Ekaterina Volkova, a young actress who's become famous for her role in a soap opera. They seem to know everyone who's anyone in politics and the media, and of all the people who flock to this soiree no one is more photographed or celebrated than they. I'm hoping that Limonov will invite me to join them for dinner afterward, but he does nothing of the kind. He also doesn't invite me to the apartment where Ekaterina lives with their baby—I learn tonight they have an eight-month-old son. Too bad: I'd have liked to see the place where the warrior relaxes between hideouts. I'd have liked to surprise him in the unexpected role of father. Above all I'd have liked to get to know Ekaterina better; she's ravishing and exudes the kind of charm I thought was the sole prerogative of American actresses: laughing a lot, marveling at everything you say, leaving you abruptly when someone more important walks by. Nevertheless I get to talk with her for five minutes at the buffet, enough time for her to tell me with a naive freshness that before meeting Eduard she'd never been interested in politics but that now she's understood: Russia is a totalitarian state, you've got to fight for freedom and participate in the protest marches, which she seems to take as seriously as her yoga classes. The next day I read an interview with her in a women's magazine where she reveals beauty secrets and tenderly embraces her famous husband, the opposition leader. What has me speechless is that, when asked about politics, she repeats what she said to me exactly, attacking Putin with as little precaution—and as little consequence—as, let's say, the Dixie Chicks had or felt when they attacked George W. Bush at exactly the same time. I try to imagine what would have happened under Stalin, or even under Brezhnev, on the fictitious assumption that such words could have been printed, and I think that there are worse things than Putin-style totalitarianism.

4

I HAVE A hard time reconciling these images: the writer-hoodlum I knew in the past, the hunted guerrilla, the responsible politician, the star the magazines' "People" sections write gushy articles about. I tell myself that to get a better idea I have to meet some party militants, some grassroots *nazbols*. The skinheads that drive me to their leader every day in a black Volga and who frightened me a bit at first are nice kids, but they don't talk much—at least I can't get them to. At the end of the press conference with Kasparov I start talking to a pretty girl, and ask if she's a journalist. She says yes, that is, she works for the website of the National Bolshevik Party. Cute as a button, sensible, well dressed: she's a *nazbol*.

Through this charming girl I meet a charming guy, the (clandestine) head of the Moscow section. With his long hair tied back in a low ponytail, his open and friendly face, he doesn't look like a fascist at all, more like a militant antiglobalist. In his little apartment in the suburbs he's got albums by Manu Chao and paintings in the style of Jean-Michel Basquiat on the walls, done by his wife.

"So your wife shares your political struggle?" I ask.

"Oh, yes. In fact she's in prison. She was one of the forty in the big 2005 trial, the one Politkovskaya covered."

He says it with a big smile, proud as can be—and as for him, if he's not in prison too, it's not his fault, it's just that *"Mne ne povezlo"*:

that's not how things worked out. Another time, maybe, it's not too late.

The two of us go to Taganskaya District Court, where, as it happens, a couple of *nazbols* are standing trial that day. A tiny courtroom, the accused handcuffed in a cage, their friends on the three benches reserved for the public, all of them from the party. There are seven in the dock: six guys with a range of looks, from the bearded Muslim student to the working-class hero in a tracksuit, as well as a somewhat older woman with tousled black hair and a pale complexion, rather beautiful in the style of a leftist history teacher who rolls her own cigarettes. They're accused of hooliganism, that is, of tussling with pro-Putin youths. Minor wounds inflicted here and there. When questioned they say it was the others who started it, and they aren't being charged with anything; the trial is purely political and if they have to pay for their convictions, so be it, they'll pay. The defense points out that the accused aren't hooligans but serious students with good grades and that they've already done a year of preventive custody, which should be good enough on its own. The judge isn't convinced. Verdict for the lot: two years. The police lead them away and they laugh as they go, clenching their fists and saying *"Da, smert'!"*: Hail death! Their friends look on with envy: these are heroes.

There are thousands, perhaps tens of thousands, like them. Enraged at the cynicism that has become a religion in Russia, they worship Limonov. This man who could be their father—or even, for the youngest, their grandfather—has led the adventurer's life everyone dreams of at twenty. He's a living legend. And at the heart of this legend is the cool heroism he demonstrated during his imprisonment, which they all want to emulate. He was at Lefortovo—a KGB fortress that is the Alcatraz of Russian mythology—in the harshest labor camp, and he never complained, never buckled. He managed not only to write seven or eight books but also to help his cellmates, who ended up regarding him as both a kingpin and a kind of saint. The day he was released, inmates and guards wrangled over who would carry his suitcase.

———

When I asked Limonov himself how it was in prison, at first he just said, "*Normalno,*" which means, roughly, Okay, no problems, nothing special. It was only later that he told me the following anecdote.

From Lefortovo he was transferred to the labor camp at Engels, on the Volga. The fruit of ambitious architectural planning, it's a brand-new model establishment that is willingly shown off to foreign visitors so they'll draw flattering conclusions about the progress of penitentiary conditions in Russia. In fact the inmates at Engels call it "Eurogulag," and Limonov confirms that the stylish architecture doesn't make it any more livable than the classic camps surrounded by barbed wire—rather less so. In any case, the sinks in this camp, made of a polished steel plate above a cast iron pipe with sober, pure lines, are exactly the same as in a hotel conceived by the designer Philippe Starck, where Limonov's American publisher put him up the last time he visited New York at the end of the eighties.

That started him thinking. None of his fellow inmates was in a position to make the same comparison. Nor were any of the elegant guests at the chic New York hotel. He wondered if many people in the world apart from him, Eduard Limonov, had lived such different lives: as a prisoner in a forced-labor camp on the Volga, and as a trendy writer surrounded by Philippe Starck interiors. No, he concluded, probably not. That was a source of pride for him, a pride that I can understand. The gap between those two lives he's lived is what made me want to write this book.

I live in a calm country on the decline, where social mobility is limited. Born into a bourgeois family in Paris's Sixteenth Arrondissement, I became a bourgeois bohemian in the Tenth. The son of a senior executive and an eminent historian, I write books and screenplays and my wife is a journalist. My parents have a vacation home on the Île de Ré—more or less the French equivalent of Martha's Vineyard—and I'd like to buy one on the Greek island of Patmos. While I don't think this is a bad thing or that it precludes rich human experiences, nevertheless from both a geographical and a sociocultural point of view, you can't say life has taken me very far from my roots—and that's true for most of my friends as well.

Limonov, on the other hand, has been a young punk in Ukraine, the idol of the Soviet underground, a bum, and then a multimillionaire's butler in Manhattan, a fashionable writer in Paris, a lost soldier in the Balkans, and now, in the fantastic shambles of postcommunism, the elderly but charismatic leader of a party of young desperadoes. He sees himself as a hero; you might call him a scumbag: I suspend my judgment on the matter. But after I was done laughing at his anecdote about the sinks in Engels, I thought to myself, His romantic, dangerous life says something. Not just about him, Limonov, not just about Russia, but about everything that's happened since the end of the Second World War.

Something, yes, but what? I'm writing this book to find out.

I

Ukraine,
1943–1967

I

THE STORY BEGINS in the spring of 1942, in a city on the banks of the Volga called Rastyapino before the Revolution and Dzerzhinsk since 1929. This new name pays tribute to Felix Dzerzhinsky, one of the earliest Bolsheviks and founder of the secret police agency that has throughout its history been known as the Cheka, GPU, NKVD, KGB, and is today called the FSB. In this book we will meet it in the form of the last three of these menacing acronyms, but Russians, in addition to the designations of each era, call it, even more ominously, *organy*: the organs. The war is raging; heavy industry has been dismantled and relocated to the hinterland, out of the theater of operations. In this way, a weapons factory in Dzerzhinsk ends up employing the city's entire population, as well as NKVD troops to watch over them. It's a time of heroism and brutality: a worker who arrives five minutes late is court-martialed, and it's the Chekists, as the secret police are called, who arrest, sentence, and execute him, if need be, with a bullet to the back of the head. One night, as some Messerschmitts on a reconnaissance flight from the Lower Volga drop some bombs on the city, a soldier standing guard over the factory uses his flashlight to light the way for a young worker, who left her post late and is hurrying to a shelter. She stumbles and catches hold of his arm. He notices a tattoo on her wrist. In the darkness lit up by the glow of fires their faces come closer. Their lips touch.

The soldier, Venyamin Savenko, is twenty-three and comes from a family of Ukrainian peasants. A skilled electrician, he was recruited by the NKVD, which plucks the best workers from every industry. So, rather than being sent to the front like most of the youths his age, he was assigned to guard a weapons factory in the countryside. He's far from home, which is more the rule than the exception in the Soviet Union: what with deportations, exiles, mass population transfers, people continually being shuffled around, the chances of living and dying where you were born are as good as nil.

Raya Zybin, for her part, comes from Gorky, formerly Nizhny Novgorod, where her father directed a restaurant. In the Soviet Union you don't own or manage a restaurant, you direct one. It's not something you can start up or buy into, but a post to which you're assigned, and not a bad one at that. Unfortunately Raya's father was dismissed for embezzlement and sent to a disciplinary battalion in the battle for Leningrad, where he died not long ago. It's a stain on the family, and in these days, in this country, a stain on the family can ruin your life. For us it's one of the most basic tenets of justice that children don't pay for the crimes of their fathers, but in the Soviet Union it's not even a formal principle, something you can appeal to in theory. The children of Trotskyists, or of kulaks, as wealthy farmers are called, or of those privileged under the old regime, are doomed to live as outcasts, barred from becoming Young Pioneers, attending university, and joining the Red Army or the Party; they have one chance to escape this fate, and that's by renouncing their parents and being as enthusiastic about the Party as possible. And since being enthusiastic means denouncing those around you, the organs have no better helpers than those with tarnished biographies—as is brought home by so many terrible stories in Orlando Figes's outstanding book *The Whisperers*, on private life under Stalin. In the case of Raya's father it may be that his death on the battlefield helped things somewhat; the fact is that like the Savenkos, the Zybins made it through the Great Terror of the thirties without mishap. No doubt they were simply too insignificant. This luck doesn't stop young Raya from being ashamed of her dishonest father, just as she's ashamed of the tattoo she got while she was at technical school. Later, she'll try to get rid of it by spraying hydrochloric acid on her wrist, because she hates not being able to wear short-sleeved dresses and, as the wife of an officer, she hates looking like a bit of a slut.

———

Raya's pregnancy coincides almost to the day with the siege of Stalingrad. Conceived in May 1942, a terrible month, the time of the most bitter defeats, Eduard is born on February 2, 1943, twenty days before the German Sixth Army capitulates and the tables turn. Repeatedly he will be told that he is a child of victory, and that he would have been born into a world of slaves if the men and women of Russia hadn't sacrificed their lives to prevent the city that bore Stalin's name from falling to the enemy. Later bad things will be said about Stalin; he'll be called a tyrant and his reign of terror will be denounced. But for the people of Eduard's generation he will remain the supreme leader of the people of the Union at the most tragic moment in their history; the man who defeated the Nazis and proved himself capable of a sacrifice worthy of the ancient Romans: the Germans had captured his son, Lieutenant Yakov Dzhugashvili, while the Russians had captured Field Marshal Paulus, one of the top military leaders of the Reich, at Stalingrad. When the German High Command proposed an exchange, Stalin responded with disdain that he didn't exchange field marshals for simple lieutenants. Yakov committed suicide by throwing himself on the electrified barbed wire fence of his prison camp.

Two anecdotes stand out from Eduard's earliest childhood. The first one, his father's favorite, is touching: the baby, for lack of a crib, lies in a shell crate, sucking on a herring's tail in place of a pacifier, smiling as if he were in seventh heaven. "*Molodets!*" Venyamin cries: "Good boy! This little guy will be comfortable wherever he goes!"

The second anecdote, less charming, is told by Raya. She's downtown, carrying her baby on her back, when the Luftwaffe launches an air raid. She takes refuge in a cellar with a dozen city dwellers, some of them terrified, others apathetic. The ground and walls shake; everyone listens to gauge how far away the bombs are falling and what buildings they're bringing down. Little Eduard starts to cry, attracting the attention, then the rage of one guy who hisses that Fritz has ultramodern techniques for pinpointing live targets, that they home in on the faintest sounds and that the baby's crying will get them all killed. He does such a good job of rousing the others against Raya that they throw her out, forcing her to seek another shelter under the falling bombs. Livid with anger, she tells herself and her baby that everything people say about helping one another, about solidarity and fraternity, is just a joke. "The truth, and never forget this, Edichka, is that men are cowards and bastards, and they'll kill you if you're not ready to strike first."

2

IN THE PERIOD following the war, cities aren't called cities but "population concentrations," and the young Savenko family, moving from place to place as the postings come, lives in barracks and army camps in various population concentrations on the Volga before settling in February 1947 in Kharkov, now Kharkiv, in Ukraine. Kharkov, a large industrial center and rail hub, was the scene of bitter fighting between the Germans and Russians, who took and lost and retook it, each occupying the city in turn, massacring the inhabitants in the process and leaving, by the end of the war, nothing more than a field of ruins. The concrete constructivist building on Red Army Street that lodges the NKVD officers and their families—called "persons in charge"—overlooks what was once the imposing main station and is now a chaos of stones, bricks, and metal surrounded by fences that you're not allowed to climb over because apart from the bodies of German soldiers, there are mines and grenades strewn amid the rubble. One little boy had his hand blown off. Despite this example, the band of rascals Eduard joins likes nothing more than raiding these ruins, hunting for cartridges whose powder they empty onto the tramway tracks, causing crackling and fireworks, once even provoking a derailment that becomes legendary. In the evening, the biggest boys tell terrifying stories: of dead Fritzes who haunt the ruins on the lookout for unsuspecting stragglers; of stew pots in the cafeteria with children's fingers at the bottom; of cannibals and trading in human flesh. Everyone is hungry in these days, there's nothing to eat but bread, potatoes, and above all kasha, the buckwheat porridge that's part of every meal served up by poor Russians and which features occasionally in the homes of fairly well-off Parisians like me, who pride ourselves on how well we make it. Sausage is a rare luxury; Eduard is so wild about it he dreams of becoming a butcher when he grows up. No dogs, no cats, no pets: they'd get eaten. Rats, on the other hand, abound. Twenty million Russians died in the war, but another twenty million brave the postwar period without a roof over their heads. Most children no longer have fathers; most of the men still alive are invalids. On every street corner you see people missing an arm, a leg, two legs. Everywhere you see gangs of children left to fend for themselves, children whose parents died in the war or are imprisoned as public enemies, hungry children, child thieves and child murderers, children returned to the state of nature who move about in dangerous hordes and for whom the age of criminal responsibility, that is, of the death penalty, has been lowered to twelve.

The little boy admires his father. On Saturday evenings he likes to watch him grease his service weapon, he likes to see him put on his uniform, and nothing makes him happier than being allowed to polish his father's boots. He plunges one arm inside, right up to the shoulder, and spreads the polish with his other hand with care, using special brushes and cloths for each step of the operation, part of a whole kit that takes up half of Venyamin's suitcase when he leaves on assignment and that his son looks after, packing and unpacking it, anxious for the glorious day when he'll have one too. In his eyes, the only men worthy of the name are soldiers, and the only children to hang around with are the children of soldiers. He doesn't know any others: the families of the officers and junior officers living in the NKVD building on Red Army Street keep to themselves and have little respect for the civvies, a sniveling and undisciplined lot who are liable to stop without warning in the middle of the sidewalk, obliging the soldier to readjust his path in order to keep to the steady, energetic, regulation four-mile-an-hour pace at which Eduard will walk until the end of his days.

To get them to go to sleep at night, the children on Red Army Street are told stories of the conflict that the Russians don't call the Second World War as we do but the Great Patriotic War, and their dreams are filled with caving trenches, dead horses, and brothers in arms whose heads are ripped off by an exploding shell. Eduard is thrilled by these stories. Still, he notices his father seems a bit embarrassed when his mother tells them. They're never about him or his adventures, but only about Eduard's uncle, Raya's brother, and the little boy doesn't dare ask, "But what about you, Dad, did you go to war too? Did you fight?"

No, he didn't fight. Most of the men his age have looked death in the eye. War, his son will write later, bit them between its teeth like a suspect coin and they know, for not having bent, that they are the real thing. Not his father. He didn't look death in the eye. He served out the war far from the front, and his wife rarely misses a chance to remind him of it.

She's hard, proud of her standing as the wife of an officer, an enemy to all tenderness. She always sides against her son and with his adversaries. If he's been beaten up she doesn't console him but lauds the aggressor: that'll make Eduard a man, not a sissy. One of his first memories is suffering from a serious ear infection when he was five. Pus dripped from his ear; he was deaf for several weeks. The way to the clinic where his mother took him crossed the railway tracks. He saw, rather than heard, the train as it approached—the smoke, the speed, the shape of the black metal monster—and he was suddenly seized by the irrational fear that she wanted to hurl him under its wheels. He started to scream: "Mommy! Mommy! Don't throw me under the train! Please! Don't throw me under the train!" In his account he insists on the importance of the word *please*, as if this politeness alone had dissuaded his mother from her dire project.

When I got to know him in Paris thirty years later, Eduard liked to say his father was a Chekist, because he knew that would cast a pall over the room. Once, after he'd gotten his kicks with this announcement, he poked fun at us: "Stop imagining such terrible things, my dad was basically a gendarme, that's all."

Really, that's all?

During the civil war, just after the Revolution, Trotsky, serving as commander of the Red Army, had been obliged to press members of the imperial armed forces into service. These were professional soldiers and weapons specialists, but "bourgeois specialists," and as such relatively untrustworthy. He created a corps of political commissars to control them, countersign their orders, and shoot them if they showed signs of resisting. That's how the principle of the "double administration" was born, based on the idea that to accomplish a task you need at least two men: one to do it and one to make sure he does it in conformity with Marxism-Leninism. This principle spread from the army to society at large, and in the process, it became clear that a third person was then needed to supervise the second, a fourth to supervise the third, and so on.

Venyamin Savenko is a modest cog in this paranoid system. His work is to supervise, control, and report. That does not necessarily imply—on this point Eduard is right—terrible acts of repression. Let's not forget, as a simple NKVD orderly he spent the war planted in front of a factory. Promoted during peacetime to the modest rank of junior lieutenant, he works as a *nacht-kluba*, which you could translate as "nightclub manager," but which here means organizing leisure and cultural activities for the soldiers—dance parties on Red Army Day, for example. The job suits him well: he plays the guitar, likes to sing, and in his own way has a taste for the good things in life. He even puts clear polish on his nails: quite the dandy, this Junior Lieutenant Savenko, who, his son says in retrospect, could have led a far more interesting life if he'd had the courage to get out from under his wife's thumb.

The life of nightclubbing NKVD-style in which Venyamin to a certain extent blossoms doesn't last, however, because the job is swiped by one Captain Levitin, who becomes without knowing it the sworn enemy of the Savenkos and a key figure in Eduard's private mythology:

the schemer who's not as good as you but is more successful, whose insolence and devilish luck not only humiliate you in front of the bosses but, even worse, in front of your family, so that the little boy, who all the while loyally parrots his parents' disdain for Levitin, can't stop thinking in secret—although he hates himself for it—that his father is kind of pathetic and that Levitin's son is, actually, pretty lucky. Eduard will later develop the theory that everyone has a Captain Levitin in life. His own will soon appear in this book in the guise of the poet Joseph Brodsky.

3

HE'S TEN YEARS old when Stalin dies, on March 5, 1953. His parents, that entire generation in fact, spent their whole lives in the Great Leader's shadow. To all of their questions he had the answer, terse and gruff, no room for doubt. They remember the days of fear and grief that followed the German attack in 1941 and the day when, overcoming his despair, Stalin spoke on the radio. Addressing the men and women of his country, he did not call them "comrades" but "my friends." "My friends": these simple, familiar words, whose warmth had been forgotten and that proved a balm to the soul in times of such terrible trouble, were as important to the Russians as Churchill's and de Gaulle's were to Westerners. The entire country mourns the man who pronounced them. Schoolchildren weep because they can't give their lives to prolong his. Eduard weeps with the rest.

At the time he's a nice, sensitive, and rather sickly young boy who loves his father, fears his mother, and is a great source of satisfaction to them both. The delegate of the soviet of Young Pioneers in his class, he's on the honor roll every year, as is only fitting for the son of an officer. He reads a lot, and his favorite authors are Alexandre Dumas and Jules Verne, both very popular in the Soviet Union. Despite all their differences, that's something our childhoods have in common. Like him, I admired the Musketeers and the Count of Monte Cristo.

I dreamed of becoming a trapper, an explorer, a sailor—or, more precisely, a whale harpooner like Ned Land as played by Kirk Douglas in the film version of *Twenty Thousand Leagues Under the Sea*. Tattooed, quick-witted, and never flustered, his chest muscles swelling his striped shirt, he towered over the learned Professor Arronax and even the mysterious Captain Nemo with his brute strength. These three figures provided me with divergent heroic models: the scholar, the rebel, and the man of action, who was also a man of the people. If it had only been up to me, this last was who I'd have wanted to be. But it wasn't only up to me. My parents made it clear early on that no, becoming a whale harpooner was out of the question, it would be better to be a scholar—I have no memory of the third option, the rebel, ever being up for discussion—especially because I was shortsighted: try harpooning a whale with glasses!

I had to start wearing them at the age of eight. So did Eduard, but he suffered for it more than I did. Because his handicap barred him not only from an action-hero career but from the one to which he had been naturally destined. The eye doctor who examined him left his parents little hope: with such bad vision their son was very likely to be declared unfit for service.

For him, this diagnosis is a tragedy. He never thought of being anything other than an officer, and now he's told that he can't even do his obligatory military service, that he's condemned to become what he's been taught to disdain since his earliest childhood: a civvy.

And perhaps that's what he would have become if the building housing the NKVD officers hadn't been demolished, its inhabitants scattered, and the Savenkos moved to the new housing complex in Saltov, on the very outskirts of Kharkov. Saltov has streets that intersect at right angles, but there's been neither the time nor the money to pave them. Four-floor concrete cubes, home to workers at three factories called the Turbine, the Piston, and the Hammer and Sickle, have just gone up and already they're run down. This is the Soviet Union and in principle it's not demeaning to be from the working class; still, most of the men in Saltov are alcoholic and illiterate, and most of their children leave school at fifteen to go to work in a factory or, more often, to loiter on street corners, get drunk, and beat one another up—and even in a society without classes it's hard to imagine how the Savenkos can see this exile as anything but a drop in status. From day one Raya bitterly misses Red Army Street, the community of officers proud to belong to the same caste, the books they passed around, the evenings when, with their uniform jackets unbuttoned, revealing white shirts beneath, the husbands led their young wives around the dance floor to fox-trot or tango records confiscated in Germany. She berates Venyamin, reminding him of more clever comrades who've been promoted three times while he's risen laboriously from junior lieutenant to lieutenant, who've been given real apartments in the center of town while the three of them have to make do with one room in this horrid suburb where no one reads or dances the fox-trot, where there's no one a refined woman can talk to, and where the streets ooze with blackish mud every time it rains. She doesn't go as far as to say she would have been better off marrying a Captain Levitin, but that's exactly what she thinks, and little Eduard, who so admired his father—his boots, his uniform, and his pistol—starts to pity him, starts to see him as honest and a bit stupid. His new friends aren't the sons of officers but of workers, and the ones he likes don't want to become laborers like their parents, but thugs. Like a career in the army, this career too has a code of conduct, has values and morals that he finds attractive. He no longer wants to be like his father when he grows up. He no longer wants anything to do with that honest and ultimately fairly dull existence; he wants a free and dangerous life: the life of a man.

He takes a decisive step in this direction the day he gets into a fight with a boy in his class, a big Siberian named Yura. In fact, he doesn't fight *with* Yura; Yura beats the living daylights out of him. He's taken home dazed and covered in bruises. True to her stoical military principles, his mother doesn't pity or console him; she sides with Yura, and it's a good thing, he thinks, because his life changes that day. He understands one basic thing: there are two kinds of people, those you can hit and those you can't—not because they're stronger or better trained, but because they're *ready to kill*. That's the secret, the only one, and nice little Eduard decides to defect to the other camp: he will become someone you don't hit because you know he can kill.

Now that he's no longer a *nacht-kluba* Venyamin is often away on assignment, for weeks at a time. Just what these assignments consist of is unclear. Eduard is starting to lead his own life and isn't really interested, but one day Raya says she's counting on him to show up for dinner because his dad's getting home from Siberia, so he decides to go meet him at the station.

In line with a habit he'll never lose, he arrives early. He waits. Finally the Vladivostok–Kiev train pulls in. The passengers get out and head for the exit. He's standing where no one can possibly escape his attention, but Venyamin doesn't appear. Eduard asks at the desk, checks the train's arrival time, which is easy to get wrong because there are eleven time zones between Vladivostok and Leningrad and departure and arrival times at each station are indicated using Moscow time—still the case today; it's up to travelers to calculate the time difference. Disappointed, he wanders from one platform to the next, in the din amplified by the station's immense windows. Old women in headscarves and felt boots, hawking pails of cucumbers and cranberries to travelers, nag him. He crosses the sidings and comes to the area reserved for freight. And it's here, in an isolated corner of the station, between two trains, that he happens upon this spectacle: men in civilian clothing, handcuffed and haggard, walk down the plank of a freight car while soldiers in greatcoats with bayonets on their rifles push them roughly into a windowless black truck. The whole operation is overseen by an officer. In one hand he holds a sheaf of papers fastened to a clipboard; the other rests on the holster of his pistol. He calls out the names in a dry voice.

This officer is his father.

Eduard remains hidden until the last prisoner has climbed into the truck. Then he goes back home, troubled and ashamed. What is he ashamed of? Not of his father being part of a monstrous system of repression. He has no idea about this system, has never heard the word *Gulag*. He knows there are prisons and camps where delinquents are shut away, and has no problem with that. What is happening, something he doesn't really understand and which explains his shame, is that his value system is starting to change. When he was a child there were servicemen on one side and civvies on the other, and even if he didn't see the heat of battle, as a soldier his father still deserved respect. According to the code of the Saltov boys he's in the process of adopting, there are hoods and punks on one side and cops on the other, and just when he chooses the punks' camp he discovers that his father is less of a soldier and more of a cop, and of the lowest rank at that: a patrolman, a screw, a petty security guard.

The scene has a nocturnal follow-up. In the family's single room, Eduard's bed is at the foot of his parents'. He has no memory of ever having heard them make love, but he does remember listening in to a hushed conversation they had when they thought he was asleep. Depressed, Venyamin tells Raya that rather than taking Ukrainian convicts to Siberia as usual, this time he brought some back in the other direction, a whole contingent that was to be shot. A change had been introduced to avoid overly demoralizing the camp guards: one year all those condemned to death in the Soviet Union are shot in one prison, the next year in another. I've looked in vain for a trace of this improbable custom in books on the Gulag, but even if Eduard misunderstood what his father was saying, it's certain that these men whose names his father called as they left the train and ticked off as they climbed into the truck were going to their deaths. One of them, Venyamin tells his wife, made a very strong impression on him. His file was coded as "particularly dangerous." He was a calm and polite young man who spoke an elegant Russian and made sure to do his exercises every day, whether in his cell or in the freight car. This refined, stoical condemned man becomes a hero for Eduard, who begins to dream that he'll be like him one day, that he'll go to prison too and impress not only lowlifes and underpaid cops like his father but women, thugs, real men— and like everything he dreamed of doing as a child, in the course of his life, he'll get the chance to do just that.

4

EVERYWHERE HE GOES he's the youngest, the smallest, and the only one wearing glasses, but he's always got a switchblade in his pocket with a blade longer than his palm is wide. That's the distance from the breastbone to the heart, which means his switchblade can kill. And he can drink. It wasn't his father who taught him but a neighbor, a former prisoner of war. In fact, the prisoner of war said, you can't learn to drink: you've got to be born with a liver of steel, and Eduard was. Nevertheless there are certain tricks: drink a little glass of oil to grease the pipes before a binge (I was taught the same thing: my mother heard it from an old Siberian priest), and don't eat at the same time (I was taught the opposite, so I pass on the advice with some caution). On the strength of his innate gifts and these helpful tips, Eduard can drink two pints of vodka every hour, at the rate of one big eight-ounce glass every fifteen minutes. This knack allows him to amaze all and sundry right down to the Azerbaijanis who come up from Baku to sell oranges at the market, and to even earn some pocket money from bets on the side. It also allows him to take part in those marathon drinking binges the Russians call *zapoi*.

Zapoi is serious business, not a one-night bender of the kind we partake in, the kind you pay for with a hangover the next day. *Zapoi* means going several days without sobering up, roaming from one place to another, getting on trains without knowing where they're headed, telling your most intimate secrets to people you meet by chance, forgetting everything you've said and done: a sort of voyage.

So it happens that one night when they've started drinking and are short of booze, Eduard and his best friend Kostya decide to break into a grocery store. At fourteen, Kostya—aka the Cat—has already done time for armed robbery in a penal colony for minors. It's on the basis of this authority that he teaches his disciple Eduard the burglar's golden rule: Act bravely and stick to your guns, and don't wait for the perfect moment because the perfect moment doesn't exist.

Take a quick look to the left and right to make sure no one's passing on the street. Ball your jacket around your fist. Smash the basement windowpane with a quick blow and there you go, you're in. It's dark, no question of switching on the light. They swipe as many bottles of vodka as can fit into their backpacks, then break open the till. Just twenty rubles, chicken shit. There's a safe in the director's office, but try opening a safe with nothing but a knife. Kostya gives it a shot anyway and while he's struggling with it Eduard looks around for something else he can steal. A coat with an astrakhan collar hangs from the hook behind the door: what the hell, they can resell it. At the bottom of a drawer is an opened bottle of Armenian cognac, no doubt the director's private stock; he doesn't sell this kind of alcohol to his working-class customers. In Eduard's personal cosmology, all storekeepers are crooks, but you've got to admit they know about the good things in life. Suddenly voices, the sound of footsteps nearby. Fear bores into his intestines. He drops his pants, crouches down, lifts the tails of the stolen coat and lets out a stream of diarrhea. False alarm.

A little later, after they've left the same way they came in, the two boys stop at one of those dismal playgrounds so loved by designers of working-class housing complexes. Sitting on the dirty, humid sand at the base of a slide so rusty that parents avoid taking their kids there for fear of tetanus, they empty the bottle of cognac. After his embarrassment passes, Eduard starts boasting that he took a shit in the director's office. "I bet that punk's going to take advantage of the burglary to say that money he embezzled got swiped too," Kostya says. Later still they go over to Kostya's place. Kostya's mother, a war widow, complains when they lock themselves in his room and keep on drinking. "Shut up, you old bitch," her son answers politely through the door, "otherwise my buddy Ed'll come out and fuck you in the ass!"

After drinking the whole night, the two boys take the remaining bottles over to Slava's place. Since his parents were sent to a camp for economic crimes, Slava has lived with his grandfather in a hut on the riverbank. In addition to Eduard and Kostya, there's an older guy at his place that afternoon, Gorkun. Gorkun has metal teeth, tattooed arms, and doesn't talk much; he's thirty and, as Slava announces proudly, he's spent half his life at Kolyma. The Kolyma work camps, on the eastern edge of Siberia, are reputed to be the harshest of all, and in the boys' eyes, having spent three five-year terms there is like being a Soviet hero three times over: respect. The hours pass slowly, spent shooting the breeze, lazily waving away the clouds of mosquitoes that hover over the silted river in July, swigging warm vodka, and eating bits of cured fat that Gorkun slices with his Siberian knife. All four are drunk, but they're past the ups and downs typical of the first day of drunkenness and have attained that somber, stubborn stupor that gives the *zapoi* its cruising rhythm. As night falls they decide to go hang out in Krasnozavodsk Park, where Saltov's teenagers get together on Saturday nights.

There, without fail, a fight breaks out—and to tell the truth, Eduard and his friends were looking for one. It starts on the outdoor dance floor. Gorkun invites a girl to dance. The girl, a redhead with large breasts and a flowery dress, refuses because Gorkun stinks way too much of alcohol and because he looks like what he is: a *zek*, as convicts are called in Russian. In an effort to impress Gorkun, Eduard goes up to the girl, takes out his knife, and presses it lightly against one of her large breasts. Trying to sound like a man, he says: "I'll count to three, and if at three you don't dance with my buddy . . ." A little later in a dark corner of the park they're attacked by the redhead's friends. The brawl turns into a rout when the police turn up. Kostya and Slava manage to escape, the cops catch Gorkun and Eduard. They throw them on the ground and start kicking them in the ribs and methodically crushing their hands: with broken hands, you can't hold a weapon. Eduard jabs blindly with the knife, cutting one policeman's pants and a bit of his calf. The others work him over until he's unconscious.

He comes to in a cell, in the stench proper to all police stations the world over—he'll get to know many more. The police commander who interrogates him is surprisingly polite, but doesn't hide the fact that attacking a police officer with a weapon could get him the death sentence if he were an adult and, since he isn't, at least five years in a penal colony. Would an adolescence behind bars have broken him, brought him back into line, or would it have been just one more episode in his adventurer's life? We'll never know; he escaped that fate because on hearing the name Savenko, the commander raises his eyebrows and asks if he's the son of Lieutenant Savenko of the NKVD, and since Lieutenant Savenko is an old friend of his he pulls a few strings, buries the file on the knife wound, and, instead of five years, Eduard gets just fourteen days. In principle he should spend them collecting garbage, but he's too bruised to move so he's put in a cell with Gorkun, who, won over by the adolescent's fervor, becomes talkative and regales Eduard with stories about Kolyma for the next two weeks.

It goes without saying that if Gorkun was in Kolyma it was for criminal offenses, otherwise he wouldn't brag about it to boys like Eduard and his friends, who, unlike us, have no respect at all for political prisoners. Having never met one, they think they're either pontificating intellectuals or boneheads who got themselves locked up without really understanding why. Gangsters, on the other hand, are heroes; in particular, they worship that criminal aristocracy known as *vory v zakone*, thieves in law. There aren't any in Saltov, whose criminals are nothing more than petty delinquents. Gorkun himself doesn't pretend to be one, but he did get to know some in the prison camp and never tires of recounting their glorious deeds, putting insane acts of bravery on a par with bestial cruelty, presenting both as equally worthy of admiration. As long as a gangster is *honest*—that is, as long as he observes the laws of his clan, as long as he knows how to kill and how to die—Gorkun sees nothing but panache and moral distinction in playing cards for a cellmate's life and bleeding him like a pig once the game's over, or persuading another to attempt a joint escape, all the while planning to eat him as soon as food runs out on the taiga. Eduard listens to Gorkun with rapt devotion, admiring his tattoos, being initiated into their mysteries. Russian, and in particular Siberian, gangsters don't just get random tattoos anywhere, anyhow. The images and their positions indicate precisely the bearer's rank in the criminal hierarchy. The right to cover your body with them is acquired progressively as you climb the echelons, and woe be it to the poseur who usurps this right: he's skinned and gloves are made from his hide.

In his last days in jail Eduard realizes something that fills him with a strange joy, a sort of plenitude he'll seek constantly in life. He went into prison admiring Gorkun and dreaming of being like him one day. He leaves convinced—and this is the source of his joy—that Gorkun isn't so impressive after all and that he, Eduard, will go much further. With his years in prison camp and his tattoos Gorkun may be able to hold sway over provincial adolescents for a spell, but once you've hung around him for a bit it's clear that he talks about big gangsters like the small gangster he is, without comparing himself with them or imagining for an instant that he could ever be in their place—kind of like how that poor fool Venyamin talks about high-ranking officers. This way of knowing and staying in your place has elements of humility and candor, but it's not for Eduard, who thinks that it's good to be a criminal—maybe in fact there's nothing better—but you've got to set your sights high and aim to be a kingpin, not some lowly grunt.

5

KOSTYA IS GALVANIZED by this new perspective as soon as Eduard shares it with him, and whereas Gorkun's only ambition when he gets out is to play dominoes, the two boys are now filled with disdain for everything around them. No facet of Saltovian society escapes their derision: dull-witted, resigned laborers, young punks destined to become laborers like their parents, engineers or officers who are nothing but upper-class laborers, to say nothing of the shopkeepers. No doubt about it: what they've got to do is become gangsters.

But how? How to find a gang and be accepted by it? There have got to be some in the city, and plucking up their courage they take the tramway downtown, bursting with excitement: Kharkov is ours! Unfortunately, when they get there they feel out of place, just as any hicks venturing into a classy part of town would. Still, Eduard lived there once, in an era that, like his mother, he tends to idealize. He gives Kostya a ritual tour of his childhood landmarks: Red Army Street, Sverdlov Avenue. But the tour is soon over and after that they have no idea where to go or what door to knock on; they hardly dare order a beer at a bar. Irritated and disappointed with themselves, they return to their apartment complex, which has nothing to do with real life, but where they just happen to live—so it goes.

Then Eduard meets Kadik, who will be his other best friend throughout his adolescence, and things change. Kadik's a year older, lives alone with his mother, and doesn't hang out with the little punks in Saltov. He knows people in town, but not the gangsters that Eduard dreams so ardently of meeting. His big source of pride is knowing a saxophonist who can play "Caravan" by Duke Ellington and, through him, having rubbed shoulders with the members of Kharkov's "Blue Horse" group: beatnik types who've been honored with an article in *Komsomolskaya pravda*—swinging Kharkov, so to speak. To escape the fate that awaits young Saltovians, Kadik aspires to be an artist. And in the absence of a clear vocation he's at least something of a hipster: he plays a little guitar, he collects records, he reads, and he puts all his energy into keeping abreast of what's going on in the city, in Moscow, in America even.

All of this is totally new to Eduard. Kadik's values and codes shatter his own. Under Kadik's influence he discovers the cult of clothing. When he was little his mother dressed him in finds from the flea market, where war booty was bought and sold: he wore the pretty suits of model German children and felt a confused pleasure in imagining they had belonged to the son of the director of Krupp or IG Farben, killed in Berlin in 1944. Now the Saltov dress code holds sway: work pants, big parka lined with synthetic fur, any deviation and it's obvious you're a faggot—so Eduard's buddies are flabbergasted to see him turn up one day in a hooded canary-colored jacket, mauve crushed-velvet pants, and a pair of shoes with metal heels that send sparks flying when he drags his feet on the pavement. He and Kadik are the only ones in Saltov who can appreciate their own dandyism, but since he's known to be quick with his knife the others laugh but don't dare call him a fag.

This dandyism is also what he likes about the jazz musicians his new friend so idolizes. He has no affinity for music, and never will. But he does start reading again. He'd stopped at Jules Verne and Alexandre Dumas; now he starts again with Jack London and Knut Hamsun, the grand vagabonds who plied every trade and embellished their novels with these experiences. His favorite prose authors are foreign, but when it comes to poetry he feels no one can match the Russians. And a boy who reads their verse very naturally becomes a boy who writes his own as well, then reads what he's written to his friends. In this way Eduard, who until that moment had never dreamed of such a calling, becomes a poet.

A cliché has it that poets in Russia are as popular as singers in the West, and like many clichés about Russia, it is, or at least was, absolutely true. Our hero even owes his slightly affected first name to his father, a simple Ukrainian junior officer, and his love for the minor poet Eduard Bagritsky (1895–1934). Readers of *Memoir of a Russian Punk,* the book from which I draw the material in this chapter, are astonished to discover in passing that while they like his poetry, Eduard's friends, the petty thugs of Saltov, also tease him for copying Blok and Yesenin. A budding poet is no more out of place in a Ukrainian industrial apartment complex than a budding rapper is today in the suburbs of Paris or New York's housing projects. Like the rapper, he can tell himself that it's his chance to escape the factory or a life of crime. Like him, he can count on his friends' encouragement and pride if he's at all successful. And it's at the urging not only of Kadik but also of Kostya and his gang that Eduard signs up for a poetry competition that takes place on November 7, 1957, the Soviet national holiday and a day, as we will see, that proves decisive in his life.

On that day the entire city gathers at Dzerzhinsky Square, which, as no Kharkovite is unaware, was paved by German prisoners and is the largest square in Europe and, after Tiananmen, the second largest in the world. There are parades, dance performances, speeches, and awards. The proletarian masses come out in their Sunday best, a spectacle that prompts sarcastic remarks from our two dandies. And, at the cinema Pobeda—Victory—there's a poetry competition. Eduard, notwithstanding the sophisticated airs he puts on, hopes with all his heart that Sveta will come and hear him read.

Kadik is confident: she'll come, she can't not come. In fact, nothing is less certain. Sveta is capricious, temperamental. Theoretically Eduard "goes out" with her, but even if he says yes when his friends ask if he's had sex with her, it's not true: he hasn't had sex with anyone yet. He hates being a virgin and he hates having to lie, something he thinks a man should never do. He hates having no claim to Sveta and knowing that she's attracted to older boys. He hates, at fifteen, looking like he's twelve, and pins all his hopes on the notebook containing his verses. He chooses the ones he will read with care, ruling out the many poems on gangsters, armed robbery, and prison, and wisely sticking to those about love.

When he and Kadik arrive at the Pobeda the whole Saltov gang is already in the crowd—but no Sveta. Kadik tries to reassure him: it's still early. Various official speakers follow one another on the platform. Unable to control himself any longer, Eduard stoops to asking if anyone has seen Sveta. And unfortunately yes, someone has: at the Park of Culture, with Shurik. Shurik's an eighteen-year-old dimwit with a scrawny mustache, and Eduard is certain he'll be a shoe salesman until he retires, whereas he, Eduard, will travel the world leading the life of an adventurer. Still, at this particular moment, he'd give a lot to trade places with Shurik.

The competition starts. The first poem deals with the horrors of serfdom, making Kadik snicker: serfdom hasn't existed for a century, guy's really on the ball! After that a bit about boxing, imitating—as none of the punks in the audience fails to see—the rising young poet Yevgeny Yevtushenko. At last it's Eduard's turn, and he fights back tears while reciting the poem he wrote for Sveta. Afterward, while the other contestants read their works onstage, his friends gather around and congratulate him, hugging him, slapping him on the back, saying "Eat your tail"—the Saltov gang's ritual greeting. Everyone says he'll win the prize, and in fact, in the end, he does. He is called back on-stage, where the director of the Stalin House of Culture congratulates him and gives him a certificate along with a present.

What present?

A box of dominoes.

Holy shit, the pricks, Eduard thinks. A box of dominoes!

As they leave the cinema, while Eduard, surrounded by his buddies, tries to put on a brave face, a guy comes up; he says Tuzik sent him. Tuzik's a well-known thug in Saltov: he's twenty, he's hiding to escape military service, and he never makes a move without a squad of armed men. And, the messenger says, he wants to see the poet. The friends exchange worried looks: this is nothing to laugh about. Tuzik is notoriously dangerous, but it would be even more dangerous to refuse his invitation. The messenger leads him to a dead end street nearby where fifteen or so sinister-looking types are waiting, and in the middle of this following, thickset, almost fat, dressed in black, is Tuzik, who says he liked the poem. And he wants the poet to write another one for him in honor of Galya, the very made-up blonde he's holding by the waist. Eduard promises to do it, and a joint of Tajikistan hash is held out to seal the deal. It's the first time Eduard has smoked and it makes him feel sick, but he inhales anyway. Tuzik then invites him to kiss Galya, on the mouth. There's good reason to be wary; everything he says seems to have a double meaning, and if he gives you a hug it could be to stab you in the gut. They say that's what Stalin was like: cuddly and cruel. Eduard tries to shrug it off with a laugh. Tuzik insists: "You don't want to kiss my girlfriend? Don't like the way she looks? Go on, use your tongue!" It's a familiar tune and it doesn't bode well, but nothing bad comes of it. They all go on drinking and smoking and taking digs at one another for a long time, a very long time, until Tuzik decides to change things up and take a walk around town. Eduard, who's not entirely sure whether he's been adopted as a mascot or a whipping boy, would like to slip away, but Tuzik doesn't let him go.

"You ever killed anyone, poet?"

"No," Eduard replies.

"Would you like to?"

"Uh . . ."

In fact Eduard gets a kick out of being Tuzik's companion and walking next to him at the head of twenty tough-ass guys ready to wreak havoc on the town. It's late, the celebrations are over, almost everyone has gone home, and all those who see the gang coming down the street under the broken lights hurry away. But lo and behold, one guy and two girls don't get away quickly enough and the gang starts to needle them. "You've got two chicks all to yourself," Tuzik says to the guy nonchalantly. "Lend me one?" The guy goes pale, knowing he's gotten himself into a tight spot. He tries to joke but Tuzik folds him in two with a punch to the gut. At his signal, the others start pawing at the girls. It looks like it's going to be rape. It is rape. They strip one of them naked. She's fat with whitish skin, no doubt a factory girl from Saltov. The guys take turns sticking their fingers in her pussy. Eduard does the same, it's cold and wet, and when he takes his fingers out there's blood on them. That sobers him up in a flash, and the excitement wanes. A few yards away ten or so guys gang-rape the other girl, one after the other. As for the guy, they beat the crap out of him. He groans more and more faintly, then stops moving altogether. The side of his face is a bloody pulp.

In all the commotion this time Eduard manages to escape. He walks quickly, his knife and notebook of poems in his pocket and the box of dominoes under his arm, not knowing where to go. Not to Kadik's place, or to Kostya's. Finally he goes to Sveta's. He wants to fuck or kill. If she's alone, he'll fuck her; if she's with Shurik, he'll kill them. No reason not to: he's a minor so he won't be shot, he'll just get fifteen years and the guys will think of him as a hero.

It's late, but Sveta's mother, who's considered more or less a whore, opens the door. Sveta's not home yet.

"You want to wait?"

"No, I'll come back."

He walks off into the night, walking and walking, racked by a mixture of excitement, rage, disgust, and other feelings he can't identify. Sveta's back when he returns. Alone. What happens next is confused; there isn't really any conversation, Eduard takes her to bed and fucks her. It's his first time. "Is that how Shurik sticks his cock in you?" he says. Once he's come—too quickly—Sveta lights a cigarette and gives him a rundown of her philosophy: women are more mature than men, so for things to work sexually the man's got to be older. "I really like you, Edik, but you see, you're too young. You can sleep here if you want."

Eduard doesn't want to; he leaves in a fury. People are there to be killed, he thinks, and that's just what I'm going to do when I'm older.

And that's how he loses his virginity.

6

THE NEXT SCENE takes place five years later, in the room occupied by the Savenko family. It's midnight; Eduard gets undressed without making a sound so as not to wake his mother, who's asleep alone in the parental bed. His father is on assignment, he doesn't know where and doesn't want to know. It's been a long time since he admired him. As tired as he is after eight hours at the factory he isn't sleepy, so he sits down at the table where a copy of Stendhal's *The Red and the Black* is lying, part of a collection of foreign classics bound in imitation leather. His mother must have taken it out to accompany her solitary dinner, removing it from the small glass-paned bookcase that protects the proof of her sophistication from the falling dust. He's already read it, and loved it. Flipping through the pages he comes to the famous passage where, one summer night under a linden tree, Julien Sorel forces himself to take Madame de Rênal's hand, and this scene that so thrilled him now fills him with a sudden, dizzy sadness. Just a few years ago it was easy for him to identify with Julien, who came from a godforsaken dump with no advantages save his charm and ambition, and to imagine himself, like Julien, seducing a beautiful aristocrat. What now dawns on him with brutal clarity is that not only does he not know any beautiful aristocrats, he also stands no chance of ever meeting any.

He had big dreams and in the last two years, everything has gone wrong. It started with Kostya and two of their other friends being condemned to death by the Kharkov District Court. One was executed; Kostya and the other got off with twelve years in a prison camp. Right after that, Kadik, who had big dreams of becoming a jazz musician, got a job at the Hammer and Sickle, and after duly making fun of him for a few months, Eduard tucked his tail between his legs and followed his example. He's a foundry worker now. It's dirty and mind-numbing, but Eduard's the sort of guy who does well in whatever field he chooses. If fate had allowed him to become a gangster, he'd have been a good one. As a worker he's good too, with his cap on his head and his lunchbox at noon, regularly listed on the honor roll, downing his twenty-six ounces of vodka on Saturday night with the other guys on his shift. He no longer writes poetry. He has girlfriends, losers like him. The ultimate catastrophe would be for him to knock one of them up and have to marry her, and, when you look at the situation dead on, more likely than not that's what *will* happen. As it did to Kadik, his guide on the path of defeat, who has just shacked up with a worker named Lydia who's older than him and not even pretty, her belly already growing rounder, while the poor guy tries to convince himself with pathetic obstinacy that with her it's happened, he's found true love and he doesn't regret—not at all, really—sacrificing his childish dreams for her sake.

Poor Kadik. Poor Eduard. Not yet twenty and already done for. A failed gangster, a failed poet, doomed to a shitty life in the asshole of the world. People have often told him how lucky he was not to have been with Kostya and the other two the night they got drunk and killed a man. But how can they be so sure? Isn't it better to die while you're alive than to live the life of a dead person? Looking back on this night, thirty years later, he'll think that it wasn't to die but to feel alive that he took his father's horn-handled razor from the bathroom shelf—he himself hardly shaves at all: to look at his skin you might almost think he was Asian, it's all but beardless and very soft, the kind of skin that deserves to be caressed by beautiful, sophisticated women. But there'll be none of that.

He presses the sharp blade against the inside of his wrist and looks up in the dim light at the familiar, ugly room where half his life has ebbed away. He was still a child when he arrived here: a tender, serious little boy. How far away that all seems . . . Ten feet away his mother snores under her covers, her head turned to the wall. She'll die of sorrow, but that trip to the grave began when he gave up his studies and became a laborer, so he might as well finish off the job. The first cut is easy, the skin slits open, it's almost painless. Things get harder when he hits the veins. He's got to turn his head away, clench his teeth, and pull the blade with a deep, sharp tug to get the blood to flow. He doesn't have the strength to have a go at the other wrist, one should be enough. He leaves his hand on the table in front of him, watching the dark stain blossom on the plastic tablecloth and soak into *The Red and the Black*. He doesn't move. He feels his body grow cold. The sound of the chair when he falls wakens his mother with a start. He wakes up the next day in the nuthouse.

A mental institution is worse than prison, because in prison at least you know the deal, you know when you'll get out, whereas here you're at the mercy of doctors who look at you from behind their glasses and say, "We'll see," or, more often, nothing at all. Eduard spends his days sleeping, smoking, eating kasha, being bored. So bored that he begs Kadik to help him climb the wall, and Kadik, good Kadik, without saying a word to his dragon Lydia, leans a ladder up against the window and manages to pry a bar loose. Once out, Eduard is determined to flee far away, but he makes the mistake of going back to his parents' place first, where the police pick him up the next morning.

It was his mother who called them, and when he asks in a rage why she did it, Raya explains that it's for his own good: if he goes back to the hospital he'll be let out very quickly, in accordance with regulations, whereas as a wanted runaway he'll always be a fugitive. Fine words, no doubt she believes them, but rather than being released he's transferred from the ward with the calm crazies to the ward with the psycho crazies, where he's attached to the bars of his bed with wet towels; and it's not even his bed—he shares it with a crackpot who spends his time whacking off morning, noon, and night, because with the psycho crazies you don't even have a bed to yourself. Once a day he's given a shot of insulin even though he doesn't have diabetes, both to teach him a lesson and to calm him down. Sure enough, it calms him right down. He becomes slow and spongy; he can feel that his sugar-deprived brain is going to crap; he no longer even has the strength to rebel. He starts wanting to get it all over with, to fall into a coma and never wake up.

After a good two months on this regime he's lucky enough to be treated by an old psychiatrist with hairy ears who, after a short conversation with this boy-cum-zombie, has the wisdom to conclude: "You're not crazy. You just want to get attention. My advice: there are better ways of doing that than slitting your veins. Don't go back to the factory. Go see these people and tell them I sent you."

7

THE ADDRESS THE old psychiatrist gave him belongs to a bookstore in the center of Kharkov, where they're looking for an itinerant salesperson. The job involves displaying used books on a folding table in a movie theater lobby or at the entrance to the zoo, and waiting for customers. The customers are scarce, they're all but giving the books away, and the seller gets a ridiculously low percentage on each. Eduard wouldn't last long at this job, which seems more like a part-time gig for a retiree, if the bookshop, *41*, where he fetches his boxes in the morning and brings back the day's haul in the evening, didn't happen to be the meeting place for all the artists and poets Kharkov can boast. They're called the "decadents": the people poor Kadik hung out with before the Hammer and Sickle and Lydia put an end to all that. Despite his timidity, Eduard starts to linger around after the official closing time. Often he misses the last streetcar and has to walk two hours through the night and snow to get back to his distant workers' suburb. Because at night, once the metal shutters have been rolled down, the group can not only drink and talk to their hearts' content but above all exchange clandestine copies of banned works called *samizdat*—literally, self-published. You're given one copy and you make a few more in turn, and that's how just about everything vital in Soviet literature circulates: Bulgakov, Mandelstam, Akhmatova, Tsvetaeva, Pilnyak, Platonov . . . On one memorable evening at *41*, for example, the extremely faint, almost unreadable copy (a fifth or sixth carbon copy, the connoisseurs judge with a frown) of *Procession*, a poem by the young Joseph Brodsky, arrives from Leningrad; twenty years later Eduard will characterize it as "a pastiche of Marina Tsvetaeva of dubious artistic merit, but one that corresponded precisely to the sociocultural development of Kharkov and the regulars at the bookstore."

I don't quite know what to think of such impertinence, for a reason it's time to admit: I have no feeling for poetry whatsoever. Like the visitors to a museum who first look at the painter's name to know if the painting is worth getting excited about, I have no personal taste in this domain, which makes the young Eduard's rapid and imperious verdicts all the more impressive to my eyes. He doesn't just say, "That I like, that I don't," but can distinguish at first glance the original from the copy; he's not taken in, for instance, by "those who imitate the Polish modernists, though they aren't exactly breaking new ground either, and are in fact imitating others themselves." I've already noted the Saltov hooligans' surprising skill at spotting when Eduard's first poems drew on Yesenin or Blok. What he discovers at *41* is that

Yesenin and Blok are good, but good in the way Apollinaire is, let's say—or to be cruel, Prévert: even people who don't know the first thing about poetry know them, and those who really know their stuff far prefer Mandelstam, for instance, or, even better, Velimir Khlebnikov, the great avant-gardist of the twenties.

Khlebnikov is Motrich's favorite poet, for example, and Motrich is considered the local genius at *41*. At thirty, Motrich hasn't published a thing and never will, but the advantage of censorship is that you can be an unpublished author without anyone suspecting you lack talent—on the contrary. On the periphery of their group, in contrast, there's a young guy who's written a collection of poems about the crew of the cruiser *Dzerzhinsky*, for which he received the literary prize of the Komsomol of Ukraine. A good start, a big print run, and the prospect of a fine career as a literary apparatchik, but not only does everyone consider him inferior to Motrich, he himself does too. And when he ventures into *41* he does his best to avoid mentioning a success that clearly marks him as a sellout and impostor. Motrich will suffer the fate all Eduard's heroes eventually suffer and quickly be toppled from his pedestal, but for the moment he's his hero—a real live poet—and, as Eduard will later judge, using a rather fine distinction, a bad but an authentic one. He reads his verses and listens to his pretentious prophecies. Under his influence he develops a passion for Khlebnikov, whose three-volume complete works he copies out by hand. And, in the hours of downtime offered by his job as an itinerant bookseller, he starts to write again, without telling a soul.

Anna Moiseyevna Rubinstein, the head saleslady at *41*, is a majestic woman with prematurely gray hair, a handsome, tragic face, and a huge ass. When she was younger she looked like Elizabeth Taylor; at twenty-eight she's already a matron to whom younger passengers give up their seat on the streetcar. Subject to fits of manic depression for which she receives a disability allowance, she proudly defines herself as "schizo" and calls everyone she respects crazy. They take it as a compliment. In the world of the Kharkov decadents, the genius not only has to be unrecognized but also delirious, a drunkard, and socially inept. Since the mental hospital is also an instrument of political repression, having spent time there is like a certificate of *dissidence*—a word still not in wide circulation at the time. Eduard certainly didn't know it when he was locked up with the psycho crazies, but he has a talent for catching on quickly and now he doesn't miss a chance to talk about his straitjacket and his bedmate who drooled and jerked off all day long. Writing this, I'm reminded that until I was quite old I too adhered to the romantic cult of madness. I got over it, thank God. Experience has taught me that this particular form of romanticism is pure stupidity, and that madness is the saddest, most dismal thing on earth. And I think Eduard always knew that instinctively, and prided himself on being pretty much anything—hard, egocentric, pitiless— but not mad. No, absolutely not. Just the opposite, if there is such a thing.

Anna, on the other hand, really is crazy, and her madness will take a tragic turn. But for the moment it can still be taken for a sort of eccentricity, a facet of her highly colorful character, just like her notorious sexual voracity. She's had the whole Kharkov bohemia, word has it at *41*, and she's a real specialist when it comes to deflowering young creative minds. Since she lives right next door, evenings at the bookstore often end up at her place. Eduard, who's not openly invited at first, imagines these nights end in orgies. In fact, as he discovers when he's bold enough to tag along, after-hours at Anna's consist, as at the bookstore, of impassioned conversations on art and literature, increasingly slurred poetic ramblings, gossiping and private jokes that leave him completely in the dark, sitting in his corner of the shaggy sofa, laughing when the others laugh, and getting drunk to overcome his shyness. Apart from the mistress of the house and her mother, who bangs on the door now and then to get them to pipe down, these gatherings are exclusively male, and all the men put their hands familiarly on Anna's neck and kiss her on the mouth, until Eduard gets the unpleasant feeling that he's the only one in the group who hasn't slept with her. Does he really want to sleep with her, or does he just want to become part of this group, which he realizes is his only way out of Saltov? She's got beautiful breasts, it's true, but he doesn't like fat women. When he jerks off to her the fantasies are never very convincing and he's afraid that if they end up in bed he'll either come too quickly or he won't get a hard-on at all. And then, one night, very late, as all the other guests leave one after the other, he stays put. Just as Julien resolved to take the hand of Madame de Rênal, he resolves to stay at all costs, if only to prove he's no sissy. The last ones out give him knowing winks as they put on their coats. He does his best to feign the calm, blasé attitude of someone who knows the score. When they're alone, Anna doesn't mess around. As expected he comes fast the first time but starts again right away; that's the privilege of youth. She seems satisfied: that's the main thing.

Because our Eduard, this Soviet Barry Lyndon, plans not only to sleep with Anna but to move in with her, in the bohemian holy of holies, thus transforming himself from proletarian clinger-on to official lover and master of the house. As the apartment they share has two bedrooms—immense luxury—Anna's mother, Celia Yakovlevna, at first pretends not to notice that he's staying the night. But she's quick to adopt him, because he knows how to handle elderly women and because she's grateful to him for putting an end to the parade of lovers the whole building was nattering about.

While the idea of this parade would plunge others into torments of retrospective jealousy, for Eduard it's a turn-on. He doesn't find Anna, in the end, especially arousing and he has to be drunk before mounting an attack on her enormous, fold-covered body, but it does turn him on to think of all the men who've preceded him. Many belong to their circle. Do they envy him, or make fun of him—the former what he desires, the latter what he dreads most in life? A bit of both, no doubt. But what is certain is that the Eduard of not even a few months ago, the foundry worker at the Hammer and Sickle, would have violently envied this Eduard, who no longer lives in Saltov but in the previously inaccessible center of town, whose friends are no longer workers and hooligans but poets and artists, who opens his door to them with the suave assurance of the man who's perfectly at home, and who enjoys keeping an open door for those who drop by at the spur of the moment. He no longer needs to raise his voice above the clamor in discussions; people listen when he speaks because he's the *khozyain*, which is to say the man of the house, but with a nuance of feudal authority: you can be the *khozyain* of a whole city; Stalin was the *khozyain* of the Soviet Union. Of course it'd be better if Anna were more beautiful, if he found her more desirable, but both of them will prosper from the stormy, affectionate partnership that unfolds over the next seven years. He'll keep her on an even keel, she'll smooth out his rough edges.

He reads her his poems, she thinks they're good and shows them to Motrich, who also thinks they're good. Very good, even. Encouraged, he reads them at the bookstore, and puts together a collection that he copies out ten times by hand. He's not yet at the point where others copy them, which is the second rung on the ladder of dissident glory—the third means being no longer *samizdat* but *tamizdat*: published *over there*, in the West, like *Doctor Zhivago*. His little collection, which circulates no wider than the immediate clientele of *41*, nevertheless allows him to be considered a poet, with everything that status entails.

And it's an enviable status. Because even if you lead a miserable life, it protects you from the disgrace associated with that miserable life, and many, once they've acquired it, sit back and don't write another thing their whole lives. Not Eduard, who's neither lazy nor easily satisfied, and who's discovered that by working a little each day, without fail, you're sure to make progress—a disciplined routine he'll stick to all his life. He's also discovered that there's no point talking about the "blue sky" in a poem because everyone knows it's blue, and that strokes of creativity like "blue like an orange" are almost worse for having made the rounds. To take readers by surprise, which is his goal, he puts the prosaic above the affected: no rare words or metaphors; call a spade a spade; if you talk about people you know give their names and addresses. In this way he forges a style that makes him, he feels, if not a great poet then at least an identifiable one.

To fully become this poet, all he lacks is a name, something that sounds better than the drab and boorish Ukrainian one he bears. One night, the little group assembled at Anna's place play at renaming themselves. Lenya Ivanov becomes Odeyalov; Sasha Melekhov, Bukhankin; and Eduard Savenko, Ed Limonov, a tribute to his acidic and bellicose humor, because *limon* means "lemon," and *limonka* is slang for a kind of hand grenade. While the others will drop these pseudonyms, he'll keep his. Even his name he wants to owe to no one but himself.

8

NOW I'VE GOT to talk about pants. It all starts when a guest notices his bell-bottom jeans and, since you can't buy clothes like that in stores, asks him who made them for him. "I did," Eduard foolishly brags, although in fact he had them made by a home-based tailor who supplied Kadik in his days as a dandy. "Could you make the same for me if I find the material?" "Of course," he answers, planning on taking the cloth to the tailor and making a small commission on the side.

Unfortunately, the day he goes to see him, no more tailor: he's vanished, disappeared without leaving an address. Just Eduard's luck, the one time he lies. And since there's no way he's going to confess, he sees only one solution: shutting himself up with a needle, thread, scissors, and his own pants as a model, and not coming out until he's produced something resembling bell-bottom jeans. Sewing a pair of jeans is no easy job, but he's inherited a real talent for any sort of handiwork from his father, and after forty-eight hours of effort, full of failures and plans as complicated as for a railway bridge, the result is a satisfied customer who pays him twenty rubles for the tailoring and spreads the word, so that the orders soon start flooding in.

That's how, totally by accident, he settles the question of his livelihood for the next ten years, and in a way he's satisfied with, because this job spares him confrontations with authority, be it in the form of a factory manager, shop foreman, supervisor, or any other kind of boss. As a home-based tailor he's dependent only on himself and the dexterity of his fingers; he can work when he likes—and when the orders come in, he can sew two or even three pairs of pants in a day and dedicate himself to poetry afterward. When Anna comes back from the bookstore he shoves his material and papers to the end of the table, her mother brings out some lovely red Ukrainian tomatoes, eggplant caviar, or a stuffed carp, and they sit down to a nice family dinner.

"All he needs is to be Jewish, your man," Celia Yakovlevna jokes. "We should get him circumcised."

"He's already learned a Jewish trade," Anna Moiseyevna replies, "let's not go overboard."

He's also happy that Anna is, as she says, "a prodigal daughter of the tribe of Israel." My friend Pierre Wolkenstein almost ended our friendship when he learned I was considering writing about Limonov—his was one of the first reactions prompted by this book. To Pierre, the Russian leader of a, let's say, dubious political faction, could not be anything but an anti-Semite. Think again. There are a lot of things you can hold against Eduard, but not that. It has nothing to do with his moral elevation, nor with his historical consciousness—like most Russians who perpetuate the memory of their twenty million war dead, he couldn't care less about the Shoah—but with a sort of snobbery. For him the fact that your average Russian—and even more your average Ukrainian—is an anti-Semite is the best reason not to be one yourself. Looking askance at Jews is something for blinkered, dull-witted rednecks, something for a Savenko. And the furthest thing from Savenkos of all stripes are the Jews. He's not indifferent to the fact that Anna's Jewish, in fact for him this exoticism is a point in her favor. And even if, as she says herself, she's a hooligan, a schizo, and a degenerate, he sees her as an Eastern princess thanks to whom he, doomed to live a donkey's life in Saltov, now floats in a house as colorful, poetic, and wildly eccentric as a painting by Chagall.

———

Eduard would not be Eduard, however, if he remained sitting cross-legged in his room, stitching together pants and poems. In addition to the decadents at *41*, he's got a new friend, a *pleyboi* (the word is starting to catch on in Russia) called Genka. Genka's the son of a KGB officer who, quicker on the uptake than poor Venyamin, switched careers and took over a chic restaurant frequented by the upper echelons of the Chekist hierarchy: so he's a pretty big man around town. With these contacts Genka could join the Party like his father, become a district committee secretary at thirty, and lead a cushy life until the end of his days: dacha, official car, vacations at lush seaside resorts in Crimea. This kind of career is all but guaranteed since everyone knows the time of purges and terror is over. The Revolution has stopped devouring its children. And power, as Anna Akhmatova quipped, has become vegetarian. Under Nikita Khrushchev the radiant future seems like a reasonable, worthwhile goal: security, a higher standard of living, peaceful development, and happy socialist families whose children are no longer encouraged to denounce their parents. There was the difficult period, it's true, after Stalin's death, when millions of *zeks* were liberated and some even rehabilitated. The bureaucrats, provocateurs, and informers who sent them to the Gulag had been sure of one thing: that they would never return. But now some were returning and, to quote Akhmatova once more, "two Russias stare into each other's eyes: the ones who were imprisoned and the ones who put them there." It might have been a bloodbath, but instead, nothing. The informers crossed paths with the informed upon, each knowing where they stood. Looking away and going about their business, *both* felt uncomfortable and vaguely embarrassed, like people who've had illicit dealings in the past that it's better not to talk about.

Some people talked about them anyway. In 1956 Khrushchev delivered a "secret report" to the Twentieth Party Congress that didn't remain secret for long, deploring Stalin's "cult of personality" and implicitly recognizing that the country had been governed by murderers for twenty years. In 1962, he personally authorized the publication of the book by a former *zek* named Solzhenitsyn—*One Day in the Life of Ivan Denisovich*—and its publication came as a shock. All of Russia snatched up issue number 11 of the magazine *Novy mir,* which contained this prosaic, meticulous story about an ordinary day in the life of an ordinary inmate housed in a camp that's not even particularly harsh. Completely taken aback, not daring to believe it, people started saying things like: it's the thaw, the reawakening, Lazarus is leaving his tomb; as soon as one man has the courage to tell the truth, no one can do anything to counter it. Few books have had such an impact, in their country or around the world. None, aside from *The Gulag Archipelago* ten years later, has *genuinely* changed the course of history to such an extent.

The powers that be understood that if it continued to be told, the truth about the camps and about the past risked sweeping everything away: not just Stalin but Lenin too, the system as well as the lies it was based on. That's why *Ivan Denisovich* marked both the height and the end of de-Stalinization. Once Khrushchev was stripped of his power, the generation of apparatchiks that emerged from the purges set up a sort of soft Stalinism under Leonid Brezhnev. The Party was hypertrophied, there was stability in leadership positions, string-pulling and graft were common, smaller and larger perks abounded, repression was moderate: a system known as the communism of the *nomenklatura*, of the "names" of the elite who benefited from it. And this elite was in fact quite large and, provided you play the game, not so difficult to join. Practically all Russians old enough to have known this leaden, resigned, and in a way comfortable stability think back on it with nostalgia today, when they're condemned to swim and often drown in the icy waters of self-serving calculation. A popular saying of this period was "We pretend to work, they pretend to pay us." It's not a particularly stimulating way to live, but it's all right. You get by, and provided you don't screw up completely you don't risk much. No need to care about anything; just adapt as best you can to a world that, as long as you're not named Solzhenitsyn, will remain as it is for centuries because it only exists thanks to inertia.

In this world, a nice slacker like Genka, to return to him, can let himself be just that, a nice slacker, and his Chekist father can go along with it too. Of course it'd be better if he joined the Party, just as in France during these same thirty years, it'd be better for a young bourgeois Frenchman to graduate from the École nationale d'administration or the Polytechnique. But if he doesn't it's not a big deal, he won't die of hunger or perish in a camp, he'll find a little bureaucratic sinecure thanks to which he won't be arrested as a parasite or a subversive, and there you go. That's how it happens that Genka, unworried about his future, spends his nights drinking for free with his buddy Eduard in clubs run by colleagues of his father, and his days, at least in the summer, at the snack bar at the zoo where he holds court, his entourage in stitches every time he chases away visitors on the pretext that an extraordinary session of the Congress of Bengal Tiger Tamers, of which he is the general secretary, is under way.

Genka's court is divided into two groups: the SS and the Zionists. The quirkiest SS member is a nice guy whose big number is reciting a speech by Hitler. He doesn't know much German but his audience knows even less, and it's enough for him to roll his eyes and spit out words like *Kommunisten*, *Kommissaren*, *Partisanen*, and *Juden* for everyone, the Zionists first of all, to laugh. None of the Zionists is Jewish. Their enthusiasm for Israel dates from the Six-Day War. Taking international politics into account, their position is somewhat perplexing, because being hooligans doesn't stop them from being good little patriots, and their country supports and arms the Arabs. But what impresses them above all is military valor, and from this perspective, hats off to Moshe Dayan's boys. Real soldiers, diehards like the Fritzes and the Japs, and it doesn't matter if they are or were the enemy: you have to respect them, unlike those big, soft, pink American jackasses whose idea of war—take Hiroshima—consists of dropping bombs that atomize everyone from miles up in the sky without risking anything themselves.

Apart from the Wehrmacht and the Israel Defense Forces, the other thing Genka and his friends adore, Zionists and SS alike, is a movie that, during this period, is being screened almost nonstop in Kharkov; they've probably seen it ten or twenty times: *The Last Adventure*, with Alain Delon and Lino Ventura. Foreign, and in particular French, films are one of the novelties of the Khrushchev years. The first scene of *The Last Adventure*, where Delon flies through the Arc de Triomphe, will inspire Eduard and Genka to commit their most memorable misdeed, when, plastered as they often are, they try to lift off in an old crate on the runway of the military air base. The affair doesn't make waves; the security guards who stop them take it as a joke, and, touched as I was the day my sons, aged three and six, tried to run away from home with some clothes bundled in a handkerchief and tied to an umbrella, end up offering them a drink to make them feel better about having failed.

And that's how Eduard's days go by. He sews, writes, spends time with Genka and his crowd in one of his fine homemade suits—he's particularly proud of the chocolate-colored one trimmed with gold thread. He does sit-ups and push-ups which make him muscular, and he's tanned summer and winter because the color lasts for ages on his olive skin. He'd pay dearly to be an inch or so taller, not to have to wear glasses, to have a more noble nose: to look like Delon, in other words, whom he tries to imitate in front of the mirror. When he neglects Anna for too long, she gets fed up and goes out looking for him. She usually finds him at the snack bar at the zoo, where she berates him in front of everyone, ranting and raving and calling him a young scoundrel: *molodoi negodia*, the title he'll give to his memoirs of this period. These scenes humiliate him as much as they delight his friends. They mock the fat ass and gray hair of this lover, who weighs twice as much as he does and could be his mother. To save face, he lets on that he uses her and that she supports him. Once he even says she turns tricks for him: in his mind, it's better to be an apprentice pimp than a good little boy.

9

AS HE HIMSELF says, a chronicle of Soviet life in the sixties wouldn't be complete without the KGB. The Western reader shudders in advance, thinking of the Gulag and psychiatric internment. But even if Eduard had to go down to the station perhaps more often than was fair, his relations with the organs in Kharkov were closer to burlesque. This is what happened.

A painter friend of theirs, Bakhchanyan, known as Bakht, met
a French guy who was passing through; the Frenchman gave him a
denim jacket and a couple of back issues of *Paris Match* magazine.
At the time—just after Khrushchev was toppled and the Brezhnev-
Kosygin-Gromyko troika assumed power—that constituted a crime,
and a pretty serious one at that. All contact with foreigners was banned,
as they were suspected both of propagating dangerous Western vi-
ruses in the form of books, records, and even clothes, and of smug-
gling dissident texts out of the country. No sooner has he left the
Frenchman's hotel wearing the jacket and carrying the copies of *Paris
Match* in a plastic bag than Bakht starts worrying that he's being followed. He shows up at Anna and Eduard's place and spills his guts.
They have just enough time to stash the jacket and magazines in a
chest on which Anna settles her callipygian posterior: the Chekist is
already knocking at the door.

Eduard lets him in and sizes him up at a glance: graying blond,
the look of a former athlete who's let himself go to seed. It doesn't
take much to see he's got a wife his age and two or three ugly kids with
no future: in short a colleague and brother of poor Venyamin's. And
he's the one who, seeing the books and paintings, seems embarrassed
to be bursting in on the artists. He senses that they lead a more interesting life than he does, which might make him turn nasty but he's
not that kind of guy. He searches because it's his job, without any particular zeal. They think he's going to leave empty-handed and he's almost at the door when his gaze lingers; he's struck by an idea. While he's
been searching, Anna hasn't moved from the chest she's sitting on. He
asks her to open it and there's a showdown. She tries to refuse, as force-
fully as if the Gestapo wanted her to rat on her network of partisans,
but in the end she yields. The game is up, the treasure confiscated.

Anna and Eduard get off with a reprimand, and as for Bakht he's
sentenced by a "court of comrades" at the Piston factory. As if they
fancy themselves art critics, these comrades decide that a donkey could
paint pictures like his with its tail and, to bring him down to more
figurative realities, send him to go dig holes on a building site for a
month, after which he returns to his provincial, outmoded abstracts

without further hassles. Eduard's conclusion: if the authorities in Kharkov had been a little more ruthless, the honest painter Bakhchanyan could have become famous the world over, just as the honest poet
Brodsky has just done: a man who was simply lucky enough to be in
the right place at the right time, and hit the jackpot by coincidence.

Let's take a closer look at this assertion, and what it says about our hero.
And let's introduce the person he'll consider his own Captain Levitin
for a large part of his life: Joseph Brodsky, the young prodigy from
Leningrad, as he was dubbed in the early sixties by Anna Akhmatova.

Anna Akhmatova, compared to Motrich, is another kettle of fish
altogether. Now that Mandelstam and Tsvetaeva have passed away,
all the connoisseurs consider her the greatest living Russian poet. Of
course there's also Pasternak, but he's rich, covered in honors, and
insolently happy. His tardy clash with the authorities will remain civilized, while Akhmatova, banned from publishing since 1946, lives on
tea and dry bread in shared apartments, which adds to her genius the
aura of resistance and martyrdom. She says: "I was in the midst of my
people, there, where, in their misfortune, my people were."

In his malevolence, Eduard likes to describe Brodsky as the eternal top of the class, forever hiding behind the teacher's petticoat, but
the truth is that Brodsky's youth was every bit as adventurous as his
own. Also the son of a junior officer, he left school early, worked on
a milling machine, dissected bodies in a morgue, and spent time as a
geological assistant in Yakutia. Along with another young punk, he
left for Samarkand, where he hijacked a plane in an attempt to reach
Afghanistan. Interned in a psychiatric hospital, he was given hideously
painful sulfur injections and a pleasant therapy known as *ukrutka*,
which consisted of wrapping the patient in a sheet, plunging him in
an icy bath, and letting him dry, still wrapped in the sheet. His fate
took an important turn when, at twenty-three, he was arrested on
charges of "social parasitism." The trial of this "Jewish pygmy in cor-
duroys, this writer of poems where gibberish and pornography fight
for the upper hand" (to quote the prosecution), would normally have
gone unnoticed. But a journalist present at the hearing wrote it all

down in shorthand, the transcript circulated as *samizdat*, and an entire generation was electrified by this exchange: "Who has enrolled
you in the ranks of poets?" the judge asks. Brodsky thinks. "Who
enrolled me in the ranks of the human race? God, perhaps . . ." As
Akhmatova commented: "What a biography they're concocting for
him, our redhead! You'd think he was the one pulling the strings!"

Banished to the Far North near Arkhangel'sk for five years, the
redhead wound up shoveling manure in a tiny village. Frozen earth,
an abstract landscape marked by cold, white expanses, and the rugged
friendship of the villagers: the experience inspired poems that, reach-
ing Leningrad by circuitous routes, became cult objects for all of the
more or less dissident circles in the Union. At the bookstore *41*, Brodsky's name is on everybody's lips, and for someone as competitive as
Eduard, it's irritating. He already didn't think much of the wave of
enthusiasm that swept the country at the publication of *Ivan Denisovich* two years earlier. But okay, Solzhenitsyn could be his father, while
Brodsky's only three years older than him. They should be fighting in
the same league, and that's clearly not the case.

Very early, the young rebel Limonov got into the habit of regarding
the dissidence born in the sixties with a mocking hostility, of pretending to put Solzhenitsyn and Brezhnev, Brodsky and Kosygin, all
in the same boat: important people, officials, sworn authorities, each
pontificating on his own side of the barrier, the first secretary's complete works on dialectical materialism stacked up next to the weighty
tomes by the longbeard who plays the prophet. That's not for us astute
lumpen punks, who've learned a thing or two and know full well that
it's a huge exaggeration to call Soviet society totalitarian: above all it's
chaotic, and anyone who's halfway clever can take advantage of the
chaos and have a good time.

According to the most serious historians (Robert Conquest, Alec
Nove, my mother), twenty million Russians were killed by the Germans during four years of war, and twenty million by their own
government during twenty-five years of Stalin's reign. These two figures are approximations, and the sets they cover must intersect somewhat. But what's important for the story I'm telling is that the first

profoundly marked Eduard's childhood and adolescence, and he did
what he could to ignore the second because, despite his taste for revolt
and his disdain for his parents' mediocre destiny, he remains their
boy: the son of a subordinate Chekist officer, raised in a family that
was spared the major convulsions of history and that, having never
experienced absolute arbitrariness, thought that if people were arrested, well then, there had to be a reason. He remains a Young Pioneer who's proud of his country, its victory over the Fritzes, its empire
that spans two continents and eleven time zones, and the holy fear it
inspires in those Western pansies. He doesn't care about anything,
but he cares about that. When people get to talking about the Gulag
he sincerely thinks they're exaggerating, and that the intellectuals
who denounce it are making a big fuss over something the nonpoliti-
cal prisoners (meaning run-of-the-mill gangsters) tend to be much
more laid back about. Added to that, the dissidents' boat is full as it is.
It's already got its stars; if he joins them he'll never be anything but
second fiddle, and fat chance of him accepting that. So he prefers to
snicker and say that people like Brodsky are full of themselves, that
his banishment to Arkhangel'sk is a nice joke, five years—reduced to
three—of vacation in the countryside with the Nobel Prize at the finish line, even if he doesn't know it yet: well done, Captain Levitin!

10

EDUARD'S NOW BEEN leading the life of a Kharkovite bohemian for
three years and he's starting to feel like he's made the rounds. That
he's surpassed everyone who once impressed him; that he's toppled his
idols one after the other. Motrich, their circle's great poet, is nothing
but a sad boozehound who, past thirty, still waits for his mother to go
out before inviting a couple of friends over for a drink. And when he
does, he has them all drink from the same glass to limit possible break-
ages. Genka the *pleyboi* will spend his life watching *The Last Adventure* without daring to venture anywhere himself. As for the Saltovians,
they're hardly worth wasting your breath on: Kostya's rotting away

in prison, poor Kadik in his factory. When they meet up every now and then he's a bitter, sorry sight. He dreamed of being an artist and living in the center of town; Eduard is an artist and lives in the center of town. So Kadik calls him a parasite, and says that it's all well and good to strut your stuff at the snack bar at the zoo in a chocolate-colored suit with golden thread, but someone's got to tighten the engine screws.

"Someone, sure, but not me," Eduard retorts, cruelly quoting a line penned by an author Kadik introduced him to and whom they both adored in the past: "You remember what Knut Hamsun said? The workers should be lined up and shot."

"He was a fascist, *your* Hamsun," Kadik grumbles.

Eduard shrugs: "Yeah, so what?"

Whether they're thugs or artists, as far as he's concerned, no one who helped the foundry worker Savenko become the poet Limonov has anything more to teach him. He considers them all failures and now makes no bones about saying so to their faces. In one of the books that he'll write later on in Paris about his youth, he reports, with his usual honesty, a conversation he had with a friend during this period. Kindly and somewhat sadly, this friend says that his habit of dividing the world into failures and successes is immature and, most important, will only result in perpetual unhappiness. "Eddie," she says, "is it really so impossible for you to imagine that a life without success or fame might be fulfilling? That you can find success in love, for example, or by building a peaceful, harmonious life with your family?" Yes, for Eddie it's impossible, and he takes pride in this fact. The only life worthy of him is the life of a hero; he wants the whole world to admire him and thinks that any other measures of success—a peaceful, harmonious family life; simple joys; a garden tended far from the public eye—are the self-justifications of the failed, the soup that Lydia serves to poor Kadik to keep him cooped up at home. "Poor Eddie," his friend sighs. Poor you, thinks Eddie. And yes, poor me if I become like you.

"To Moscow! To Moscow!," Chekhov's three sisters sighed from deep in the provinces, and a century later, Eddie dreams of going there himself. Anna's also tempted by the adventure, fearing nevertheless that once there her seductive young scoundrel will find someone better and escape. One evening at *41*, a friend of her ex-husband's comes to visit, a painter born in Kharkov who's long since found a place for himself in the capital. This Brusilovsky is elegant, on a first-name basis with famous people, sometimes even calls them by their nicknames. In Limonov's tongue-in-cheek description, he's the kind of guy who lets on in the provinces that he's very well known in Moscow, and in Moscow that he's very well known in the provinces. Eduard's intimidated and feels uncomfortable, all the more so when Anna pushes him to read his poems to the guest. Adopting a paternal attitude, the artist deigns to compliment them. "But why leave?" he asks. "Life's good in Karkhov. Here you can let your work mature, far from the tainted, superficial hustle and bustle of the capital. The bright lights only make you unhappy. Real life, calm and slow—that's what's best for an artist. You know what? I envy you."

Yeah right, jerk, Eduard thinks to himself. If Kharkov's so great why'd you leave in the first place? Still, like the polite child whose role he plays so well, he keeps his thoughts to himself, and listens deferentially to the Muscovite who after vaunting life in the provinces, starts in on his friends the Smogists. "What, you don't know the Smogists? You don't know the SMOG? The Smartest Modern Organization of Geniuses? You don't know Gubanov? He's only twenty, but everyone who's anyone in Moscow swears by no one but him." And, his eyes half closed, Brusilovsky recites some verses by the young genius: "It is not I who drown in the Kremlin's eyes, but the Kremlin that drowns in mine."

Fucking twenty-year-old Gubanov, Eduard fumes. I'm almost twenty-five, Brodsky's already passed me by, no one in the world knows I exist. Something has to change.

II

Moscow, 1967–1974

೫

I

AROUND THIS TIME my mother, Hélène Carrère d'Encausse, who's since become a renowned historian in her own right, published her first book, *Marxism and Asia*. The fact that my mother had written a book impressed me a lot. I tried to read it, but I got stuck on the very first four words, which read: "Marxism, as everyone knows . . ." This lead-in became a source of hilarity for me and my sisters: "No they don't," we would repeat. "Everyone doesn't know that Marxism. We don't. You should have thought about us!"

The book was about how the Muslim peoples of Central Asia had adapted to the Soviet ideology and power, a subject that had until then been little explored and to which my mother had dedicated her early years as a researcher. I was six months old when she left on a long research trip to Uzbekistan, traveling undercover with a group of scholars who were researching sheep epizootics. From Bukhara, Tashkent, and Samarkand she brought back photos of mosques, of domes, of ascetic, haughty beggars in turbans with jet-black eyes. These photos are bathed in a spellbinding, coppery light that both attracted and frightened me a bit as a child. I would have liked to go with my mother to this mysterious country she called *Youessessar*. I didn't like it when she left; it was hard for me to deal with her being gone, and one of my happiest memories is the day she decided I was big enough to go along with her to a history conference in Moscow.

I remember each detail of this enchanted voyage. My mother took me everywhere. At a lunch given by the French cultural attaché, I sat next to her at the table; I listened politely to the adult conversation, so enthralled that more than forty years later I can still recite like a mantra the names of the other guests. There was a professor of Byzantine history called Gilbert Dagron, a certain Néna (not Nina or Lena), who was the wife of the moviemaker Jacques Baratier, and a boy who, although Russian, had a French name: Vadim Delaunay. Very young, very handsome, very nice, he was a sort of ideal older brother who immediately took a liking to me. If I'd liked games I'm sure he'd have played some with me. Since I liked to read, he asked me about my favorite books. Just like me, he knew absolutely everything about Alexandre Dumas.

That was in 1968; I was ten. That's the year Eduard and Anna moved to Moscow. Changing cities on one's own initiative was no mean feat in the Soviet Union. Ever since the Revolution—and this is still true today—you need a residency permit, the *propiska*, which is difficult to obtain; they in fact didn't get one, which condemned them to a clandestine life, ever at the mercy of subway checkpoints. They lived in small rooms on the outskirts of town and moved often to avoid attracting attention. Their belongings amounted to a suitcase for clothes, a typewriter for poems, and a sewing machine for pants. They also started making two-handled handbags out of cheap calico, copied from a model they'd seen in one of Bakht's old issues of *Paris Match*. Production cost: one ruble. Sale price: three. Their first winter in Moscow was the harshest of the decade: even when they wore all their clothes, pulling piece after piece on, one on top of the other, they were cold all the time; and they were hungry all the time too. At the cafeteria where they ate their meals, they scraped together leftover mashed potatoes and sausage skins from the dirty plates.

Brusilovsky, the Kharkovite painter who'd made a career in Moscow, was, in those early days, both their protector and the center of their social life. Dirt poor as they were, his huge studio with animal hides on the couches, lampshades made of maps, and imported alcohol, was a den of luxury and warmth, and as long as they were prepared to admire his success, Brusilovsky wasn't a bad guy at all. He's the one who recommended that Eduard begin his conquest of Moscow by attending Arseny Tarkovsky's poetry seminar—the way a French Brusilovsky would have sent an ambitious young man from the provinces to hear Gilles Deleuze at the University of Vincennes around the same time. "But there's a hitch," he warned, "it's really crowded. If you're not part of the inner circle you'll never get in. Ask for Rita."

One Monday evening, Eduard slips his notebook of poems into the inside pocket of his skimpy coat—"fish fur," they say in Russian—and takes the subway to the headquarters of the Writers' Union, an old patrician residence that served as the model for the Rostov family's house in *War and Peace*. He's an hour early but there are already lots of people there. Like him they stand around stamping their feet; it's twenty below. He asks for Rita and is told she hasn't arrived yet but that she'll come. She doesn't. A black Volga glides alongside the snowy sidewalk. The master gets out, muffled up in an elegant fur-lined coat, his white hair slicked back, smoking aromatic tobacco from an English pipe. Even his slight limp is distinguished. A disdainful beauty who could be his daughter walks at his side. The doors open and close behind them, together with a handful of the chosen. Eduard says he stayed outside with the rank and file six Mondays in a row. That strikes me as a lot but it's not like him to exaggerate, so I believe him. On the seventh Monday Rita shows up, and he penetrates the inner sanctuary.

Today Arseny Tarkovsky is far less well known than his son Andrei, who at that time was just beginning his career as a genius of world cinema. We'll see soon enough what Eduard thought of the filmmaker Nikita Mikhalkov, but as far as I know he's never mentioned Tarkovsky junior. This surprises me, because even though I admire Tarkovsky as everyone else does, I can easily imagine the brutal paragraph our brutal boy might write about this cultural sacred cow: his grave imperviousness to any form of humor, his stiff-necked spirituality, his contemplative shots invariably accompanied by Bach cantatas . . . Be that as it may, Tarkovsky senior, then a highly reputed poet and one of Marina Tsvetaeva's former lovers, rubs him the wrong way from the moment he sets eyes on him. Not because he looks like a jackass—on the contrary—but because the only possible role up for grabs in his circle is quite obviously that of the devoted disciple. And young though he is, Eduard is clear on that: no thanks.

Every time the group gets together, one member reads his poems. This week it's a certain Mashenka, dressed—and here I'm quoting Eduard—in loose-fitting, shit-colored clothes, with the sort of passionate, melancholic face then common to all female poets in Soviet literary circles. Her poems suit her appearance: modeled on Pasternak's, delicately lyrical, totally predictable. In Tarkovsky's place Eduard would advise her to throw herself under the subway, but the master just warns her in a paternal way against all-too-perfect rhymes and recounts a related anecdote about his late friend Osip Emilyevich. Osip Emilyevich is Mandelstam, and anecdotes about Osip Emilyevich and Marina Ivanovna (Tsvetaeva) are dished up every week. Eduard boils with disappointment and rage. What he wants is to read his poems, and for everyone to be blown away. The next Monday it's the same thing. And the Monday after that. He senses full well that he's not the only one who's frustrated at having to wait endlessly for his turn, so even if a couple of beers at forty-two kopeks a glass means not eating the next day, he goes out for a drink with a few others after the group breaks up and tries to whip up a revolt in the style of one of his heroes, the sailor in *Battleship Potemkin* who shouts, "We've had enough of rotten meat!" At first the poets don't take this provincial boy seriously, with his snub nose and his squeaky voice, but then he takes out his notebook and starts to read and soon the whole group's listening, in an increasingly dumbfounded silence. Legend has it that's how the Parnassians listened to the arrogant, uncouth adolescent with big red hands who'd come up from the Ardennes and went by the name of Arthur Rimbaud. Among those present was Vadim Delaunay.

2

I CAME ACROSS Delaunay's name reading *Book of the Dead*, in which Limonov gathers portraits of famous or obscure people he met during his lifetime, who have one thing in common: they're all dead. He describes Vadim Delaunay as I remember him: very young—barely twenty—very handsome, very kind. Everyone liked him, he says. He was a descendant of the Marquis de Launay, commander of the Bastille garrison in 1789, whose head was paraded around the streets of Paris on a stake. His family emigrated to Russia to escape the French Revolution, and it's no doubt these origins that allowed Vadim to come and go at a foreign diplomat's place, quite an exceptional thing under Brezhnev. He wrote poems and was the youngest of the Smogists, that avant-garde movement that Brusilovsky had blabbered on about to Eduard and Anna in Kharkov. I checked the dates: there's nothing to prevent me from believing that after spending all of lunch discussing the three musketeers with a little French boy at the cultural attaché's, Vadim Delaunay headed off to Arseny Tarkovsky's seminar and witnessed, on that same day, the poet Limonov's début in the Moscow underground.

There were the official writers. The engineers of the soul, as Stalin had called them. Socialist Realists who toed the line. The Sholokhovs, Fadeyevs, and Simonovs, with apartments, dachas, trips abroad, and access to stores reserved for high Party officials, whose complete works were bound, printed in the millions, and crowned with the Lenin Prize. But these privileged writers couldn't have their cake and eat it too. What they gained in comfort and security they lost in self-esteem. In the heroic era of socialist construction they could believe what they wrote and be proud of who they were. But in the days of Brezhnev, of soft Stalinism and the *nomenklatura*, such illusions were no longer possible. They knew full well that they wrote in the service of a corrupt regime, that they'd sold their souls and that everyone else knew it too. Solzhenitsyn, their collective conscience, said it: one of the most pernicious aspects of the Soviet system was that short of being a martyr you couldn't be honest. You couldn't be proud of yourself. To the extent that they weren't half-wits or cynics, the official writers were ashamed of what they did, ashamed of who they were. They were ashamed of writing long articles in *Pravda* denouncing Pasternak in 1957, Brodsky in 1964, Sinyavsky and Daniel in 1966, and Solzhenitsyn in 1969, while deep in their hearts they envied them.

They knew that these authors were the true heroes of their time, the great Russian writers to whom the people turned, as they had turned to Tolstoy in former times, for answers to the questions What is good? What is bad? How should we live? The most spineless of them sighed that if they'd had the choice they'd have followed these high-minded examples, but what can you do, they had families, children still in school, all the excellent reasons collaborators have for not living a life of dissidence. Many became alcoholics; some, like Fadeyev, killed themselves. The cleverest, who were also the youngest, learned to play both sides. That was becoming possible: those in power needed these moderate semidissidents, exportable types of the kind the Communist poet Louis Aragon specialized in welcoming with open arms in France. Yevgeny Yevtushenko, whom we will meet again, excelled in this capacity.

But to do justice to the era, there was also a broad swath of those who were neither heroes, nor sellouts, nor scammers. The people of the underground, who were fortified by two convictions: that the books that were published, the paintings that were exhibited, and the plays that were staged were inevitably compromised and mediocre; and that a true artist was necessarily a failure. The artist was not to blame, it was simply a time in which it was noble to be a failure: as a painter, to earn your living as a night watchman; as a poet, to shovel snow in front of a publishing house where you wouldn't submit your own poems if your life depended on it, and when the director gets out of his Volga and sees you shoveling in the courtyard, he's the one who feels vaguely like a douchebag. To have led a shitty life, but not to have buckled or betrayed. To have kept warm in the company of failures like yourself, spending entire nights in endless argument, passing around the *samizdat* and drinking *samogonka*, vodka made at home in a bathtub from sugar and drugstore alcohol.

All of this was memorialized by one man, Venichka Erofeev. Five years older than Eduard and like him from the provinces, he followed the career path shared by all sensitive types at the time (a fervent, then alcohol-soaked adolescence, a dull job that he gradually stopped turning up for, and a period of living by his wits) before coming to

Moscow in 1969 with a prose manuscript he nevertheless called a "poem," in the manner of Gogol's *Dead Souls*. He was right: *Moscow to the End of the Line* is the grand poem of the *zapoi*—that long-distance bender which life itself tended to resemble under Leonid Brezhnev. It tells of the jinxed, catastrophic odyssey of the drunkard Venichka between Kursk Station in Moscow and the village of Petushki in the far-flung outskirts. Two days of traveling to cover seventy-five miles, without a ticket but with the help of God knows how many pints of booze: vodka, beer, wine, and above all cocktails invented by the narrator, who provides the recipes as the drinks progress. "Tear of a Komsomol girl," for example, is a mixture of lavender toilet water, lemongrass oil, nail polish, mouthwash, and lemon soda. An alcoholic hero, a tanked train ride, pissed passengers: everyone's sloshed in this book that rests on the conviction that "all Russian men worth their salt drink like fish in the sea." Out of despair, and because in a world of deceit only drunkenness does not lie. The emphatic, deliberately burlesque style parodies Soviet doublespeak; the sentences give a new twist to quotes from Lenin, Mayakovsky, the masters of Socialist Realism. All of the "under," as the members of the underground called themselves, recognized themselves in this treatise on the spirit of "Why bother?" and the alcoholic coma. Recopied diligently, read and recited in the circles Eduard traveled in, translated in the West, *Moscow to the End of the Line* has become a sort of classic and Venichka a legend: a metaphysical failure, a sublime drunk, the spectacular incarnation of everything powerfully negative that the era had to offer. People went on pilgrimages to Petushki Station and still do; a couple of years ago a statue was even erected in his honor.

A punk ahead of his time, Venichka was disdain and resignation personified. In that sense he was the opposite of the dissidents, who persisted in believing in the future and the power of truth. Forty years later these distinctions become somewhat blurred, and certainly the members of the underground read the dissidents and passed around their writings, but with rare exceptions they didn't take the same risks or—above all—share the same faith. For them Solzhenitsyn was like the statue of a commander whom as luck would have it they had no chance of running into: he lived in the provinces, in Ryazan, worked day and night, and only mixed with former *zeks* whose accounts—the material on which *The Gulag Archipelago* would be based—he gathered with immense caution. He had no contact with the small, gregarious, warm, taunting world in which Venichka Erofeev was a hero and Edichka Limonov a rising star, and if he had he would have disdained it. His determination and courage were vaguely inhuman, inasmuch as he expected from others what he demanded of himself. He considered it cowardice to write about anything but the camps: that amounted to *hushing up* the camps.

In August 1968, a few months after my lunch with the French cultural attaché, the Soviet Union invaded Czechoslovakia and bloodily crushed the Prague Spring. To protest the invasion, a group of dissidents had the extravagant audacity to stage a demonstration on Red Square. There were eight of them, whose names I make a point of recording here: Larisa Bogoraz, Pavel Litvinov, Vladimir Dremliuga, Tatiana Baeva, Viktor Fainberg, Konstantin Babitsky, Natalya Gorbanevskaya—who came pushing her baby in a carriage—and Vadim Delaunay. The latter bore a placard on which he'd written the words FOR YOUR FREEDOM AND OURS. No sooner were the demonstrators arrested than they were condemned to prison sentences of varying lengths: Vadim got two and a half years. After his release and new tangles with the KGB, the young man with whom I'd so happily chatted about Athos, Porthos, and Aramis emigrated. He moved to Paris, where I could have seen him again, if I'd known. He died in 1983, aged thirty-five.

3

EDUARD KNEW ALL these people well. They take up a lot of space in his *Book of the Dead*, because with the help of alcohol most of them died young. He liked Vadim Delaunay a lot, Erofeev much less. His supposed masterpiece struck him as overrated, as did *The Master and*

Margarita by Bulgakov, whose posthumous cult was then growing. Eduard doesn't like cults dedicated to anyone but himself. He thinks the admiration paid to them is stolen from him.

The worst in this respect was Brodsky. Back from his exile in the great North, he lived in Leningrad but came to Moscow from time to time and appeared, though sparingly, in the kitchens of the underground. He was literally venerated. Everyone knew his poems, his rejoinders at his trial, and the list of personalities who'd supported him—from Shostakovich to Sartre to T. S. Eliot—by heart. Dressed in baggy pants and an old sweater full of holes, his long, tangled hair already thinning, he arrived at parties late and left early, staying just long enough for people to notice his discretion and the simplicity of his manners. He always sat in the darkest corner, and everyone circled around him. That wasn't at all to the liking of the young poet Limonov, whose insolence and crushed-velvet jackets had made him the star until Brodsky appeared on the scene. To reassure himself, he tried his best to believe that Brodsky's aura wasn't natural, that he'd *created* a persona for himself. My friend Pierre Pachet, who knew him a little, thinks there's some truth to this remark. Then again, he says, who doesn't do the same? What simplicity is truly simple? Brodsky, in any event, had securely settled into the posture of an uncontrollable— not even a dissident; less anti-Soviet than a-Soviet—a rebel. Unperturbed, he rejected the publication offers that his more obsequious colleagues like Yevtushenko dangled in front of him, with their promises of "Join us, just say the word." This perpetual conscientious objection became so annoying that the KGB finally ordered him to pack his bags in 1972. Good riddance, Eduard must have thought.

Luckily for his sense of pride, there were plenty of mere mortals in the small world of the underground with whom he and Anna made friends—lots of friends. The best among them, the most valiant of these underground artists, was the painter Igor Voroshilov, a lyrical and sentimental lush whose specialty was *labardan*, a dish for the penniless made from fish heads. Eduard and Anna shared everything with him: bottles, rough patches, and the rare summertime house-sitting godsend, when people they knew went off on vacation and asked them to look after their apartments. Eduard liked him all the more because he wasn't remotely jealous of him, as evidenced by the following story. One night, Igor calls him for help: he's going to commit suicide. Eduard crosses Moscow to talk him out of it and finds him drunk, of course. They talk. Igor cries a lot and explains that he's shed his illusions, that he feels like—what's more he knows—he's a second-rate painter. Eduard takes this seriously: even if you don't commit suicide—and Igor isn't about to—it's terrible to come to terms with the fact that you're a second-rate artist, and maybe even a second-rate human being. That's what he himself dreads the most in the world. And, he adds, the worst thing is that Igor's right. The market will confirm it: he was the best of guys, but a second-, even third-rate painter.

What I find terrible is the cruel calmness with which Eduard states this. Later he'll meet a few figures of the New York underground— Andy Warhol, people at the Factory, beatniks like Allen Ginsberg and Lawrence Ferlinghetti—and even if they don't make a very big impression on him, he recognizes that their names will go down in history. It makes sense when people say: I knew them when. Whereas, he says, nothing at all remains of the Smogists, of their leader Lenya Gubanov, of Igor Voroshilov, Vadim Delaunay, Kholin, Sapgir, and others about whom I took down pages of notes whose details I will spare you. An outdated avant-garde in a stagnant little fishbowl; extras in a small chapter of Eduard's turbulent life. But they spent their whole lives in this fishbowl, and that's sad.

This blend of disdain and envy doesn't make my hero very likable, I know. And I know several people in Moscow who, having rubbed shoulders with him in those days, remember an unbearable young man. These same people acknowledge, nevertheless, that he was a good tailor, a very talented poet, and, in his way, an honest fellow. Arrogant but utterly loyal. Pitiless but attentive, curious, and even helpful. After all, even if he thought that his friend Igor was right to consider himself a washout, he spent the night taking great pains to try to lift his spirits. Even those who didn't like him thought he was someone you could count on, someone who didn't leave people in the lurch, who took care of them if they were sick or unhappy, even if he didn't have anything good to say about them. And I think a lot of self-proclaimed humanists with nothing but kindness and compassion on their lips are in fact more selfish and more indifferent than Eduard, who has spent his whole life casting himself in the role of the villain. Just one detail: when he emigrates he'll leave behind thirty or so collections, which he himself compiled and bound: works by *other poets*. Because, he says in passing, "It's part of my program in life to show an interest in other people."

4

THEY'VE SETTLED INTO life in Moscow, orders for pants are flooding in, they're leading quite the happy bohemian existence, but what Anna was most worried about when they left Kharkov is coming to pass: the young scoundrel doesn't cheat on her, because conjugal fidelity is part of his moral code, but he's seductive, bursting with health and happy to be alive, and she's a fat wreck of a woman, slowly yielding to the madness she's long kept at bay. She makes scenes, and it's not the first time. Worse still: her mind goes blank, she has periodic nervous breakdowns and starts falling down in the street. One day she stares at him and says, "You're going to kill me, I know it, you're going to kill me."

She ends up in a psychiatric ward for a couple of weeks. Most of the time when he comes to see her she's haggard and dazed by strong sedatives, but occasionally he finds her tied to her bed because she's fought with other inmates—you think of them as inmates, not patients, that's how much like a prison it is.

When she gets out, she's sent to rest with friends of friends who have a small house by the sea in Latvia. Eduard accompanies her and gets her settled in; behind her back, he and Dagmar, who owns the house, settle on when she should take her medication. Dagmar's father, a bearded old painter with the head of a satyr, offers to teach her how to paint with watercolors to calm her down. Good idea, Eduard agrees, and he heads back to Moscow, where, on June 6, 1971, he goes to his friend Sapgir's birthday party.

Like Brusilovsky, Sapgir is one of the few people they know who has done pretty well for himself. The author of stories full of bears and water nymphs read by children across the country, he's got a nice apartment, a dacha, and friends in both the underground and the world of official culture. At his place you meet people like the Mikhalkov brothers, Nikita and Andrei, both talented filmmakers. Famous abroad, they maneuver between obedience and audacity as tactfully as their father, a famous poet himself, does. Between the dawn and twilight of his long career, this father will compose national anthems for both Stalin and Putin. Eduard detests the Mikhalkovs, just as he detests anyone who inherits anything. Another of Sapgir's friends is a similar type: Viktor, a balding, elegant, high-cultural apparatchik in his fifties, who arrives that same day in a white Mercedes and introduces his new fiancée, Tanya, to the crowd.

A lanky twenty-year-old brunette dressed in a leather miniskirt, tights, and high heels, Tanya's the kind of girl Eduard's only ever seen on the covers of foreign magazines like *Elle* and *Harper's Bazaar* that people pass around under their coats; never in real life. He's thunderstruck, afraid to go anywhere near her. When she looks at him, he buries his nose in his plate. Finally, amused by his timidity, she's the one who goes up and speaks to him. A couple of weeks later she'll tell him that with his white jeans and red shirt, unbuttoned to reveal his tanned chest, he was the only person among the well-fed, blasé group who was really alive. He breaks a couple of Venetian glasses while uncorking a bottle of champagne, making her shriek with laughter. There's nothing particularly astonishing about the fact that he's a poet; the streets are full of them. But after egging him on to recite one of his verses, she opens her eyes wide. At Viktor's prompting she's also written a few poems: they're bad but Eduard doesn't say so. He also doesn't say that he finds her little dog grotesque. They spend the time talking, laughing, and stuffing the little dog with caviar, while Viktor and the other important people his age compare privileges and congratulate one another loudly. When they leave, Viktor asks Tanya if she had a good time in the tone of a father picking his daughter up after kindergarten. Sapgir, who's more attentive and has been watching the two young people out of the corner of his eye, takes Eduard aside: "Don't do anything stupid," he says. "She's not for you."

At the beginning of the summer, Viktor goes to Poland to give a series of lectures on socialist art's exalted goal of fostering friendship among peoples. Eduard, meanwhile, has a stroke of luck: friends of his are going to spend some time at their dacha and leave him to look after their three-bedroom apartment in the heart of the city.

It's Tanya who beds him—out of curiosity—rather than the other way around, and the first time is nothing special. He'll make up for it later, but at twenty-seven his sex life has been anything but sensational: his first flings in Saltov were followed by six years of monogamy with a woman who didn't really turn him on and who was less a lover than a partner in survival. For him, Tanya's an extraterrestrial. Her willowy, luxurious body, her incredibly soft skin without a single rough spot, wrinkle, or blemish: it's what he's dreamed of all his life without ever knowing it existed. Now that he holds her in his arms, she's got to belong to him and only him, forever. Unfortunately, he quickly understands that she doesn't see things the same way at all. She has taken advantage of Viktor's absence to sleep with this muscular, energetic boy who's both timid and insolent, but in her milieu, sleeping with someone doesn't really mean much. Everyone more or less sleeps with everyone else, and she sees no reason to hide the fact that the young poet isn't the only one she finds attractive: she's also got her eye on an actor, one of the privileged bunch who drink champagne and drive around in a Mercedes.

Days pass and there's still no news from Tanya; Eduard is in agony. One night he can't take it anymore and goes over to her place. He rings, his heart thumping. No one's home. He decides to wait on the landing. It's summer, the building is occupied by *nomenklatura* who've all left for the countryside, so there are no suspicious neighbors to poke their noses out and ask what he's doing there. One in the morning, then two, soon the whole night's gone by. He falls asleep, wakes up in fits and starts, his forehead on his knees. Just before dawn he hears Tanya laughing in the lobby three floors down, a man's laughter answering hers.

He hides on the landing one floor up, from where he sees the elevator stop and her get out, still laughing, with the well-known actor who kisses her on the mouth as they enter the apartment. Eduard's in pain, it seems to him he's never been in this much pain in his entire life. For a guy from Saltov, the sole remedy for such suffering is to do what he didn't have the chance to do to Sveta and her dimwit Shurik ten years earlier: kill them both, her and her lover. He's still got his knife on him. He takes it out, walks down to their floor, rings again. No answer. There's no way they could be screwing already. He rings again and again, then bangs on the door with menacing thuds the way the Chekists do when they come to arrest people in the middle of the night. Times may be tame, but still, Tanya gets scared. He hears her come to the door. Her voice shaking, she asks who's there. "Eddie?" Reassured, she laughs. "Do you know what time it is? You're nuts!" She refuses to let him in, asks him to go, nicely at first, then not so nicely. Fair enough! He slashes his wrists on the landing. There's no alternative but to open the door and take care of him. They carry him into the kitchen, where the little dog happily licks the blood as it drips from his wrist.

Any other girl would have broken up with him on the spot. Not Tanya, who's less put off by this scene than impressed by the young poet's love for her. No one in her circle knows how to love like that: so savagely, so intransigently. He takes everything too seriously, but compared to him everyone else seems lukewarm. Moreover, after the first flights of emotion he turns out to be a remarkable lover, and they spend the summer screwing every which way, in every hole; soon she looks forward to their meetings as impatiently as he does. Viktor returns from his tour in Poland, and they go back to the apartment where Eduard's charged with watering the plants. Summer in Moscow is terribly hot. They spend all afternoon naked, taking showers together and turning themselves on gazing at his tanned body and her very white one in the mirrors. At the end of August the owners come back from their dacha and there's no getting around letting them have their apartment back, but, fresh stroke of luck, a friend is looking to sublet her room. One hundred square feet just five minutes from Tanya and Viktor's place on the other side of Novodevichy Convent—a blessing like that is definitely nothing to sneeze at. For Eduard it's the hand of fate, and when Anna gets back from Latvia he does something he's normally loath to do: he lies. He says that the room where they were staying before the summer is no longer free, and that he's sleeping on a couch at some friends' place while he waits for something better. Unfortunately, he says, he can't ask her over, but in the meantime he's found her a place on another couch with other friends.

He could talk to her, tell her he's fallen in love with someone else. He should, the lie weighs heavily on him, but he doesn't dare: he's afraid of her reaction, of her madness, of destroying her. Nevertheless Anna's looking great, she's relaxed, the summer on the Baltic has clearly done her good. But he feels she's changed, and not just because she's doing better. This impression is confirmed when they go to bed: she no longer moves the same way. As in love as he is with another woman, it still bothers him. The next morning, while she's still sleeping, he digs around in her suitcase and discovers a notebook in which she's been keeping a diary. She talks about nature, the sea, the flowers, her new calling as a painter—and, in passing, she reveals her wild sensual passion for Dagmar's father, the bearded old artist with a satyr's head. Eduard is devastated, beside himself with jealousy. When she wakes up, Anna goes about her business in the room: how calm she is, the lying cheat! What a clear conscience she seems to have!

He says nothing, but persuades her to go back to Kharkov for a while, to give him time to find a room suitable for the two of them. The next day he goes with her to the station; the whole time he can't stop thinking about the knobby old painter penetrating her fat, deformed body, and not even the knowledge that he possesses the slender, luxurious body of the little rich girl can calm him: the fact is he knows full well that he doesn't possess it, that she does what she wants with it without giving him a second thought. It's torture. He buys Anna something to eat and drink for her journey and settles her in. In principle this is just a temporary separation, but he knows it's over. She'll never come back to Moscow.

All that fall he's consumed by his passion for Tanya. They take long walks in Novodevichy Cemetery—a Mecca of literary pilgrimages for fans of Chekhov and other bearded nineteenth-century authors. Since she's in love with a poet, Tanya thinks she should show thoughtful reverence at their graves, at which point he—clean-shaven, young, and full of life, not a fan of literary pilgrimages nor of bearded nineteenth-century authors—gives her a delicious shock by putting his hand on her ass. The little dog that drank his blood trots along behind them and whines dolefully while they have sex in the single bed in his little room in the *kommunalka*. As for Tanya, she comes at full volume. The babushka next door later gives them bawdy winks. "You can see right away she's not from your world," she tells Eduard, "but it's just as clear that you've got what it takes in your pants. You must do things to her that her rich-boy lovers don't even know exist." Eduard likes the babushka, and he likes playing the big-dicked stud who drives the princess wild with pleasure and her well-heeled suitors crazy with jealousy. They're all in love with her, but it's him she loves, and it's for him that she decides to leave Viktor over the course of the winter. It's him she marries, in the church. And it's with him that she consents to live in poverty in a little room, or in apartments lent to them by friends.

He's won. Everyone envies him: both in the little world of the underground where no one has ever seen such a beautiful, sophisticated woman, and in the exclusive circles where the rich are shocked to see their princess ravished by this insolent poet in white jeans. For several seasons he and Tanya rule over the Moscow bohemia. If there ever was something resembling a Soviet glam scene in the seventies, in the grayest days of the gray Brezhnev era, they were it. There's a photo that shows him, long-haired, standing triumphantly in what he calls his "national hero vest"—a patchwork of 114 pieces of multicolored cloth he's sewn together, and, at his feet, Tanya, naked: ravishing, slender, with the small, light, firm breasts that drive him wild. He's kept this photo all his life, carried it everywhere he's gone, and hung it on the wall like an icon wherever he's set up camp. It's his lucky talisman. It says that no matter what happens, no matter how low he stoops, he was once that man. And she was his woman.

5

PARALLEL LIVES OF illustrious men: Aleksandr Solzhenitsyn and Eduard Limonov both left their country in the spring of 1974, but the departure of the first made more of an international splash than that of the second. Since Khrushchev's fall, an open conflict had broken out between the authorities and the prophet of Ryazan, who, thanks to a typically Soviet contradiction, was considered the most important writer of his era and as a result was banned from publishing. I know few tales as beautiful as that of this solitary, medieval, rustic man who escaped both cancer and the camps, and who was filled with the certainty that he would see the truth triumph in his lifetime, because those who lie are afraid and he was not. This man who, when his col-leagues voted to ban him from the Writers' Union because, among other reasons, "his works fail to deal with the topic of comradeship between writers," was able to respond tranquilly: "Once and for all, I proclaim the established literature, the magazines and novels that are published, null and void. It's not that talents cannot grow in this field (there are some). But they are doomed to perish because the soil is in-fertile, because there is a consensus *not to say* the vital truth, the truth

that jumps out at you without there even being any need for literature." That vital truth is of course the Gulag. It's also that the Gulag
existed before and after Stalin, that it's not a sickness of the Soviet
system but its essence, its purpose even. Solzhenitsyn spent ten years
secretly writing up the accounts of 227 former *zeks* in his tiny script,
burying and microfilming his manuscripts to have them sent to the
West, putting together the monumental *Gulag Archipelago*, which was
ultimately published in France and the United States and read out on
Radio Liberty at the beginning of 1974.

Yuri Andropov, then director of the KGB, understood that this
bomb was more dangerous for the regime than the entire American
arsenal, and took the initiative by convening an urgent meeting of the
Politburo. The minutes of this crisis meeting were made public in 1992
when Boris Yeltsin declassified the archives. It's a genuine drama that
deserves to be acted out onstage. By then Brezhnev has more or less
lost his hard edge and doesn't really see the danger. Of course he's in
favor of denouncing this attack against "all we hold most sacred" as
bourgeois propaganda, but, ultimately, he prefers to let things ride:
this'll all die down, just like the protests against the invasion of
Czechoslovakia. Podgorny, the chairman of the Presidium, doesn't
share his fatalism. Fuming with rage, he deplores that the system is so
neutered that the most reasonable solution is no longer even considered: a bullet in the back of the head, period. Look at Chile—there
they don't pussyfoot around. Sure, things may have gone a bit too far
under Stalin, but now they're being taken to the opposite extreme.
More diplomatic, Kosygin proposes sending Solzhenitsyn up past
the Arctic Circle. As these tirades progress one imagines Andropov
sighing and looking up at the ceiling, then he finally takes the floor:
"All of that is well and good, my dear friends, but it's too late. The time
for a bullet in the head was ten years ago; now the whole world is
watching, impossible to touch a hair on Solzhenitsyn's head. No, the
only option is expulsion."

Solzhenitsyn is destined for big things: forcibly put on a plane bound
for Frankfurt two days after this meeting and, on his arrival, greeted

by Willy Brandt like a head of state. But what his expulsion shows, and what so rightly grieved the irate Podgorny, is that the Soviet system had lost the will and the power to inspire fear. It now bared its teeth without true conviction, and instead of persecuting unruly elements, it preferred to let them go make trouble elsewhere. Elsewhere meant in Israel, a destination for which passports were liberally distributed in those years. In principle you had to be Jewish to get one, but the authorities weren't exactly sticklers; they tended to consider any known pain in the ass a kind of Jew—making Limonov eligible.

When I asked him about the circumstances of his departure, he told me about being summoned to the Lubyanka, the Moscow headquarters of the KGB: a sinister building if ever there was one, a building you entered without being sure you'd ever leave and whose very mention made everyone turn pale—everyone except him, of course. He said he went there with his hands in his pockets all but whistling: his father was one of the boys, and the Chekists, in any case, weren't as malicious as the dissidents made them out to be, easygoing if lethargic officials who could be won over with a good joke. He also mentioned having met none less than Andropov's daughter through a college classmate of hers. She was quite pretty, in fact, and he had her in stitches the whole night, first flirting a bit with her and then finally putting her to the test: could she persuade her dear old dad to let her take a look at the file of the poet Savenko-Limonov? She gallantly took up the challenge and a few days later—although there's no telling if she was telling the truth or if she was just teasing him—she came back with the answer: "Antisocial malcontent, staunch anti-Soviet."

What is certain is that unlike other antisocial, anti-Soviet malcontents like Brodsky or Solzhenitsyn, who had to be kicked out by force and would have given an arm and a leg to stay in their native land, speaking their native tongue, Eduard and Tanya *wanted* to emigrate. Eduard because, according to a pattern we're now starting to recognize, he was convinced that after seven years he'd made the rounds of the Moscow underground, just as seven years earlier he'd made the rounds of the Kharkov decadents, and Tanya because her head was filled with foreign magazines, with their stars and famous models, and she wondered, "Why not me?"

Sometimes she dragged Eduard to visit an old woman called Lilya Brik, who was the great-aunt of one of her friends. A living legend, Tanya said respectfully, because she'd been Mayakovsky's muse in her youth. And her sister, what's more, had been Aragon's muse in France under the name of Elsa Triolet. It was a real mystery to Eduard how men of that caliber could have been ensnared by two such plump, ugly little women.

These visits bore him. The only living legend that interests him is himself, and he likes neither the past nor these apartments so typical of the old Russian intelligentsia, full of books and paintings, samovars and carpets and dust-covered medicine on the bedside tables. What he likes is a chair and a mattress, and even those he considers more of a luxury than anything else: on a military campaign all you need is a good coat. But Tanya puts her foot down, because she loves celebrities and because the octogenarian Lily flatters her shamelessly, always raving about how beautiful she is. She promises that as soon as Tanya lands, the West will be at her feet. If they go to Paris they'll have to go see Aragon, and if they go to New York, her old friend Tatiana, who'd also been Mayakovsky's mistress back in the old days and who now reigned over the fashionable set in Manhattan. Each time they come she shows Tanya a beautiful, heavy bracelet that Mayakovsky had given her. Twisting and sliding it on her desiccated old wrist, she smiles: "You'll be the one to wear it when I'm dead, my dove. The day before you leave it'll be yours."

For people like us, who come and go and take planes as we please, it's hard to understand that for a Soviet citizen the word *emigrate* meant a voyage of no return. It's hard for us to understand the word, as simple as the blow of an ax: "forever." And I'm not talking about defectors, artists like Nureyev and Baryshnikov who took advantage of a tour abroad to demand political asylum: those of whom it was said in the West that they had "chosen freedom" and whom *Pravda* called "traitors to their country." I'm talking about people who emigrated legally. That had become possible in the seventies, though it was difficult, and applicants knew that if it worked they could never return. Even to visit, even for a short trip, even to kiss a dying mother. That made you think twice; it's why relatively few people wanted to leave, and it's no doubt what the authorities were counting on when they opened this safety valve.

The last days were poignant. Laughing with a friend, sitting under a linden tree, riding up the escalator between the rows of lamps at the Kropotkinskaya subway station and emerging into the open air among the flower kiosks, full of the smells of Moscow in the spring. Everything you'd done a thousand of times without a second thought you were now doing, you realized in a kind of stupor, for the very last time. Each part of this so familiar world would soon be definitively out of reach: a memory, a turned page that you could no longer flip back to, the stuff of incurable nostalgia. Leaving this life that you'd known for so long for another of which you knew nothing but the high hopes you placed in it was a way of dying. If they didn't curse you, those left behind tried their best to be happy for you, but they were like the faithful accompanying their nearest and dearest to the doors of a better world: do you rejoice because those leaving will be happier there than here, or cry because you'll never see them again? When in doubt you could always drink. Some of these farewells turned into such frenetic *zapoi*s that those would-be emigrants only emerged from them, bleary-eyed, after the plane had taken off. There wouldn't be another one, the door had closed and wouldn't open again, nothing for it but to have another drink, without knowing if it was to drown a despair that was now beyond remedy or, as their friends kept repeating with a prod in the ribs, to thank their lucky stars that they'd escaped such a close shave. "We're better off here, aren't we? Together. At home."

As unsentimental as Eduard is, as much confidence as he had in the radiant future that awaited him and Tanya in America, he must inevitably have felt this wrenching of the soul. I imagine he went with her to say goodbye to her family—a family of soldiers, but of far higher rank than his own—and I know for certain that she took the train to Kharkov with him and met not only Venyamin and Raya—who were flabbergasted by their son's boldness and dismayed to be losing him—but also Anna, who, on learning through the grapevine that her former companion was passing through, showed up at the Savenkos's place to pitch a hysterical fit in the best Dostoyevskian tradition: throwing herself at the feet of the seductive girl who stole her young scoundrel, kissing her hands through tears, repeating that she's beautiful, that she's good, that she's noble, that she's everything that God and the angels love, while she, Anna Moiseyevna, is a poor, ugly, fat Jew, lost and unworthy of existing or touching the hem of her dress. Not wanting to be outdone, and perhaps remembering Nastasya Filipovna's manners in *The Idiot*, Tanya lifted up the poor woman, kissed her elatedly, and with a theatrical gesture removed the beautiful bracelet she was wearing, a family heirloom, insisting that Anna take it to remember her by, topping it all off with "Pray for me, dear, dear soul! Promise me that you'll pray for me!"

In the train on the way back, as his parents' slumped silhouettes receded on the platform, both waving their handkerchiefs in the certainty that they would never see their only son again, it crossed Eduard's mind that if Tanya had been bold enough to give her beautiful bracelet to crazy old Anna, it was because she was counting on another one, more beautiful still.

The day before they left they went to say goodbye to Lilya Brik, and the old bat really did provide them with the letters she'd promised ("I entrust you," she wrote to her former rival Tatiana, "with two marvelous children. Take care of them. Be their fairy godmother"). But for the first time since they'd started coming to see her she wasn't wearing her precious bracelet. And that whole visit, she never once brought it up.

III

New York,
1975–1980

☙

I

FRENCH PEOPLE ARRIVING in New York for the first time aren't surprised, or if they are it's because the city is so much like what they've seen in films. For Eduard and Tanya, children of the Cold War and a country where American films are banned, all the familiar imagery is new: the steam rising from the manholes, the metal fire escapes clinging like spiders to the dirty brick buildings, the jumble of neon signs on Broadway, the skyline seen from a field in Central Park, the nonstop hustle and bustle, the sirens of the police cars, the yellow taxis, the black shoeshine boys, the people having conversations with themselves on the street without anyone stopping to talk some sense into them. Coming from Moscow, it's like stepping out of a black-and-white movie into Technicolor.

Their first few days they walk all over Manhattan, clasping each other's hands, each other's waists, looking around greedily, then looking at each other, bursting into laughter and kissing even more greedily. They buy a map of the city in a bookstore the likes of which they've never seen: instead of being locked away behind the counters like drugs at a pharmacy, the books are at your fingertips. You can pick them up, flip through them, even read them—all without having to buy them. As for the map, they're blown away by its accuracy. If it says that the second street on the right is St. Mark's Place, well, then it's St. Mark's Place, something that's inconceivable in the Soviet Union where city maps are inevitably wrong—that is, if you can find one at all—either because they date from the last war or because they anticipate large-scale construction projects and show the city as it should be in fifteen years, or simply because they're designed to mislead visitors, who are always more or less suspected of espionage. They walk and walk, venturing into boutiques that are way too expensive, diners, fast food restaurants, and small movie theaters with double features, some of which show porno films, and that too enchants them. She gets turned on in the seat next to him and tells him, and he makes her come. When the lights come up they look around and see an audience of loners who were probably more turned on by Tanya's moans than by the film, and Eduard bursts with pride: at having such a beautiful wife, at being the envy of these poor bastards, at being in the theater not because he's sexually deprived but because he has that taste for curious and erotic experiences that denotes the true libertine.

She spoke a little English when they left Moscow; he didn't speak a word and could only read the Cyrillic alphabet. But during the two months they spent in a transit center for emigrants in Vienna, where they had to use every last ounce of cunning to avoid ending up in the line for Israel, they picked up the basics and learned to get by on the broken English that a surprising number of foreigners make do with in New York. Plus they're good-looking, young, and in love, and people are happy to lend them a smile and help them out. When they walk arm in arm down a snowy street in Greenwich Village, they know they look like Bob Dylan and his girlfriend on the cover of the album containing "Blowin' in the Wind." Back in Kharkov this record was the most precious treasure in Kadik's collection. He must still have it, given what good care he took of it, and sometimes, after he's done at the Hammer and Sickle, he must still listen to it while Lydia's back is turned. Does he think about his audacious friend Eddie, who left for distant shores? Of course he thinks about him, and will do all his life, with admiration and bitterness. Poor Kadik, Eduard thinks. And the more he thinks of Kadik and all those he left behind in Saltov, Kharkov, and Moscow, the more he thanks heaven he is who he is.

They have two contacts: Tatiana Liberman, Lilya Brik's friend and ex-rival, and Brodsky, whose address is passed out to anyone who emigrates to New York from the little world of the underground, the way poor peasants from Brittany or Auvergne who seek their fortune in Paris are given the address of a cousin who's apparently made it big there. Because after being expelled three years earlier, Brodsky's become the darling of the entire Western high intellectual *nomenklatura*, from Octavio Paz to Susan Sontag. He did a lot to open the eyes of his new friends—though for the most part they're still Communist sympathizers—to the reality of the Soviet regime, and even the fanfare that greeted Solzhenitsyn's arrival didn't weaken his position, because Solzhenitsyn is terrible company while Brodsky, with his air of an absentminded professor, proves to be the king of poetic conversation and a master at befriending the greats of the literary world. Like the Jorge Luis Borges interview, the Brodsky interview became a literary genre in itself. Even today the legendary Russian Samovar on Fifty-second Street in Manhattan is proud of his patronage. The Russian émigrés in New York respectfully called him *nachal'nik*, the boss—what the Chekists, incidentally, called Stalin.

He no longer remembers exactly who Eduard is when he calls— so many of these Russians who can't even speak English are sent his way—nevertheless he arranges to meet in a tearoom in the East Village, a cozy, dimly lit place that does its best to exude a *Mitteleuropa* charm conducive to long discussions on literature that always cover the same ground: whom do you prefer, Dostoyevsky or Tolstoy, Akhmatova or Tsvetaeva; these are his favorite sport. Just like the apartments of old Moscow intellectuals, it's the sort of place that our Limonov detests, and things don't get any better when he finds out they don't serve alcohol. Luckily Tanya's there too. Brodsky likes pretty women, she turns on the charm—without having to force herself, she later admits—and they start talking, feeling more and more relaxed. Eduard observes the poet from the sidelines. His reddish, disorderly hair already going gray, he smokes and coughs a lot. They say he's in poor health, heart trouble. Hard to believe he's not yet forty, you'd think he was fifteen years older. And although he's not much younger than Brodsky, in his presence, Eduard feels like he's been assigned the role of the petulant child before the wise old man. The wise but cheeky old man, that is, who's much more friendly and approachable than he was in Moscow, even if you sense behind his good cheer the condescension of someone who's made it and is well aware that although one wave may follow the next, the newcomers will still have to row for a long time in their lifeboat before they can compete with him for a first-class cabin.

"America's a jungle, you know," he says, turning finally to Eduard. "To survive here you need the skin of an elephant. That's what I've got. You, I'm not so sure." You old prick, Eduard thinks with a benign smile. He's waiting for the rest: the tips, the contacts, and it all comes without their having to ask. Eduard needs to earn a living. Since he knows how to write, he should go see Moishe Borodatikh, editor in chief of *Novoye russkoye slovo*, a Russian daily for émigrés. "Not the kind of paper that chases Watergate scoops," Brodsky quips, "but it could help you out while you're learning English." And if the opportunity strikes he'll take Eduard and Tanya to see his friends the Libermans, where they'll meet everyone . . .

As an invitation it's pretty vague, and Eduard takes a great deal of pleasure in saying that they're already in contact with the Libermans, in fact they're even going to a party at their place next week. A silence, then Brodsky concludes cheerfully: "Well then, we'll see each other there."

The thing to do would be to describe the party at the Libermans' as Flaubert describes the ball at the château La Vaubyessard in *Madame Bovary*, right down to the smallest spoon and dimmest lamp. That's what I want to do, but words fail me. Let's just say that the party takes place in a penthouse on the Upper East Side, and that the guest list is an ideal blend of wealth, power, beauty, glory, and talent—in short, a soiree straight out of *Vogue*'s society pages. As soon as they're introduced by the butler, Tanya decides that from now on her goal in life is to make a place for herself in this world; at the same moment, Eduard decides that his is to reduce it to ashes. Still, before burning it all down, it sure is great to see it up close, great to think that the kid from Saltov has made it this far. No one in Saltov has seen or ever will see such an interior. None of the Libermans' guests has the slightest idea what Saltov is like. He alone knows both worlds, that's his strength.

No sooner has he let this proud thought go to his head than he's brought down to earth when he notices, in the middle of one of the other rooms, at the center of attention—at the center of everything, in fact, because wherever he goes he's at the center—no less a man than Rudolf Nureyev. Rotten luck: just when you think you're a Mongol conqueror whose calm, cruel, and swarthy presence alone will soon make a mockery of the blandness of all these exquisitely civilized people, you run into Nureyev, who comes from even farther away, from the murky depths of a backwater in Bashkiria, who's lifted himself to remarkable heights and is now the radiant and demonic embodiment of barbarian seduction. Others do their best to approach him and catch his eye, Tanya would clearly like to try. Not Eduard, who leaves the room in a disgruntled fit and finally takes refuge in the bathroom, whose walls feature drawings by Dalí dedicated to Tatiana Liberman.

And speak of the devil, there's Tatiana, who's making a big fuss over the two wonderful children with a kind of Slavic exuberance that's only a little over the top. She's not young, but she's younger than Lilya Brik and infinitely better preserved. She emigrated at the right time and became one of France's most celebrated beauties in the twenties. An eccentric woman with a cigarette holder and a Louise Brooks hairstyle in the days of jazz and Scott Fitzgerald, she married a French aristocrat, was widowed during the war, and got married once again, this time to a Ukrainian émigré, Alex Liberman, whom she followed to New York, where he became the artistic director of Condé Nast Publications—that is, of *Vogue* and *Vanity Fair*, to name two of the corporation's flagships. From this command post, Alex and his wife have for the last thirty years been making and breaking the careers of photographers, models, and even artists who at first glance have nothing to do with the fashion world. They made Brodsky's, Tatiana confesses to the young Limonovs. Although he had the good sense to steer clear of Israel when he left the USSR, the poor fellow followed who knows what silly advice and accepted an invitation from the University of Michigan at Ann Arbor, where he was almost buried for life among pipe-smoking, cardigan-sporting professors of

Russian literature: a dreadful fate from which the Libermans saved him by bringing him to New York and introducing him to their friends. "And now you see . . . ," she says, indicating him with a nod: the last to arrive as always, and as always dressed in an old, tired vest and wrinkled pants, uncombed, looking every bit the dreamer but still paying close attention to what an immense, gorgeous, elegantly curved girl is saying. Tanya whispers ecstatically to her husband that it's the model Verushka. Exchanging glances with the mistress of the house, the poet shoots her a tender, grateful, and—Eduard thinks cruelly—slightly obsequious smile, as as if he's dedicating an elegy. Then, recognizing the two young Russians at her side, he raises his glass to them as if to say, "Good luck my children, here you are, it's all up to you."

They have no trouble imagining themselves adopted as the Libermans' godchildren and becoming, like Brodsky, firmly embedded in the jet set. The prospect of coming and going in this patrician palace takes the edge off Eduard's first reflex, which was to burn it all down. A modeling contract for Tanya, a successful book for him, and the patronizing Captain Levitin had better watch out.

In fact, at first, that's exactly how it seems things will turn out. The Libermans love youth, insolence, and everything Russian, and are soon fawning all over them. The first season they invite them to other, no less sumptuous parties where Andy Warhol, Susan Sontag, Truman Capote, not to mention congressmen of all allegiances, rub elbows. One day Tatiana introduces Tanya to the great photographer Richard Avedon, who gives her his card and says she should call him, another day to Salvador Dalí, who, in an English almost as primitive as hers, declares himself enchanted by her "ravishing little skeleton" (she's slender, it's true, skinny even) and speaks of doing her portrait, perhaps with Grace Jones. One weekend the Libermans take them to their manor in Connecticut, piling them into the back of their car as if they were their own kids. Visiting the study where Tatiana's daughter devotes herself to literature, Eduard wonders what books can be born in such calm, comfortable, and, to his eyes, dead environs. To write interesting things you've first got to experience interesting things, he thinks: adversity, poverty, war—but he refrains from saying so, raving prudently about the countryside, the interior decoration, the jams at breakfast. He and Tanya are two adorable young Russians, nothing more than pretty little pets, and it's still too early to test the boundaries of this role, as he realizes when he hazards a remark about the vanity that Brodsky conceals under his absentminded air. Tatiana stops him with a lifted brow: even that's going too far.

The Libermans drop them off on the way back from the countryside. Alex is amused to know that the Limonovs live on Lexington: "So we're neighbors," he says. But whereas he and Tatiana are on Seventieth Street between Lexington and Third, the Limonovs' apartment is down at number 233, that is to say worlds away. The rich old couple insists on seeing the poor young couple's place, and say they're charmed by the tiny bedroom that gives onto a dark courtyard and by the combination kitchen-bathroom swarming with cockroaches. But even the thin-skinned Eduard isn't incredulous at their remarks. Instead he finds them encouraging; after all, they too—or at least Alex—had a difficult start, and Alex does seem sincere when he repeats, "Good, good, this is how you have to start out. You have to fight and be hungry when you're young, otherwise you'll never amount to anything."

A few days later Alex has a television set delivered to their place, to help them learn English faster. When they turn it on Solzhenitsyn appears, the sole guest on a special talk show, and one of Eduard's most cherished memories is having fucked Tanya in the ass under the bearded prophet's nose as he harangued the West for its decadence.

2

NOVOYE RUSSKOYE SLOVO is a Russian-language daily founded in 1910, a little before *Pravda*, whose format and type it so resembles that it's hard to tell the two apart. Its offices take up one floor of a rundown building not far from Broadway, and even if this magic name fired Eduard's imagination until his first visit, it's like being in a quiet neighborhood in a small Ukrainian village. Journalism as a career also fired his imagination—he thought of Hemingway, Henry Miller, Jack London, who all started out as journalists. But as Brodsky said, the day to day at *Novoye russkoye slovo* isn't exactly gripping. Eduard's work consists of compiling and translating articles from New York papers for Russian subscribers who, since they get their news three days late anyway, are not at all picky when it comes to a story's freshness. In addition to this so-called information, the newspaper contains an interminable serialized novel called *Princess Tamara's Castle*, cooking recipes that are all more or less variations on kasha, and, especially, letters or articles (the distinction is by no means clear) by obsessive anti-Communists. The editors are old Jews in suspenders who barely speak English, although they've been living here for almost fifty years. Most of them emigrated right after the Revolution, and the eldest of them still remembers Trotsky's visits to the paper before that. Lev Davidovich, the old man says to anyone who wants to listen, lived in the Bronx and eked out a living lecturing on the world revolution to empty halls. The waiters in the little restaurants where he ate hated him because he thought it offended their dignity to leave tips. In 1917 he bought two hundred dollars' worth of furniture on installment and then disappeared without a trace. When the loan company finally tracked him down he commanded the army of the largest country in the world.

Even if throughout his childhood he never stopped hearing that Trotsky was an enemy of the human race, Eduard is enchanted by the grand spectacle of his life. He also likes listening to Porphyry, a somewhat younger Ukrainian who, during the war, started out in the Red Army but then, after joining the Vlasov Army—that is, the White Russians fighting alongside the Germans—ended up guarding a camp in Pomerania. A nice little stalag, he adds, not an extermination camp. Still, he did kill a few people, and talks about it without bragging. Eduard admits to him one day that he's not sure he'd be able to do the same. "Sure you would," Porphyry assures him. "If your back's to the wall you'll do it like everyone else, don't worry."

The atmosphere at *Novoye russkoye slovo* is easygoing, old-fashioned, very Russian. Coffee in the morning, tea with lots of sugar at all hours, and a birthday practically every other day that serves as an excuse for bringing out the vodka and pickled cukes and the Napoleon cognac the linotypists cherish. Everyone calls him "my dear" and "Eduard Venyaminovich," the patronymic long as an arm. All in all it's a warm and reassuring atmosphere for someone who's just arrived and doesn't speak English. But it's also something of an old folks' home, where the dreams of émigrés—who must have come to America believing a new life awaited them, before they got bogged down in the tepid coziness, the trifling quarrels, the nostalgia and the vain hopes of going back—slowly ebbed and died. Their collective pet peeve, even more than the Bolsheviks, is Nabokov. Not because *Lolita* shocks them (okay, a little), but because he stopped writing émigré novels for émigrés and turned his broad back on their stale little world. Eduard doesn't like Nabokov any more than they do, out of class hatred and a disdain for "literary" literature. But he wouldn't want to hate him for the same reasons they do, or spend too long hemmed in by these walls that smell of tombs and cat piss, for anything in the world.

To become known, a writer has, by and large, the choice between inventing stories, telling true ones, and giving his opinion about the world as it is. Eduard has no imagination, and the columns about Kharkov thugs and the Moscow underground that he tries to pitch—not to mention his poems—don't interest a soul. That leaves him a career as a polemicist. The chance to try his hand comes up when Sakharov wins the Nobel Peace Prize.

This great physicist, father of the Soviet hydrogen bomb, rallied dissidents behind him for several years, publicly campaigning in favor of the Helsinki Accords, that is, in favor of human rights in his country. There isn't a single account of Andrei Sakharov that does not depict him as a man of irreproachable intellectual rigor and moral rectitude that verges on sainthood. And although there's no reason not to believe all that's been reported, at this point in our story there's also no reason to be surprised that this golden legend exasperates our Eduard. So he locks himself away for two days to explain with a furiously witty pen that the dissidents are cut off from the people, that they only represent themselves and, in Sakharov's case, the interests of their caste, the high scientific *nomenklatura*; that if by chance they—or politicians committed to their ideas—did come to power, it would be a catastrophe, far worse than the current bureaucracy; that life in the Soviet Union is gray and boring, but it's not the concentration camp they make it out to be; and finally, that the West is no better, and that the émigrés incited by these irresponsible rabble-rousers to turn against their country end up being cruelly duped when they leave it, because the sad truth is that no one needs them in America.

Here he's talking about himself: this is just what he's starting to fear after languishing for six months at *Novoye russkoye slovo* and playing walk-on parts on the fringes of the jet set. The confident euphoria of their arrival has dissipated—his article is aptly called "Disillusion." It's turned down by *The New York Times* and several other prestigious newspapers—or rather, *The New York Times* and the other prestigious newspapers don't even acknowledge receiving it. Finally it appears in an obscure magazine, more than two months after the fact. That is to say, it goes completely unnoticed by the people it targeted: New York's intelligentsia. But it does shake up the small world of the émigré community, troubling the sweet torpor at *Novoye russkoye slovo*. Even those who admit there's some truth to his analysis don't see the need to shout it from the rooftops: Isn't that playing into the Communists' hands?

One morning, the editor in chief Moishe Borodatikh calls Eduard to his office. His finger trembling with indignation, he points to a newspaper unfolded on the desk. Eduard leans over: his picture is spread over half a page. The photo is old, and was taken in Moscow; nevertheless it shows him at the foot of a New York skyscraper. It's a

Soviet newspaper, *Komsomolskaya pravda*, and under the photomontage Eduard reads: "The poet Limonov reveals the whole truth about the dissidents and emigration." He glances through the article, and lifts his head with a smile that's half uncomfortable, half resigned, trying to pass it off as a joke. Moishe Borodatikh doesn't think it's a laughing matter. After a pause he says, "They say you work for the KGB." Eduard shrugs: "What, is that a question?" He leaves the office without waiting to be kicked out.

Togetherness is comfort in adversity, but they're together less and less. Tanya slips away from him. Buoyed by Lilya Brik's predictions, she imagined she'd become a famous model, but Alex Liberman, who could open the doors of *Vogue* for her with a single word, doesn't. All he does is compliment her on her beauty with a gallantry that starts to verge on perversity. Avedon's assistants don't call her back, nor do Dalí's. She discovers the humiliating condition of the proletarian in a world of luxury. To get in the door at a modeling agency you need a portfolio, and of course this pretty young foreigner in need of a portfolio is prey to no end of hustlers passing themselves off as photographers. More and more frequently she's not there when Eduard gets home at night. She calls to say he should have dinner without her because they still haven't finished shooting. He hears music in the background and asks if she'll be home soon. "Yes, yes, I'll be home soon." "Soon" is rarely before two or three in the morning, and then she's wiped out, complains she's drunk too much champagne and snorted too much coke in an irritated voice, as if to say, "At least I work!" It's winter, it's cold in their apartment, she goes to bed completely dressed and wants him to hug her as she falls asleep, but no longer has the strength to make love. She snores, her nose clogged. As she sleeps her face contracts slightly with displeasure. And he, awake until dawn, tortures himself thinking that he can't afford such a beautiful wife, that she's going to leave him as he left Anna, because the market has better on offer. It's inevitable, it's the law, he'd do the same in her place.

———

He questions her, she's evasive. He wants to talk, she sighs, "What do you want to talk about?" When he confesses his worries, she shrugs and says his problem is that he's too serious.

"What's that supposed to mean, too serious? Too in love with you?"

No. He doesn't know how to have fun. He doesn't know how to enjoy life.

When she says that, her mouth twists so bitterly that he shoves her over to the bathroom mirror and says: "Look at yourself. You think you look like you enjoy life? You think you look like you're having fun?"

"How do you expect me to have fun with you?" she answers. "You're always making scenes, and you interrogate me like the KGB."

Scene after scene, interrogation after interrogation—in the end, she lets the cat out of the bag. Like all women in her situation, she first tries to downplay it—"What difference does it make who it is?"—but he keeps badgering her until he finds out that his name is Jean-Pierre. Yes, he's French. A photographer. Forty-five. Good-looking? Not really: he's bald, got a beard. A loft on Spring Street. Not loaded, not a superstar, but he does all right. An adult, that's all, not a screwed-up little Ukrainian who blames everyone else for his failures and is always sulking and crying.

That's how she sees him now, and in fact he does cry a lot. Eduard, Mr. Tough Guy, cries. As in Jacques Brel's song "Ne me quitte pas," he's ready to become the shadow of her hand, the shadow of her dog, so that she won't leave him. "But I don't want to leave you," she says, touched to see him in so much pain. He pulls himself together: so everything'll be fine. As long as they stay together, everything'll be fine. She can even have a lover, no big deal. She can be a whore, he'll be her pimp. It'll be thrilling, just one of many thrilling escapades in their lives as debauched but inseparable adventurers. He's enchanted by this pact, wants to drink champagne to celebrate. Relieved, Tanya smiles evasively and says yes, yes.

They make love that night and fall asleep exhausted. No longer tied to a desk, he has a sole obsession: to stay at home with her, to stay in bed, to never stop fucking her. He doesn't feel safe unless he's inside her. It's the only firm ground he knows, all around is quicksand. He stays hard for three or four hours; he doesn't even need the dildo that used to relieve his cock to give Tanya the endless multiple orgasms they both loved. He holds her face in his hands, looks at her, asks her to keep her eyes open. She opens them wide, he sees as much terror as love. Afterward, worn out, haggard, she rolls over on her side. He wants to take her again. She pushes him away, says sleepily that she can't anymore, her pussy hurts. He falls back into withdrawal as into a well. He gets up, goes over to the nook that serves as both kitchen and bathroom. Under the yellow bulb he digs through the laundry basket and takes out her underwear, sniffing and scratching it with his fingernail, looking for traces of the other man's sperm. He beats off into it for a long time, unable to come, then goes back to bed where the sheets smell like sweat, fear, and the cheap wine they spilled drinking from the bottle. Leaning on his elbow, he looks at the slender, white, curled body of the woman he loves, her small, pointed breasts and the thick socks at the bottom of her long legs. She complains of poor circulation, her feet are always freezing. He so loved to take them in his hands and rub them softly to warm them up. How he loved her! How beautiful she was to him! Is she really that beautiful? Could it be that the old bitch Lilya Brik was just playing a cruel trick when she said that everyone in the West would be at her feet? If Alex Liberman doesn't do anything for her, if the agencies don't call her back, there's got to be a reason, and that reason jumps out at you when you look at the photos in her portfolio. She's pretty, yes, but pretty in a gauche, provincial way. She managed to dupe people in Moscow, but that's just the point: Moscow's the sticks. Once you see that, it's pathetic, the contrast between her femme fatale pose and the truth of the matter: she's a would-be model who sleeps with third-class photographers and doesn't stand the slightest chance of ever making it. That seems clear to him now, and he wants to wake her up and tell her. He gets ready to say it with the cruelest possible words—the crueler they are the truer they seem to him. The thought gives him a pained kind of pleasure, and at the same time an immense wave of pity wells up inside him; he sees a frightened, unhappy little girl and he wants to protect her, take her back to the home they should never have left. His eyes turn to the icon that like all Russians, even nonbelievers, they've hung in a corner of this dreary room, adrift in a strange world, and it seems to him that as she holds the little baby Jesus with an oversized head to her breast, the Virgin is looking at them sadly, that tears are flowing down her cheeks, and he pleads with her to save them, though he can't even believe in the prayer himself.

She wakes up; it's hell all over again. She wants to go out, he doesn't want her to, they quarrel, drink, come to blows. She gets mean when she drinks and because he asked her to tell him everything and not hide a thing, all right, she doesn't, she tells him the things that will hurt him the most. For example that Jean-Pierre got her into sadomasochism. That they tie each other up, that he bought her a collar that's spiked like a dog's and a dildo like theirs only bigger, that she sticks in his ass. It's this detail—the dildo she sticks in Jean-Pierre's ass—that makes him flip out. He pins her against the bed and starts squeezing her neck. He feels her fragile vertebrae beneath his strong, nervous hands. At first she laughs and dares him, then her face turns red, her expression switches from taunting to one of disbelief, then from one of disbelief to one of pure terror. She arches her back to try to push him off, but he crushes her under his weight and sees in her eyes that she understands what's happening. He squeezes, squeezes, his knuckles go white, and she struggles, she wants air, she wants to live. Her terror and the heaving of her body turn him on so much that he comes, and as his cock finally empties in long spasms, he releases his grip, opens his hands, and lets them fall to his side as he sprawls on top of her.

Much later they'll talk about it. She'll tell him that she was turned on by it too, but that she thought that if he did it again he'd go all the way and that's why she left him. "You're right," he'll admit. "I would have done it again, I'd have gone all the way."

In any case, the day he finds the cupboards empty when he comes back from doing some shopping, he's not surprised. He looks for some trace of her in the drawers, under the bed, in the garbage can, and places what he finds—a stocking with runs in it, a tampon, unflattering photos she ripped up—under their icon. He lights a candle. If he had a camera he'd take a snapshot of this memorial—the Memorial of Saint Helena, he thinks with a snicker. He sits there in front of it for a moment, the way the Russians sit for a short prayer before going off on a journey.

Then he leaves.

3

THE MAN WHO remembers everything remembers nothing of the week that followed. He must have walked the streets, waited in front of Jean-Pierre's place, fought with Jean-Pierre or someone else—a couple of black eyes bear witness—and above all drunk until he blacked out. A total, kamikaze, extraterrestrial *zapoi*. He knows that Tanya left on February 22, 1976, and that he woke up on the twenty-eighth in a room at the Winslow Hotel, with the good Lenya Kosogor at his bedside.

He doesn't leave this room, or even this bed, for the first few days. He's too weak, too battered and anyway, where would he go? No more wife, no more work, no more friends or relatives. His life extends no further than this room, four paces long and three wide, worn linoleum floors, sheets changed every fifteen days, the smell of bleach vying with piss and vomit, exactly what a guy like him needs. Until now he's always trusted in his lucky stars, sure that his adventurous life would lead him somewhere, that the film would have a happy end. Happy meaning that one way or another he'd become famous, that the world would know who Eduard Limonov is, or at least was. But with Tanya gone he no longer believes it. He believes that this sordid room isn't one film set among many, but the last, the one all the others were leading up to. The end of the line, nothing left but to let himself sink. To drink the chicken broth prepared for him by the good Lenya Kosogor. To sleep and hope he never wakes up.

The Winslow Hotel is a sort of refuge for those Russians—Jews for the most part—who like him are part of the "third wave" of emigrants in the seventies; he can recognize them on the street, even from behind, by the aura of lassitude and misfortune that surrounds them. They're the ones he had in mind when he wrote the article that cost him his job. In Moscow or Leningrad they were poets, painters, or musicians, staunch members of the underground who kept warm in their kitchens—and now in New York they're dishwashers, house painters, or movers, and although they force themselves to believe what they believed at first, that it's just for the time being and that their true talent will be recognized one day, they know full well it's not true. So, always hanging around together, always speaking exclusively in Russian, they get drunk, gripe and groan, talk about their country, and dream of being allowed to go back, but they won't be allowed to go back: they'll die here, trapped and swindled.

There's one guy like that at the Winslow. Eduard's gone to his room a few times, maybe for a drink or to borrow a buck, and he's sure he has a dog because it smells like dogs, there are chewed bones in a corner and even lumps of dog shit on the floor, but no, he doesn't have a dog, he *doesn't even have a dog*, he's so lonely he could die and he spends days on end rereading the few letters his mother has sent him. Another taps all day long at a typewriter without ever publishing a thing, and lives in terror because he thinks his neighbors are eyeing his room. It's no use explaining to him that that's a delusion imported from the USSR, where the seediest room is very precious and where people may well spend months hatching twisted plots to do in their neighbors in order to get their hands on one hundred square feet, which four of them will then squeeze into. It's no use explaining to him that that's not how things work in America, because he holds dearly to this delusion, it's his last link to the grimy *kommunalka* that he regrets having left, though he can't admit it. And then there's Lenya Kosogor, the good Lenya Kosogor, who spent ten years at Kolyma and takes pride in the fact that his name is right there, in black and white, in *The Gulag Archipelago*. All the émigrés call him "the guy Solzhenitsyn talked about," and since ten years is more time than Solzhenitsyn did, Lenya tells himself that he too could write about the Gulag and become rich and famous, but of course he doesn't. Ever since he found Eduard lying on the sidewalk, practically unconscious and half dead from the cold, he hasn't left his side. It's his good deed. Perhaps his real desire to help is mingled with secret satisfaction at seeing this arrogant young man—who always avoided him whenever their paths crossed for fear that he brought bad luck—hit rock bottom. Perhaps he's not unhappy to induct him into the fraternity of losers by taking Eduard to the welfare office, where he's allocated $278 a month.

The cheapest room in a hotel as squalid as the Winslow costs two hundred dollars a month. He's got seventy-eight left over. It's not much but he doesn't want to look for work. He's okay with getting pissed on California wine at ninety-five cents a half-gallon, rummaging through restaurant garbage cans, hitting up his compatriots for cash, and when worst comes to worst, swiping purses. He's a piece of shit, he'll live like a piece of shit. He spends his days aimlessly wandering the streets, though he prefers poor and dangerous neighborhoods where he knows he risks nothing because he's poor and dangerous himself. He breaks into abandoned buildings with rusty fences and boarded windows. There he'll always find vagrants he can talk to, though they rarely speak the same language, crouching in puddles of piss. He also likes to seek shelter in churches. One day during a service he digs his knife into the back of a pew and starts twanging it. The worshippers watch him warily out of the corner of their eyes, but no one dares approach him. Sometimes at night he splurges on a porno film, less to get turned on than to cry softly, thinking of the days when he went there with his beautiful wife and made her come, making all the losers jealous; he's the loser now.

Where is Tanya now? He has no idea, and he's given up trying to find out. Since the mega *zapoi* that followed her departure he hasn't gone near the loft where she may be living. When he goes back to the hotel, he jacks off thinking about her. What works best isn't imagining that he's screwing her, but that she's being screwed, and not by him. By Jean-Pierre, or with a huge dildo by Jean-Pierre's lesbian friend with whom, as she told him to make him even more jealous, they had a threesome. What does Tanya feel when she gets fucked up the ass cheating on her husband Limonov? To feel it himself he puts a candle in his own ass, lifts and spreads his legs and starts panting and moaning like she does, saying what she said to him, what she must say to the others, things like "Oh, that's good, it's so big, it feels so good." He comes and lies there, his stomach sticky with sperm. No point wiping himself off with a Kleenex, the sheets are dirty anyway. He dips his finger in it, licks his finger, swishes it down with a little cheap red wine, manages not to gag, and starts over. Legend has it that the poet Yesenin wrote poems in his own blood. Will legend say that the poet Limonov got drunk on his own come? More likely there won't be any legend at all; sadly, no one will know who the poet Limonov was, this poor Russian boy lost in Manhattan, friend in misfortune to Lenya Kosogor, Edik Brutt, Alyosha Shneerson, and others who will die as they lived, in complete obscurity.

Filled with self-pity, he looks at his beautiful, vigorous young body that nobody needs. Many women would want to caress it if they saw him alone and naked on the bed; so would many men. Since Tanya cheated on him he's often thought that it's better to have a pussy than a cock, that it's better to be chased than to chase, and that what he really wants is to be taken care of like a woman. When you think about it, it'd be great to be a faggot. At thirty-three he still looks like a teenager, he knows men are attracted to him, they always have been. True to the Saltov code of honor he's always spurned their advances, but now he couldn't care less. He needs to be protected and pampered, even if he could never totally respect anyone who would protect and pamper him. He needs to be Tanya to replace Tanya.

He talks this over with a gay Russian guy, who introduces him to a gay American guy. The gay American guy is named Raymond, he's in his sixties, wealthy and elegant, with dyed hair and a friendly manner. In the chic restaurant where their first meeting takes place, Raymond watches him devour his shrimp cocktail with the tender smile of a good Samaritan buying a warm meal for a poor little boy. "Don't eat so fast," he says, stroking his hand. Eduard has no doubt about what the waiters think, and he's happy to be taken for what he's decided to be: a little slut. The only thing that worries him is that poor Raymond also seems to be looking for love, looking to receive love, that is, he isn't just inclined to give it. In Eduard's mind, there's the one who gives love and the one who receives it, and he thinks he's given enough.

After lunch they go back to Raymond's place and sit down next to each other on the couch; Raymond starts stroking Eduard's cock through his jeans.

"Come with me," Eduard hears himself say, and, taking him by the hand, he leads him into the bedroom, onto the bed. While Raymond busies himself undoing the buckle of the heavy army belt Eduard inherited from Venyamin and the NKVD, Eduard rolls his head from side to side with his eyes half closed the way he's seen Tanya do it. He tries to do everything like Tanya, but he doesn't get hard. Raymond, who's finally managed to get Eduard's shriveled dick out of his jeans, uses his hands, his mouth, a lot of goodwill and tenderness, but it's no use. Both a little embarrassed, they zip themselves back up and return to the living room for a drink. When Eduard leaves, they exchange promises to call each other again that neither believes.

It's summer again, and he often spends entire nights outside. In the streets, on benches. Now he's in a park, in the playground. A sand-box, swings, a slide. He remembers one night in a similar playground, just a bit dingier because everything's dingier in the Soviet Union, with Kostya, aka the Cat, who's since killed a man and served twelve years in prison. Where's Kostya now? Dead or alive? He's playing with the sand, pouring it from one hand into the other, when he sees the flash of two eyes staring at him from the shadows at the base of the slide. He's not afraid, it's been ages since he knew what that was. He moves closer: it's a young black guy curled up in a ball, wearing dark clothes, probably stoned.

"Hi," Eduard says. "My name's Ed. You got something to smoke?"

"Fuck off," the guy growls. Not at all offended, Eduard crouches down next to him. With no warning the guy jumps on him, punches him. Their entwined bodies roll in the sandbox, they wrestle. Eduard manages to free a hand and reaches for the knife in his boot, and he might well have used it if, just as unexpectedly as he attacked, his adversary hadn't all of a sudden let go. They lie there, their bodies pressed together, catching their breath on the humid sand.

"You turn me on," Eduard says. "You want to fuck?"

They start to kiss and stroke each other. The young black guy has soft skin, and under his smelly clothes he's got a compact, muscular body, pretty similar to Eduard's. He rocks his head as well, his eyes half closed, murmuring, "Baby, baby . . ." Eduard bends forward, undoes his belt, impatient to know if what they say about black guys' cocks is true. And it is: it's bigger than his own. He takes it in his mouth and, stretching out on the sand, getting a big hard-on of his own, sucks him for a long time, going slowly as if they had all the time in the world. There's nothing furtive about it, it's untroubled, intimate, majestic. I'm happy, Eduard thinks: I've got somebody. The other guy lets it all happen, confident and unrestrained. He strokes Eduard's hair, gasps softly, and finally comes. Already familiar with the taste of his own sperm, Eduard loves the taste of this guy's and he swallows it all. Then, his head resting against the drained cock, he starts to cry.

He cries for a long time; it's as if all the accumulated suffering since Tanya left him is being released, and the young black guy takes him in his arms and comforts him. "Baby, my baby, you're my baby . . . ," he repeats, like an incantation.

"I'm Eddie," Eduard says. "I'm totally alone. Will you love me?"

"Yes, baby, yes," the guy says.

"What's your name?"

"Chris."

Eduard's tears subside. He imagines their life together in the slummiest parts of town. They'll be dealers, live in squats, and never leave each other. Later, he pulls down his pants and underwear and makes the gesture with which Tanya offered herself. "Fuck me," he says to Chris. Chris spits on his cock and sticks it in. It's bigger than the candle, but Eduard's training serves him well: it doesn't hurt too much. When Chris comes, they slump onto the sand and fall asleep where they lie.

He wakes up a little before dawn. Chris groans softly as Eduard slips out of his arms, feels around for his glasses, and leaves. He walks through the city as it rouses itself, totally happy and proud. I wasn't afraid, he thinks, I got screwed in the ass. *Molodets!*" as his father would say: good boy.

4

IT'S SUMMER AND he tans on his tiny balcony on the sixteenth floor of the Winslow Hotel, eating cabbage soup from a pot. Cabbage soup is good: a potful costs him two dollars and lasts three days, it's as good cold as it is hot, and even without a fridge it doesn't go bad. Across from him are office buildings with tinted windows, behind which suited businessmen and secretaries from the suburbs must wonder about this tanned, muscular guy, who sits out in the sun on his balcony in little red underpants, or even butt naked. It's Edichka, the Russian poet who costs you $278 a month, dear American taxpayers, and who cordially despises you. Every two weeks he goes to the welfare office, where he waits with other social outcasts to receive his check. Every two months he has a meeting with a case officer who inquires about his prospects. "I look for job, I look very much for job," he says, exaggerating his bad English to account for why he still hasn't found work. In fact he doesn't look for job at all, though he does make a little extra cash helping Lenya Kosogor out every once in a while.

Lenya works as a mover for a Russian Jew specialized in moving Russian Jews: rabbis, intellectuals with boxes full of the complete works of Chekhov and Tolstoy, whose dark green Soviet bindings and glue always smell a bit like fish.

Concerned that he's not integrating fast enough, the welfare office pays for him to take English lessons. Apart from him there are only women in the class, black, Asian, Latino. They show him pictures of their children, all dressed up as the children of poor people so often are, and sometimes bring him samples of their native cuisine—sweet potatoes and plantains—in thermal food containers. They talk about their countries, he talks about his own, and they open their eyes wide when he says that education and health care are free there. Why did he leave such a great country?

Just what he's asking himself.

Every morning he walks to Central Park and lies down on the grass, using a plastic bag with his notebook in it as a cushion. He stays there for hours looking up at the sky and, below the sky, the terraces of buildings for the superrich on Fifth Avenue. That's where people like the Libermans live; he's stopped seeing them altogether and their refined world seems to him like part of a very distant former life. Just a year ago he went to their place as a promising young writer, the husband of a pretty woman on her way to becoming a famous model—and now he's a bum. He looks at the people around him, listens to their conversations, and calculates the chances of each one escaping his or her present condition. The bums, the real ones, you can forget. The employees and secretaries who come to eat a sandwich on a bench at lunchtime will get promoted but won't go far, and in fact they never imagined they would. The two young intellectual types, who seem to take themselves very seriously as they talk and scribble on the typed pages of what must be a screenplay, must have great faith in their bullshit dialogue and their bullshit characters, and maybe they're right, maybe they'll make it, maybe they'll get as far as Hollywood: the pools, the starlets, the Oscars. That group of Puerto Ricans, on the other hand, who've set up a whole camp of blankets, transistor

radios, babies, and thermoses on the lawn . . . they'll stay where they
are for sure. Unless . . . who knows? Maybe, thanks to their sacrifices,
that wailing baby in its shit-filled diaper will excel in school and win
the Nobel Prize in medicine or become secretary-general of the UN.
And what about him, Eduard, with his white jeans and his black
ideas: what will become of him? Is he living out one chapter of a romantic life—as a bum in New York—or is this chapter the last, the
end of the book? He takes out his notebook and, propping an elbow
on the grass and smoking a joint he bought from one of the small-
time dealers he knows, he starts writing down everything I've just
related: the welfare office, the Winslow Hotel, the lost souls of the Russian émigré scene, Tanya, and how he got where he is now. He writes
it all down as it comes to him, without worrying about style, and soon
he's onto the second notebook, the third. He knows it's becoming a
book and this book is his only chance.

He thinks of himself as homosexual but he's barely active, it's more
a style he's adopted. One afternoon, while he's drinking on a bench
with a whimpering Russian expat—abstract painter in Moscow and
house painter in New York—a young black semivagrant asks them for
a smoke and Eduard flirts with him mostly to get a rise out of his
friend. He says, "I want you," takes him by the shoulders, kisses him;
the guy laughs and doesn't do anything to stop him. They go off to
have sex on the stairway of a building. The painter sits dumbfounded
on the bench, then tells the story to people he knows. "So it's true,
that son of a bitch Limonov is a fag now! And he lets black guys fuck
him up the ass!" A rumor circulates that he works for the KGB, another alleges that he killed himself after Tanya left him. He lets people talk, gets a kick out of it. Still, he prefers girls. The problem is
meeting them.

In the park where he spends his days writing, he talks to a girl who
hands out leaflets for the Socialist Workers Party. One good thing
about people who hand out leaflets—whether they're leftists or Jeho-
vah's Witnesses—is that they're used to getting the brush-off, so they

like it when someone's happy to talk with them. The girl's name is Carol; she's skinny, not pretty, but right now Eduard can't be picky. The Socialist Workers Party, Carol explains, represents American Trotskyists, partisans of the world revolution. Eduard's all for the world revolution. On principle he sides with the reds, blacks, Arabs, fags, derelicts, drug addicts, Puerto Ricans, and all those who, since they have nothing to lose, are—or at least should be—agitators for the world revolution. And he's all for Trotsky too—which doesn't mean he's against Stalin, but he suspects it's better not to say that to Carol. Impressed by his fiery spirit, she invites him to a "Solidarity with Palestine" meeting, warning him that things could get dangerous. Terrific, Eduard says with enthusiasm, only to be sorely disappointed the next day. It's not that the speeches are insufficiently vehement—but when it's over everyone goes off on their own, people head home or form little groups and go talk in coffee shops, nothing on the agenda but the meeting next month.

"I don't get it," Carol says, perplexed. "What did you want?"

"Well, I wanted the group to stick together. I wanted us to go get weapons and attack a government building. Or hijack a plane. Or bomb something. I don't know, something."

He clings to Carol with the vague hope of sleeping with her, but it turns out she's got a boyfriend who's as ardent a speaker and as prudent a tactician as she is, and once again he goes back to his hotel alone. He thought revolutionaries lived together in clandestine squats, not separately in little apartments where at most they have one another over for coffee. Nevertheless he sees Carol and her friends again: they're a group after all, a family, and he's desperately in need of a family, to the point where when he sees the Hare Krishnas shake their bells and tambourines and chant their bullshit in the park, he surprises himself by thinking it wouldn't be so bad to join them. He goes to meetings of the Socialist Workers Party and agrees to hand out leaflets. Carol lends him the collected works of Trotsky, whom he's beginning to like more and more. He likes it that Trotsky said, "Long live civil war!" without beating around the bush, that he disdained lame, pious speeches on the sacred value of human life, that he said that by definition the winners are right and the losers are wrong and belong in the dustbin of history: manly words. And even more than all that, he likes what the old guy at *Novoye russkoye slovo* said: that in a few short months the person who said them went from being a down-and-out émigré in New York to generalissimo of the Red Army, rolling from one front to the next in an armored train. That's the sort of destiny Eduard wants for himself. Unfortunately he stands no chance of fulfilling it, not with these American Trotskyist wimps, who can talk for hours about the rights of oppressed minorities and political prisoners but are terrified by the streets, by the ghettos, by the real poor.

As much as he wants to be part of a community, he's had enough of them. And since he's also had enough of the Russian émigrés, he takes his suitcase from the Winslow Hotel, their headquarters, and carries it over to the Embassy Hotel, which is shabbier, if that's even possible, but inhabited exclusively by blacks, drug addicts, and prostitutes of both sexes: a more elegant crowd. He's the only white person, but he doesn't feel out of place because as Carol said—though coming from her it didn't sound like a compliment—he dresses like a black guy. As soon as he's earned a dollar or two helping to move some rabbi or another, he puts it into secondhand but eye-catching threads: pink-and-white suits, lace-collared shirts, mauve crushed-velvet jackets, and ankle boots with two-tone heels that earn him the respect of his neighbors. And, as his most loyal companion Lenya Kosogor tells him, knowing it'll make him happy, rumors still abound among the émigrés. Before they said he was a queer, a Chekist, or that he'd killed himself; now that he lives with two black hookers and he's their pimp.

His window at the Embassy gives onto the roof of a small house on Columbus Avenue shared by Gennady Smakov and two dancers, all three gay. In Leningrad, Smakov was best friends with Brodsky, who speaks of him in his published conversations with the utmost warmth. Generous, erudite, gossipy, Smakov is fluent in five languages and knows fifty ballets by heart; he's a prototype for the opera- and dance-loving queen, and Brodsky and Limonov, seeing eye to eye for the first time, like him all the more because he comes from a family of total bumpkins somewhere in the Urals. For Brodsky it's a rule: only someone really provincial can become a true dandy.

Less sought after than his illustrious friends Brodsky and the star ballet dancer Mikhail Baryshnikov, Smakov rides their coattails in New York, benefiting from their contacts to cadge jobs translating or writing articles on the great Russian choreographers. Eduard is put off by this all-too-brilliant world, where he's reduced to playing a bit part even though he continues to see himself in the starring role. Still, Smakov and his roommates are really just satellites orbiting the real stars, so not too intimidating. And any time, day or night, all he has to do is cross the street to find generous Russian hospitality, which warms him up when he can't take being alone any longer. They serve him comfort food—Smakov's a marvelous cook—flatter and console him, tell him he's cute and adorable, and, all things considered, give him everything he expected from a homosexual relationship, and he doesn't even have to take the plunge himself. "You're like Goldilocks with the three bears," Smakov laughs as he cuts the coulibiac.

Eduard has so much confidence in Smakov that he gives the manuscript of *It's Me, Eddie*, to him first; this is the book he wrote that summer on the meadows of Central Park. And Smakov is thrilled—or at least impressed. He finds Eddie oh so terrible, but terrible like Raskolnikov in *Crime and Punishment*. And in fact he starts calling him Rodion, like Raskolnikov, and the book *It's Me, Roddie*. And what this tasteful aesthete also believes is that of all the talented Russian émigrés, this little scoundrel is the only one who's truly modern. Nabokov's a great artist but he's a university professor, half stuffy poet and half debauched hypocrite. "And even Joseph," Smakov says, lowering his voice as if aghast at his own blasphemy, because he owes everything to Brodsky, without Brodsky he's nothing in New York, "is a genius, sure, but like T. S. Eliot or his friend Wystan Auden, an old-school genius." When you read his poems it's like listening to classical music, Prokofiev or Britten, while what the bad boy Eddie writes is more like Lou Reed: a walk on the wild side, Smakov confides. "I'm not saying Lou Reed's better than Britten or Prokofiev—personally I prefer Britten and Prokofiev—but let's face it, a performance by Lou Reed at the Factory is more modern than a staging of *Romeo and Juliet* at the Met, you can't argue with that."

These compliments please Eduard without really surprising him: he already knows his book is brilliant. So he lets Smakov pass around the manuscript like *samizdat* to people he knows, starting with his two heroes, Brodsky and Baryshnikov.

Eduard's wary of it being shown to Brodsky, and rightly so. The great man takes ages to read it, no doubt doesn't finish it, and is slow getting back with his precious impressions, which are none too favorable. He too was reminded of Dostoyevsky, except that in his opinion the book could have been written not by Dostoyevsky or even Raskolnikov, but instead by Svidrigailov, the most perverse, violent, sick character in *Crime and Punishment*, which makes a huge difference. Baryshnikov, on the other hand, was fascinated. As soon as he had a free moment during his ballet rehearsals he sneaked away and lost himself in the manuscript. Unfortunately, he's so influenced by Brodsky that he doesn't dare contradict him.

And as neither of them is near at hand, Eduard vents his anger on the good, generous Smakov, calling him a courtesan, a parasite, and a spineless toady to the rich and famous. "You could have given my book to Rostropovich while you were at it, the king of the opportunists, the third member of the infernal troika of émigré godfathers who—it goes without saying—would be the general secretaries of the writers', composers', and dancers' unions if they'd stayed at home, and would be doing all they could to smother truly revolutionary artists, just as they are here."

Crestfallen, Smakov hangs his head in shame.

5

ONE WINTER NIGHT, to get Eduard's mind off things, Smakov insists on taking him to a reading by a Soviet poet at Queens College. Eduard isn't thrilled by the idea. All this reciprocal brownnosing between American professors and Russian intellectuals is fine for Brodsky but not for him. Still, he's tired of pacing the four walls of his flophouse, so he goes. The two sit down in the packed auditorium not far from Baryshnikov, who pretends not to recognize Eduard—or, possibly, really doesn't recognize him. It's just what he was afraid of: a humiliating evening spent holding back his rage, and his mood doesn't get any better when the reading starts.

Like Yevtushenko, the poet Bella Akhmadulina is part of the sixties generation convinced, to quote Eduard,

> that the destiny of a poet may be forged by a trip to Paris, a party at the Writers' House, and a couple of irreverent poems kept tucked in their pockets. They specialize in parting shots at the long-dead Stalin; they're the beneficiaries of concerned Western intellectuals who sign petitions as soon as they're refused a tour abroad or when a collection of their works is published at home in a print run of just a hundred thousand copies instead of a million; they idolize the Holy Trinity: Tsvetaeva who hung herself in a godforsaken backwater, Mandelstam who died crazed with fear next to the garbage cans of a prison camp where he'd been foraging for bones to chew on, and above all Pasternak, a likable poetic talent but a compromised and servile man, a dacha philosopher, a lover of the great outdoors, comfort, and old books, translating an entire collection of songs about Stalin from every conceivable language and scared to death by his own *Doctor Zhivago*, that hymn to the cowardice of the Russian intelligentsia . . .

And so on.

There's a party after the reading. It's not clear just who's invited and who isn't, so Eduard follows Smakov and they hop into a car heading for the poshest districts, winding up in a four-story townhouse with a garden on the East River, a kitchen the size of a ballroom, and decorations right out of a magazine: it's even more beautiful than the Libermans' place. The buffet is in keeping with the rest: champagne, vodka that's so chilled it goes down like oil. Thirty or so guests, Russians and Americans, the only one Eduard knows is Baryshnikov, whom he steers clear of. A young woman named Jenny with a round, likable face welcomes everyone. Eduard wonders if she's the lady of the house. No, not old enough, more likely the daughter. Some kiss her, others don't. He regrets not having had the balls to kiss her when he arrived.

With the help of the vodka he starts to relax, takes out the Jamaican weed he's always got in his pocket, and starts rolling joints. Soon a little group forms around him in the kitchen. Jenny, who bustles from one room to the next making sure everything's all right, takes a toke each time she passes, and each time she passes he jokes with her more familiarly, as if they've known each other for ages. You wouldn't call her beautiful, but there's something open about her, something accessible, almost homespun, which puts him at ease, especially in the midst of such luxurious surroundings. He gets drunker and drunker, friendlier and friendlier. He puts his arm around people's shoulders, says he didn't want to come, but he was wrong, it's been a long time since he had such a great night. He has the feeling everyone likes him. Later the poet and her husband go to bed in the room reserved for them upstairs, the last boozers leave, and he helps the staff clean up. Then it's their turn to leave. He and Jenny are the only ones left in the kitchen. They talk about the night, like a couple after all the guests have gone home. He rolls one last joint, passes it over, and kisses her. She doesn't stop him, laughing a little too loudly he thinks, but when he wants to go further she shies away. No matter how much he insists, she won't give in. As a last resort he suggests they sleep together "without doing anything." She shakes her head: no, no, no, she's heard that before, it's time for him to go home.

Go home! If she only knew what that meant! It's a cruel trek back under the icy February rain, and his room's a thousand times more sordid than when he left it just ten or so hours ago. He's got her telephone number, however, and she said he should call, which he does the very next day. But no, today won't work, they have guests. And me, he thinks without daring to ask, can't you invite me too? Two days later it won't work either because Steven's sister is there for the week. He has no idea who Steven or his sister are, and his English is still bad enough that he can't understand half of what she's saying on the phone. But he thinks she's giving him the cold shoulder and despairs. He stays in bed for a week without getting up. He cries nonstop. Behind the wall he hears the screech of the elevator where people piss as they please, and thinks of the life he'd lead if only he could seduce this rich heiress.

Finally one Sunday afternoon she says he can come over. She's at home alone. It's stopped raining, they go drink a coffee in the small private garden with a view of the river. She's wearing sweatpants that reveal what he thinks are astonishingly thick ankles for a rich heiress, but he decides it must be because she's of Irish descent. Hoping she'll be moved, he tells her a few anecdotes from his sentimental life: his crazy first wife, the second wife who left him because he didn't have any money, his mother who had him locked up in a psychiatric ward. It works, she's moved, they sleep together.

Her room on the top floor is smaller than he'd imagined. Her rustic pussy is no match for Tanya's gracious one. She makes love with bovine placidity and shocks Eduard, who considers himself so difficult to shock, by saying matter-of-factly that she's been turning him down for two weeks not because she finds him unattractive but because of a urinary tract infection. But the next morning she makes him a magnificent breakfast: freshly squeezed orange juice, pancakes with maple syrup, bacon and eggs—and he thinks that, all in all, it must be fantastic to wake up every day beside a loving wife, in a warm bed with well-ironed sheets, Vivaldi in the background, and the smell of toast rising from the kitchen.

6

IN *HIS BUTLER'S STORY*, the book where he recounts all this, there's no big scene where the hero discovers his mistake. And reading it over, I'm astonished that it could take such an observant person almost a month to understand that his rich heiress is in fact the housekeeper. She did nothing to hide it from him. She probably had no idea of either the misunderstanding or, once it was cleared up, how badly he had been deceived. For a moment he believed he'd penetrated the inner sanctum of those who had it made, and in fact he had—but as the maid's lover.

Since Eduard's now her boyfriend, Jenny thinks she can introduce him to her boss. He's forty years old, good-looking, a bon vivant and a multimillionaire. In his book, Limonov calls him Steven Gray, a name I'll use as well. He also calls him Gatsby, but that's wrong because Steven inherited his wealth; he's smooth as silk and sure of his place in the world, the opposite of Gatsby. He has a sumptuous manor in Connecticut where he lives with his wife and three children and, when he's not skiing in Switzerland or diving in the Indian Ocean, he sometimes comes and stays in his New York pied-à-terre on Sutton Place, watched over by the precious Jenny. She's the only one who lives there full time, but each day a secretary charged with looking after the mail and a Haitian cleaning lady come help her out. This small team (there are a good ten of them in Connecticut) spends the time waiting and, it must be said, dreading the visits of the master of the house, who, fortunately, comes seldom, and rarely for longer than a week—though it'd be even better if he never came at all, Eduard thinks.

Not that he's a tyrant. Just impatient, always in a rush, liable to fly into a rage over a trifle, for which he apologizes later; he takes pains to demonstrate what a liberal boss he is. He calls Jenny Jenny, she calls him Steven, and Eduard is invited to do the same. Steven wouldn't use a bell to summon Jenny or have his breakfast brought to him on a tray for anything in the world. Of course it goes without saying that it has to be ready and waiting, the tea perfectly brewed and the toast right out of the toaster whenever he wakes up; nevertheless he goes down to fetch it in the kitchen himself. And if, as is more and more often the case, he finds Eduard there reading *The New York Times*, he pushes politeness to the point of asking if he minds if he takes the paper. Just once Eduard would love to answer, "Yes, I mind," but of course he says, "No, Steven, it's waiting for you."

Because Eduard has become a frequent house guest. Steven likes him a lot right off the bat. He's friends with artists, takes pride in having lost a million dollars producing an avant-garde film, and adores all things Russian. His grandmother was Russian—White Russian of course. She emigrated after the Revolution and spoke Russian to him when he was a child. All that's left is a smattering of words which, like me, he speaks with the accent of the former regime. That's why he plays host to Russians passing through New York, and that's why he's delighted to have an authentic Russian poet as an all but live-in guest, with whom he can talk about the harshness but also the authenticity of life in the Soviet Union. Eduard tells him about his time in a psychiatric hospital and his tangles with the KGB. He embroiders a bit, teasing out the most popular version of political internment. He knows which refrains are the crowd-pleasers and dishes them up with all the required deference.

He smiles pleasantly and puts the cups in the dishwasher, but what he thinks to himself, as Steven, enchanted by their discussion, goes back upstairs to put on a ten-thousand-dollar suit to go have lunch at a restaurant where the cheapest meal would feed a family of Puerto Ricans for a month, is that it would be nice to see how Steven would make out if, instead of having inherited his mountain of wealth, he had to get by on his wits alone, parachuted into the jungle with noth-ing more than his cock and a knife. It's the first time in his life that Eduard's been able to observe someone so high up on the social lad-der at such close quarters, and he's got to admit that Steven's really quite a humane, civilized specimen; he doesn't at all resemble the Soviet caricature of the capitalist: potbellied, cruel, sucking the blood of the poor. Still, that doesn't answer the question: why him and not me?

There's only one answer to this question: revolution. Real revolution, not the chatter of Carol's friends or the vague reforms advocated by generation after generation of social traitors. No, violence. Heads on spikes. Things seem to have got off to a bad start in America, Eduard thinks. It'd be better to go join the Palestinians, or Gaddafi— whose photo he's got taped up over his bed, next to those of Charles Manson and himself dressed as a "national hero" with Tanya naked at his feet. He wouldn't be afraid to do that. He wouldn't even be afraid to die. What'd really be a bitch would be to die unknown. If *It's Me, Eddie* were published, if he had the success he deserves, well then, okay. The scandalous author Limonov, killed in a burst of Uzi gunfire in Beirut: that would make the front page of *The New York Times*. Steven and people like him would read about it over their pancakes and maple syrup and think to themselves, That guy must have really lived. That would be worth it. But the death of an unknown soldier, no.

Steven asks about his projects. He's written a book? Why not have it translated, at least in part? Why not show it to an agent? He knows one he can introduce him to. Eduard follows his advice, and puts his meager allowance into having the first four chapters translated, up to and including the scene where he and Chris fuck in the sandbox. The agent submits them to Macmillan. The answer doesn't come immediately, but it seems that's normal. One morning he goes to have a look at the building where his fate will be decided. Two black postal workers at the entrance push a cart full of large envelopes. Seventy to a hundred cubic feet of manuscripts, he gauges with horror. And what's even more horrible is to think that up there, somebody he doesn't know will open one of these envelopes, read the English title *It's Me, Eddie,* and start to read. Of course it's always possible that he'll be thrilled, and that when he gets to the end of the fourth chapter he'll barge unannounced into the big boss's office and say that in the midst of all this slush he's discovered a new Henry Miller. But it's just as possible that the guy will shrug and drop the manuscript onto the reject pile without a second thought. If he could at least see him, at least know what he looks like, the guy whose tastes, moods, and whims will determine whether or not Eduard Limonov will rise above the nondescript mass of losers . . . What if it's that young man who's just going into the building now, with the hurried walk of someone who knows the place inside out? Suit, tie, thin frameless glasses, a total egghead . . . It's enough to drive you crazy.

Judging from the number of glasses she finds on the coffee table in front of the fireplace, Jenny knows whether to prepare one breakfast or two. Because Steven's often not alone when he comes home, awakening in Eduard an ardent and painful curiosity. I'm a bit embarrassed to report it, but he's gotten into the habit of grading women: A, B, C, D, F, as in school, and this classification is at least as social as it is sexual. With the one stunning exception of Tanya, whom he's always considered an incomparable A—all the while wondering if he hasn't overrated her—he's had a lot of D's in his life, even F's: women you sleep with and don't brag about afterward. Jenny? Let's say a C. The women who rise from Steven's bed are like the ones you meet at the Libermans' parties: nothing but A's, straight across the board. Like the English countess, not so pretty but extremely chic, who, Jenny assures him, has a castle with three hundred servants.

"Three hundred servants!" she repeats with pride, as if she were the one who had them, and what Eduard really doesn't get is that she seems sincerely delighted, for the countess and for herself, the one lucky enough to serve her. He, on the other hand, could have died of shame when Steven cordially introduced him to her as "our dear Jenny's boyfriend." On a desert island, there's no doubt the countess would find him seductive. But here, as the boyfriend of the thick-calved maid, from a sexual point of view, he's a zero. He's become transparent, and he resents Jenny terribly for it. He can no longer stand her cheerfulness, how content she is with her lot, how she spreads her fat thighs when she sits down, how she doesn't even wait until she's alone to squeeze the blackheads on her nose. He can't stand her two best friends, who turn up at the house as soon as Steven's back is turned to smoke joints and talk about their chakras and macrobiotic diets. They're not even real hippies like Charles Manson's family: one's a secretary, the other a dental assistant. All in all he even prefers Jenny's parents, real midwestern rednecks to whom she insists on introducing him when they come to the big city for a week. Her father, a former FBI agent, looks astonishingly like Venyamin. When Eduard tells him that, adding that his father worked for the KGB, Jenny's fathers nods, then declares sententiously that there are good people all over the world: "America and Russia are full of good people. It's just their leaders that mess things up. And the Jews." He says proudly that J. Edgar Hoover sent presents when each of their children was born, and, learning that Eduard writes, wishes him as much success as Peter Benchley had with *Jaws*. Beer, checked shirt, straightforward, free of malice: Eduard thinks he's loads better than his daughter.

He could take the long view, as Jenny does: She's got the perfect job. She's in a magnificent house in the midst of all the luxury imaginable and, aside from the few days each month when Steven's there—then, of course, it's all hands on deck—she lives like a princess. She can have anyone she wants over, she doesn't pay a thing, and in exchange for being flexible and patient, she benefits from all the pleasures of wealth without needing to bother about any of the worries. Because the wealthy, she thinks, are burdened with worries: it's a good thing we're not in their place.

Of course Eduard could look at things like that. He could consider his place in this house, where he now more or less lives, as a marvelous gift of fate. "Except for Christ's sake, Jenny, you're the maid! And I'm the maid's lover!" He says that to her one day, and it's as if he were spitting in her face. He wants to get a rise out of her. But he doesn't get a rise out of her. More surprised than really hurt, she looks at him as if he were crazy, and rather than getting annoyed she responds calmly, "No one's forcing you to stay, Ed." A simple answer, but a good one. It's true, no one's forcing him to stay. Except now that he's got a taste for luxury, at thirty-five having almost never lived in even decent surroundings, he's got no desire whatsoever to return to the Embassy Hotel and idle away his days on the meadows of Central Park, having sex God knows where. Too bad Steven's not gay, he thinks.

7

SMAKOV, WHO KNOWS everyone, fills him in on how Tanya's doing. Eduard imagined her evolving in a world that was closed to him—lofts, champagne, cocaine, international artists and models—but in fact she's only just getting by. She's split up with Jean-Pierre, and had other lovers that treated her rather badly; the last one even dumped her.

They arrange to meet up. She lives in a grim studio apartment, hardly better than their dive on Lexington. She sniffs, her eyes are red, the fridge is empty. She hardly asks how he's getting along: better that way, he doesn't want to have to admit he's a sort of lackey-in-law. They go out for a walk and, knowing it's a magical remedy for both of them, he suggests they go buy some clothes at Bloomingdale's. "Pick whatever you like," he says. She looks at him suspiciously: Does he have the money? No problem, he just got his welfare check. All right. And what does Tanya choose? Panties. Cute little hookers' panties for the pussy that he no longer has the right to touch or penetrate. She tries them on and leaves the changing room topless in her high heels, with the underwear pulled over her stockings. The layers are so thin you can see her pubic hair.

He wonders if, as a model, she's really used to walking around like that without a second thought, or if she's doing it on purpose to turn him on and frustrate him. He despises her: she's a slut, a failed model, a fallen woman who will come to a bad end, but from the depths of this disdain a wave of love and pity washes over him. His Russian

princess has become this pathetic, vulgar creature who's mean because she's terrified, and that makes her even more precious in his
eyes. Now more than screw her he wants to take her in his arms, to
cuddle and console her. He wants to say, "Let's cut all this crap and
get out of here before it's too late, let's give ourselves a second chance.
The only thing that counts is love, being able to trust someone, and
you can trust me. I'm loyal, good, and strong, once I've put my faith in
someone I don't take it back. We can't go back home, but we can leave
this big city that demeans us, we can go somewhere quiet. I'll find
a normal job, I'll become a mover like Lenya Kosogor, then I'll buy a
truck, two trucks, I'll be the boss of a moving company. We'll have
a family, you'll serve the soup, I'll talk about my day, and at night
we'll snuggle up together, I'll tell you I love you, that I'll always love
you, I'll care for you when you're sick, and you'll do the same for me."

After paying a hundred dollars for two pairs of panties he suggests
they go have a drink. She knows a place not far away and of course it's
horribly expensive. She leaves him alone at their table for a minute
because there's someone she's got to call. While she's gone he goes
over in his mind what he's decided to say to her, he can't wait to say it,
but when she comes back from the telephone she asks if it's all right if
a friend of hers joins them, and five minutes later the friend's there.
He's in his fifties, orders a drink, and acts like her negligent master.
They talk in front of Eduard about people he doesn't know, they laugh,
then Tanya gets up, says they've got to go, leans down to her ex-husband
and kisses him lightly on the corner of the mouth, saying thank you,
that was so nice, it was great seeing you, and she heads off with the
guy, leaving Eduard to pay for all three drinks.

He walks home along Madison Avenue looking at the passersby,
above all the men, and judging them. Better than me? Worse? Most
are better dressed: this is a rich part of town. A lot of them are taller.
Some are more handsome. But he alone has the hard, determined
look of someone who's able to kill. And all of them, when they happen
to make eye contact, look away in fright.

When he gets back to Sutton Place he goes to bed and falls sick.

For two weeks Jenny looks after him like a child. She's happy to, and when he's better she says with regret, "It was like you were human."

It's summer again, and now it's been a year since he wrote his book lying on the grass in Central Park. Jenny asks him if he wants to go away on vacation with her to the West Coast and he accepts, a bit out of curiosity, a bit out of cowardice, because he can't live at Sutton Place when she's not there and he's got no desire whatsoever to spend August at the Embassy Hotel. As soon as they're off the plane and in a rented car with Jenny's brother and her two best friends—the ones he can't stand—he realizes it's going to be a nightmare. Not that he dislikes California, but you've got to be there arm in arm with Nastassja Kinski, he thinks, not with these middle-class kids playing at being hippies, who drink carrot juice in cheap coffee shops where they calculate how to split the bill on a corner of the paper tablecloth, and guffaw in prolonged fits of laugher so that everyone will know they're "having a great time," as they so love to say. After three days of sulking and letting himself be looked after, he can't stand it anymore and decides to go back. Jenny doesn't try to stop him: her credo is that everyone should do what they want, as long as they're not hurting anyone else.

New York is like a sauna, he thinks, he should have stayed out on the West Coast—if you're going to be on the street in August it's better to be in Venice than Manhattan—but it's too late now. He starts writing again. Not poems or a story this time, but short prose pieces, rarely longer than a page, in which he jots down everything he's got in his head. What he's got in his head is ghastly, but you've got to admire the honesty with which he unloads it: resentment, envy, class hatred, sadistic fantasies, but no hypocrisy, no embarrassment, no excuses. Later this will become a book, one of his best in my mind, *Diary of a Loser*. Here's a sample:

> They will all come: the hooligans and the timid (who are good in fights), drug dealers and those who hand out flyers for whorehouses. Masturbators and lovers of porno magazines. Those who wander

alone in the halls of museums, and those who leaf through books alone in public Christian libraries. Those who drink just coffee for two hours straight at McDonald's and stare sadly out the window. Those who have lost in love, money, and work, and those who were unfortunate enough to be born in poor families. The retirees who wait in the supermarket line for people with fewer than five items. The black punks who dream of screwing a high-class white girl and, since they never will, rape her instead. The gray-haired doorman who'd so love to trap and torture the arrogant rich girl from the top floor. The brave and the strong from all walks of life, they'll come to distinguish themselves and find glory. The homosexuals, walking in pairs, hugging each other; young men and women in love will come. The artists, and musicians, and writers whose work doesn't sell. The grand, heroic band of losers. They'll all come, they'll take up arms, they'll occupy city after city, they'll destroy the banks, the factories, the offices, the publishing houses, and I, Eduard Limonov, will lead the march and they will all know me and love me.

When she gets back from her vacation, Jenny tells him in a serious voice that they have to talk. He didn't see it coming, didn't even sense there was anything between her and the mustachioed hick in the checked shirt who invited them for a barbecue the night before his hasty departure, but now he learns that Jenny's going to move out to California to be with him, marry him, have his children. In fact she's already pregnant. "You and I weren't really in love," she says kindly to Eduard, "we were just really good friends and there's no reason to stop being friends just because we're on opposite sides of the country." Ever the good girl, she doesn't want him to suffer. He plays the part of the understanding guy, the guy who wishes her well and agrees that things are better like that, but in truth he suffers a kind of pain that surprises and devastates him. He thought he'd be the one to leave her, not the other way around. Though he didn't love her, he was positive that she loved him, and this certainty reassured him. Someone was waiting for him, he had a refuge; and now he's got nothing. Just the hostile world again, and the cold wind outside.

He's still welcome at Sutton Place, for a cup of coffee but nothing more. Steven is gauche enough to pat him on the shoulder when he sees him, as if to console him for getting dumped—him, Limonov, dumped by that cow! Steven asks what he's going to do now. The book's still at the publisher's, a bad sign. Knowing Eduard is good with his hands, Steven tells him that one of his friends is looking for someone to do some work under the table at his country house. That's how he winds up on Long Island for two months, working with a shovel and trowel for four dollars an hour. The rich New Yorkers with houses in these elegant beachside villages only come on weekends in the fall. During the week there's no one around. The house is un-heated and unfurnished. Eduard camps out on a foam mattress that he shields from the humid floor with a tarp as best he can, stirs up instant soups on a hot plate, puts on sweater after sweater, never get-ting warm. Sometimes he takes advantage of a sunny spell to go scare some seagulls on the beach or drink a beer at the deserted bar in the nearest village, inevitably getting soaked to the skin on his way back. Shivering, he slides into his sleeping bag and dreams of Jenny and her mustachioed hick making love. If anyone had told him when they were together that one day he'd jerk off to thoughts of her . . .

Apart from the owners of the bar and the little supermarket where he buys his groceries, he doesn't talk to a soul for weeks on end. Although he gave the number there to the few human beings he still considers himself close to—Smakov, Lenya Kosogor, Jenny—the phone never rings. No one thinks about him, no one remembers he exists. Except his agent, who calls him up one day to announce that Macmillan has rejected his manuscript. Too antagonistic. And they've got a point: it ends with the words "Fuck you, cocksucking bastards! You can all go straight to hell!" Without believing it himself, the agent says that he won't give up, that he's thinking about other pub-lishers. He's in a hurry to end this unpleasant conversation, in a hurry to hang up. He hangs up. Eduard sits on his bag of cement, alone in the empty living room, alone in the world. The rain falls in torrents, so hard that it hits the windows sideways, as if he were in a plane. He tells himself that this time he's toast. He tried; he failed. He'll stay a working stiff, boring holes in concrete, painting rich people's houses in the off season and flipping through porn rags. He'll die without anyone knowing he was alive.

I feel like I've already written this scene. In a work of fiction you've got to choose: your hero can hit rock bottom once, it's even recommended, but a second time is one too many; you risk repeating yourself. In fact I think Eduard hit bottom several times. More than once he was completely in the dumps, in genuine despair, with no way out. And it's something I admire about him: the fact that he's always gotten back on his feet, picked himself up, and comforted himself with the idea that when you've chosen the life of an adventurer, getting lost, being totally alone and washed up, is simply the price you have to pay. When Tanya left him, his survival tactic was letting himself sink: into misery, the street, savage sex, all of which he took in as novel experiences. This time he has a different idea. Jenny's going to join her fiancé in California soon and Steven, who's very sad to be losing her, still hasn't found a replacement. He, Eduard, has been acting as a kind of handyman and helper for months, repairing a table leg here, oiling the garden tools there, preparing a borscht that all the guests loved. He knows the house perfectly. Above all, Steven's a snob: the idea of having a Russian poet as a butler will enchant him.

8

AS PREDICTED, STEVEN is enchanted by the idea, and then not just by the idea, because the Russian poet turns out to be a model butler. He's exacting with the Haitian cleaning lady and gets on well with the secretary, although she can be difficult at times. Suspicious of anyone who rings at the door, he can switch naturally from supreme wariness to supreme deference if the stranger turns out not to be a stranger after all. At ease with the delivery people. Reserving the best cuts of meat at Ottomanelli's, the priciest butcher in New York. An expert cook, not just of borscht and beef Stroganoff but also of the vitamin-charged veggies so loved by the rich—fennel, broccoli, arugula—whose very existence this potato and cabbage eater had previously ignored. So trustworthy he can be sent out to pick up ten thousand dollars in cash at the bank. Seeing to everything, neglecting none of his master's tastes or habits. Serving him his whiskey at the right temperature. Unostentatiously averting his eyes when a naked woman leaves the bathroom. Knowing his place, but sensing which guests will take kindly to his wearing a Che Guevara T-shirt under his livery and joining in on the conversation. In short, a gem. Steven's friends envy him. Eduard is the talk of Manhattan.

This lasts one year, after which a French publisher accepts Eduard's book, and he flies to Paris with the sincere blessings of his former boss. His books will soon be translated Stateside, by the publishers who refused them at first, and I try to imagine now what Steven thought when he read *His Butler's Story*, which was brought out by Grove Press in 1987.

What did he learn? First off, that as soon as his back was turned, his butler left his room under the roof and took possession of the master bedroom on the main floor. That he sprawled out on his boss's silk sheets, smoked joints in the bathtub, tried on his clothes, and walked barefoot over the soft carpets. That he rummaged through his drawers, drank his Château Margaux, and, of course, brought home girls he'd picked up here and there, sometimes in pairs, girls he fucked, girls who fucked each other while he watched in the large Venetian mirror inclined opportunely over the king-size bed, telling them he was the master of the house, or at least that he was one of the master's friends, his equal. Maybe I'm wrong, but I don't think these breaches of conduct particularly troubled Steven. Because, and maybe I'm wrong here too, I think all servants dream more or less of precisely that— screwing in the boss's bed—and that some of them even do it and that the people who employ servants, if they're not idiots, know it and turn a blind eye. Provided everything's neat and tidy afterward and the sheets spin in the washing machine; and Eduard could be counted on for that.

No, what must have really bothered Steven isn't what his butler did in his absence, but what he thought in his presence.

He wasn't naive enough to imagine that the Russian poet liked him. Maybe he thought he liked him *well enough*. And in fact Eduard did like him well enough, finding him neither stupid nor unbearable. He had nothing against him *personally*. But when Steven was around he acted like the muzhik who serves his master while waiting for his day to come and who, when it does, will walk into the master's art-filled manor and trash all the art, rape his wife, hurl his master to the floor, and kick the shit out of him while laughing in triumph. Steven's grandmother had told him how astonished the czarist nobles were when they saw their loyal, devoted Vanyas, who'd witnessed their children's births and been so nice to them, run riot in this way. And I think he must have felt the same astonishment reading the book by his former servant. For almost two years he'd trusted and lived along-side this calm, smiling, likable man who, in his heart of hearts, was his enemy.

I imagine Steven reading it and remembering the day—previously completely forgotten—when he blew up at his butler over a pair of pants that was late coming back from the cleaners. Eduard took it all with a pale face, walled behind his impassive Mongol's countenance. An hour later Steven apologized, the matter was closed, they laughed about it—at least Steven did. He didn't suspect that if his outburst had lasted a few seconds longer, his butler would have gotten the chef's knife from the kitchen and bled him from ear to ear (at least that's what he says).

And the day of the reception at the UN senior official's! He lived next door and Steven paid a neighborly visit. Drinking champagne in the candle-lit garden, he spoke with diplomats, their wives, congress-men, a couple of African heads of state. What he didn't suspect—how could he?—was that his butler was watching them from his top-story window, and that this party filled with the high and mighty, to which he would never be invited, had so enraged him that he went down to the basement to get his master's hunting rifle, took it from its rack, loaded it, and let the sights wander from one guest to the next. There was one he recognized because he'd seen him on TV: Kurt Waldheim, the UN secretary-general whose Nazi past was uncovered twenty years later. Steven exchanged a couple of words with him that evening, and his butler took aim at them as they talked. When they parted Eduard kept the crosshairs trained on Waldheim as he moved from group to group. His finger twitched on the trigger. It was terribly tempting. If he pulled it he'd become famous overnight. Everything he'd written would be published. His *Diary of a Loser* would become a cult classic, a bible for all the hate-filled losers on the planet. He toyed with the idea, riding the cusp of the fateful gesture like the cusp of an orgasm, then Waldheim went inside, and, after an instant of agonized despair, the butler thought: Better that way, I guess. I'm not there yet.

But the worst is what the butler writes about the little boy with leukemia. He was five, the son of a different set of neighbors, a charming couple. Everyone in the neighborhood adored him, and everyone followed the course of his illness with a lump in their throats. Chemotherapy, a ray of hope, a relapse. Steven knew the parents well enough to visit. Each time he came back with a haggard look on his face. Of course he was thinking of his own children. One day the father told him all hope was lost: it was a matter of days, more probably hours. Steven came downstairs and announced the news to Jenny, who burst into tears. Eduard, who was in the kitchen as usual, didn't cry but also seemed moved in his stoic, military way. All three remained silent, and Steven retains a strangely vivid memory of this moment. The social barriers had fallen; they were just two men and a woman around a table, waiting together for a little boy to die. All that bound them now was sadness, compassion, and something fragile; perhaps love.

Eduard writes:

Let the rich boy die. I'll be glad even. What the hell, why must I pretend that I'm moved, that I sympathize, that I'm sorry. I'm not moved, I don't sympathize, and I'm not sorry! My own life—my real life, the only one—is held down by all these fuckers. Go ahead, die, doomed boy! No amount of radiation therapy or money will help you. Cancer won't defer to money. Even if you give it a billion, it won't retreat. And that's as it should be. At least there everyone is equal.

(What an asshole! Steven thinks, and I think the same thing, and no doubt you do too, reader. But I also think that if anything could have been done to save the little boy, especially if that something was hard or dangerous, Eduard would have been the first to attempt it, and he would have given it everything he had.)

9

ONE DAY STEVEN asks his butler to prepare the best room for his illustrious compatriot, the poet Yevgeny Yevtushenko. Eduard has no respect for this two-faced semidissident showered with dachas and privileges, who's both had and eaten enough cake to make you sick, but of course he doesn't say a word. Yevtushenko arrives, tall, handsome, self-satisfied, in a mauve denim jacket, a camera with a huge zoom lens slung over his shoulder alongside bags from the big department stores full of all the gadgets you can't get back home: a Siberian boor who's come to the capital, to borrow Brodsky's description, one whose accuracy I too, having met Yevtushenko twenty years later, can confirm. Steven, delighted to have this oh-so Russian Russian at his house, throws a cocktail party in his honor. Eduard serves, dressed in his livery. He dreads the humiliating ordeal of being introduced to the great man, and sure enough the moment comes. But to his great surprise, Yevtushenko asks, "Limonov?" He's heard about his book. "*Edichka*, right?" They say it's terrific. He'd like to read it.

Everyone leaves, first for the Metropolitan Opera, where Nureyev's dancing, then out to dinner at the Russian Samovar on Fifty-second Street. Eduard clears up, puts things away, goes to bed early: when Steven's in town there's nothing better to do. At four in the morning, the inside phone rings in his room. It's Yevtushenko, who asks him to come down to the kitchen. He and Steven are sitting at the table with a bottle of vodka in front of them, very drunk, their bow ties undone; they invite him to have a drink with them. Coming back from the Russian Samovar, Yevtushenko read the first page of the manuscript that Eduard had dutifully laid out for him in his room, then the second, sitting on the toilet seat, then fifty more, and after that there was no question of sleeping. He dragged Steven to the kitchen so they could all keep on drinking and celebrate his discovery, and now, his speech slurred but enthusiastic, he repeats: "It's not a good book, my friend, it's a great book! A fucking great book!" Thinking it cosmopolitan and emancipated, Yevtushenko prefers to say "fucking" twice where once will do. He's going to go out of his way to see that it gets published, he says. Steven, who gets as sentimental when he's drunk as the moneybags in *City Lights*, affectionately hugs the young prodigy in his arms. They drink toast after toast to the masterpiece and our Eduard certainly feels new hope, letting himself be swept along to a certain extent by the general euphoria, but that doesn't stop him from thinking deep in his dark heart that an American multimillionaire and an official Soviet poet belong to the same class—that of the masters—and he, Limonov, who has a thousand times more talent and energy, will never be one of them. And though they're drinking to his genius, he's the one who's going to clean up their mess when they finally go off to sleep. But when the tables turn they can count on him to have a bullet with their names on it.

After warm goodbyes—a bit less effusive in the sober light of day— Steven and Yevtushenko leave to go skiing in Colorado. A couple of weeks pass without any news: Eduard was right to be on his guard. That's when he gets a call from a guy called Lawrence Ferlinghetti. He's heard the name before: a poet himself, Ferlinghetti is also the

legendary publisher of the San Francisco beatniks. His friend Yevgeny told him about this "great book," one of the best written in
Russian since the war—point for Yevtushenko—and he wants to read
it. He's just passing through New York, where he's staying with his
friend Allen Ginsberg—guy's got nothing but famous friends. Since
Steven's away, Eduard invites him to come around to "the place"
for lunch.

Ferlinghetti's getting on in years; he's bald, bearded, and he
makes a good impression. His wife's not bad either. Even though
they've been around, the luxury at Sutton Place leaves them speechless. Yevtushenko didn't tell them what this poet did for a living, but
he must have gone on at some length about the dirtiest bits of his
book, and without daring to ask they visibly wonder how this boy
they were told was more or less a derelict, who sleeps with black guys
on the streets of Harlem, could live in such a place. Does he have a
millionaire lover? Is *he* a millionaire, haunting the slums of New
York as Caliph Harun al-Rashid haunted the back alleys of Bagh-
dad, disguised as a poor beggar? Their distinguished faces are two
question marks. Eduard thoroughly enjoys the misunderstanding,
and to his great surprise he's treated to an even bigger kick when he
resigns himself to dispelling it. Because instead of being disappointed or looking down on him, Ferlinghetti and his wife burst out
laughing. They can't get over the trick he's played on them—they're
even more blown away than before. What a card! What an adventurer! Now Eduard no longer sees himself as a lackey, but as a writer
like Jack London, who among a hundred romantic livelihoods—
sailor, gold digger, and pickpocket—was himself a servant too. For
the first time, he can play the role he so excels at, that of a relaxed
cynic surfing the waves of life, to an audience of connoisseurs. It's a
triumph. They get him to talk about his adventures, and he instinctively senses that the roguish version will go down better with his new
audience than the dissident version. Ferlinghetti's wife laps it up. "But
really," she asks, "you're gay?"

"I'm a bit of everything," he replies negligently.

"A bit of everything! Fantastic!"

When they say goodbye, tipsy and delighted, publication seems like no more than a formality. So the shock when the manuscript comes back from San Francisco a month later is all the greater: there's a letter from Ferlinghetti, who neither accepts it nor rejects it outright, but suggests a tragic ending: Eddie should commit a political murder, like De Niro in *Taxi Driver.*

Eduard shakes his head, dismayed. Ferlinghetti didn't understand a thing. God knows he's thought about it. In fact he almost did it, when he had Waldheim in his rifle sights. But if he didn't do it, it's because he still hopes to get out of this mess in another way. He takes it all, the shitty jobs, the publishers' refusals, the loneliness, the girls who don't merit anything better than an F, because he's counting on entering the drawing rooms of the rich by the front door and screwing their virgin daughters one day, and being thanked for it. He knows full well what goes on in a loser's head when he's pushed to the limit and decides to pick up a gun and fire into the crowd. But because he's capable of writing it, he's not that loser, and there's no way his double on the page will be that loser either.

The letter ends with a PS: "Now, living as he does in such a rich and beautiful home and possessed as he is of such a soft job, and no longer on the bottom of bourgeois society but already to a certain extent accustomed to its blessings, hasn't the protagonist of your book become more loyal to that society and civilization, calmer and more contented?"

What a prick, holy shit, what a prick.

False hopes, the knockout punch, it all seems hopeless again. And then, as it happens, everything picks up. Someone in Paris tells Jean-Jacques Pauvert about the book. Eduard still has no idea that Pauvert is a legendary, heretical publisher, Ferlinghetti's equal: the publisher of the Surrealists, of the Marquis de Sade and *Story of O.* He's been convicted ten times for breach of moral standards or insulting the head of state, and ten times he's risen up gleefully from the ashes. On the basis of a couple of translated chapters he's won over, and decides to publish it. Things are a bit complicated because his publishing company's just gone bankrupt again and he's got to find refuge at another, but who cares, what counts is that *It's Me, Eddie* is published in France in the fall of 1980 under the sensational title that Pauvert came up with: *The Russian Poet Prefers Big Blacks.*

IV

Paris,
1980–1989

∽

I

WHEN LIMONOV ARRIVED in Paris, I'd just returned from two years abroad, in Indonesia. The least you can say is that before this experience I had not lived a very adventurous life. I'd been a well-behaved child, then an overly cultured adolescent. My sister Nathalie sketched this portrait of me when she was given the essay topic "Describe your family": "My brother is very serious, he never gets into trouble, he reads books for grown-ups all day long." At sixteen I had a circle of friends who, like me, were passionate about classical music. We spent hours comparing different versions of a Mozart quintet or a Wagner opera, and did our best to imitate *The Music Critics' Tribune*, a legendary radio program on France Musique whose participants enchanted us with their erudition, their guile, and the evident pleasure they took in forming, in a world of barbarians devoted to binary rhythms, a small, petulant, and ironic enclave of civilization. I spent most of the seventies despising rock, not dancing, getting drunk to calm my nerves. And dreaming of being a great writer. In the meantime I became a sort of wunderkind of film criticism, publishing long articles in the magazine *Positif* on horror films or Tarkovsky, or, when I thought the movie wasn't up to snuff, short pans whose malevolence would make me blush today. Politically I tended distinctly to the right. If I'd been asked why, I suppose I would have said it was out of a sense of dandyism, a desire to be in the minority, and a disdain for the herd mentality. And I would have been surprised if I'd been told that, as a sworn enemy of what was not yet known as "political correctness," I was in fact merely parroting the opinions of my family with a submissiveness that might have been used to illustrate the theses of Pierre Bourdieu.

I'm sorry to talk with so little empathy about the adolescent and

very young man I was then. I'd like to like him, to make my peace
with him, but I can't. It's as if I lived in terror: of life, of those around
me, of myself, and the only way to stop the terror from paralyzing me
altogether was to adopt the position of the reserved, blasé ironist, and
to look down on any sort of enthusiasm or commitment with the
snicker of the guy who's not going to be duped, who's been around
the block a few times—but hasn't been anywhere else.

But finally I did go somewhere, and—my biggest stroke of luck—
with someone. I met Muriel at the Institut d'études politiques de
Paris. She was a knockout, with curves like a *Playboy* model and a way
of dressing that left nothing to the imagination. She electrified rue
Saint-Guillaume, where in those days students of both sexes wore
waxed cotton jackets, which the girls combined with Hermès scarves
and the boys with shirts fastened with a golden clip underneath the
tie. In my defense, I wore a beat-up pair of Clarks and an old leather
jacket. I was a rather unmotivated student, lazy and with a taste for
irony, loyal to the "whatever" values of high school, which of course
no longer made sense in a place where everyone already saw themselves ruling France. I wrote science fiction stories and reviewed films,
and in this capacity got invitations to private screenings I could bring
girls along to. And I suppose it was this set of artistic and bohemian
traits, this general tendency to conscientious objection, that allowed
me, despite my timidity, to go out with the sexiest and at the same
time least presentable girl in my class.

Like my fellow students, the classical music crowd found Muriel
somewhat vulgar. She had a loud voice and a loud laugh, punctuated
her sentences with "y'know" and "y'see," and rolled joints with a small
metal machine that she gave me and that I still have, on the back of
which she'd written "Don't forget" in English with a felt pen. I never
open it without thinking of her with gratitude and wondering what
turns my life would have taken if we'd stayed together longer. She was
a real hippie, and she turned me into a real hippie too. At the end of
an adolescence spent reading right-wing authors from the interwar
years and dreaming of going to the Wagner Festival in Bayreuth one

day, I found myself on an isolated farm in the Drôme department in the south of France, smoking grass, listening to John Coltrane, throwing the three coins of the *I Ching* onto frayed kilims, and, best of all, making love to a girl who loved to laugh, was free of spite, and who, naked from dawn till dusk, offered me the sight and the pleasures of an almost supernaturally splendid body. And at twenty, coming from where I did, it was without question the best thing that could have happened to me.

Military service was mandatory at the time, and for young urban sophisticates like myself who didn't want to be either soldiers or reserve officer cadets, there were two solutions: to be declared unfit for service or to work overseas with the French Peace Corps. After graduating, I opted to go overseas, and was sent to be a teacher at the French Cultural Center in Surabaya, an industrial port at the eastern tip of Java which served as the setting for Joseph Conrad's novel *Victory*, and whose exotic name inspired Bertolt Brecht and Kurt Weill to compose the song "Surabaya Johnny." Like rue Lauriston in Paris, home to the Gestapo during the Second World War, the beautiful Dutch manor that housed the cultural center had served the Japanese as operations headquarters during the occupation. Enough horrible things had happened there to give it the reputation of being haunted. An exorcist came twice a year, and we had endless trouble hiring caretakers. Apart from that, the garden was enchanting. I taught French to well-off Chinese women who'd raised their children, were a bit bored, and for whom these classes were a tasteful pastime, like bridge. We translated articles from *Vogue* on Catherine Deneuve and Yves Saint Laurent. They liked me, I think. Soon Muriel came and joined me. We took long trips on my motorbike, intoxicated by the swarms of people and the smells of Asia. It's in Surabaya that I wrote my first novel, inspired by our experiences with magic mushrooms. In those days it was almost a literary minigenre: the Peace Corps worker's first novel. Each fall three or four came out. A young man from a good family, dreaming vaguely of literature, wound up in Brazil, Malaysia, or Zaire for a couple of years, far from his family and friends, took himself for an adventurer, and told his story, spicing it up a little or a lot—in my case a lot.

As soon as I had a few days' vacation, Muriel and I went to Bali, where we were less attracted by the Balinese way of life—local celebrations, traditional music, ancestral rites—than by that of the Westerners who lived in the lodges of Kuta Beach and Legian: surfing, shrooms, and torch-lit parties on the waterfront. This cool, hedonistic society was divided into castes. There were the commoners, passing tourists with cameras around their necks, who were invisible to us; the penniless backpackers, whose obsession with not being ripped off and paying the *real* price for everything made them paranoid; the Australian surfers, uncomplicated guys who drank beer, listened to hard rock, and often had pretty girls with them; and finally the aristocracy, those Muriel and I called the *chic babas* and dreamed of joining. They arrived from Goa, rented beautiful wooden beach houses for the season, and left for Formentera. Their linen and silk clothing was more refined than the items in the local shops that the tourists wore. Their grass was better. They did yoga, and went about business that never seemed pressing. The revenues that allowed them to lead this ideally nonchalant life came from trade about which they remained evasive: drugs for the most audacious (drug traffickers risked life imprisonment under appalling conditions, or even hanging), precious stones, furniture, fabric for the smaller fry.

Thanks to her beauty and kindness, Muriel was soon adopted into this milieu, which I knew I didn't stand a chance of entering without her. I started getting jealous, pretending to disdain what I in fact envied: that was when things began to sour. But the more we went to Bali and hung around with the *chic babas*, the less we felt like returning to Paris and going back to school or getting a job at the end of my stay. On good days I imagined myself writing on the terrace of a bamboo house by the sea. Bare-chested, with a sarong around my waist, I took a drag from a joint that Muriel handed me before she went for a swim. Looking at her swaying hips as she walked off down the beach, blond, suntanned, ravishing, I said to myself that really, this was the life for us. So we started to look around for a way to lead it, and made, for starters, a prudent choice. In the shops of Kuta we found bikinis—

the quality was fairly mediocre, but they were nice enough looking—sewn with golden thread. After asking around at several manufacturers it turned out that we could get them for a dollar each and, according to Muriel, sell them in Paris for ten times that much. So we invested all the money we had, plus the allowance Peace Corps workers are entitled to at the end of their service, and ordered five thousand bathing suits, which were to be sent to France at the expense of the French Foreign Ministry and would serve to prime the monetary pump thanks to which we would be able to divide our time between Paris and Bali, especially Bali.

I'll be brief. By the time the manufacturer delivered the boxes, it had been a month since Muriel had left me for an older *baba*, more sure of himself, cooler, for whom the tormented and increasingly odious young man I was becoming was of course no match. That's how, after dreaming of the life of an adventurer on distant shores, I returned to Paris alone, unhappy, burdened with a manuscript for a first novel about an enchanted love story and five thousand bathing suits sewn with golden thread that served as a reminder of the failure of this love and, I thought, of my life as a whole. I retain an atrocious memory of the winter that followed. I've never been particularly heavy, but I'd shed twenty pounds in the heat of the tropics and what could pass for a kind of graceful Asian slenderness back in Bali looked like serious malnutrition or even serious illness in the drab light of Paris. The space allotted to me on earth dwindled; passersby ran into me on the streets without even noticing. I was afraid they'd walk right over me. In the studio apartment where I lived there was a mattress on the floor, a couple of chairs, and two crates full of bathing suits, which served as tables. Whenever a girl came over I said she should help herself, take five or ten, as many as she wanted. They weren't a big hit; I don't even remember when or how I got rid of them. I no longer felt anything but disgust for my novel, which didn't prevent me from sending it to a couple of publishers whose rejection letters punctuated that winter. I'd dreamed that the triumph of the writer would avenge the failure of the adventurer and lover, but obviously all three were complete flops.

2

TWO YEARS EARLIER, my mother had become famous. Until then a university professor esteemed by her peers, at the request of an intelligent publisher she boiled down all the research she'd done since the start of her career into a book that became a bestseller. The central idea of *Decline of an Empire* was new and audacious when the book came out. People were wrong, my mother said, to identify the USSR with Russia. It was a mosaic of peoples loosely lumped together, and the ethnic, linguistic, religious, and predominantly Muslim minorities were so numerous, so quick to reproduce, and so dissatisfied with their lot, that they would end up forming a majority and menacing the Russian hegemony. All of which led her to conclude: people were equally wrong to believe, as everyone or almost everyone did in 1978, that the Soviet empire would last for another couple of generations. It was fragile, ravaged by its nationalities as if by termites, and might ultimately collapse under its own weight.

Although it didn't collapse exactly as she predicted, the dawning decade nevertheless fully confirmed my mother's intuitions, granting her a status as a kind of oracle that she's since taken pains not to imperil with rash predictions. *Decline of an Empire* made enough of a splash to merit a front-page article in *Pravda*, denouncing the "notorious" Hélène Carrère d'Encausse as the inspiration behind a new and particularly pernicious form of anticommunism. That didn't stop my mother from going to Moscow the next year and meeting the author of the *Pravda* article, a historian who asked her with sparkling eyes, "Did you bring your book along? No? What a shame, I'd so love to read it, they say it's remarkable"—a sign that the twilight years of the Brezhnev era were vegetarian indeed.

Now that she was an uncontested specialist on the Soviet Union, people started sending my mother anything that dealt with it in any form whatsoever. That's how, one Sunday during this cruel winter, sifting through the latest arrivals while having lunch at my parents', I stumbled upon a work with the intriguing title *The Russian Poet Prefers Big Blacks.* The flyleaf was signed in an awkward hand, unused to the Latin alphabet: "For Carrère d'Encausse, from the Johnny Rotten of literature." Despite what was then my chronic bad mood, I smiled, thinking that the author of this inscription must have known as little about "Carrère d'Encausse," to whom his publisher had told him to send the book, as my mother knew about Johnny Rotten. I asked her if she'd read it. She shrugged her shoulders and answered, "Flipped through it. It's boring and pornographic"—two words all but synonymous in my family. I took the book with me when I left.

I didn't find it boring—quite the opposite. But it hurt me to read it; it wasn't what I needed. My ideal was to become a great writer, I felt like I was light years from achieving that goal, and other people's talent offended me. The classics and the great dead writers are one thing, but people not much older than me . . . As far as Limonov goes, it wasn't first and foremost his talent as a writer that impressed me. I grew up worshipping Nabokov, so it took me some time to appreciate the Russian poet's straightforward, no-frills prose, and I must have found his style rather lax. The story he told—his life, that is—affected me more than his way of telling it. But what a life! What energy! Unfortunately, instead of spurring me on, this energy only dragged me down, page after page, into depression and self-hatred. The more I read, the more I felt that I was made of dull and mediocre stuff, and that I was doomed in this world to play the role of a walk-on, and a bitter, envious walk-on at that, one who dreams of playing lead roles knowing full well he'll never have them because he lacks charisma, generosity, courage—that he lacks everything, in fact, but the horrible lucidity of the loser. I could have comforted myself with the thought that Limonov had felt just what I was feeling, that like me he divided humanity into the strong and the weak, the winners and the losers, the VIPs and the masses, that he was tormented by the fear of belonging in the latter category and that it's precisely this fear, so bluntly expressed, that made his book as forceful as it was. But I didn't see that. All I could see was that he was both an adventurer and a published writer, while I wasn't either and never would be, the sole adventure in my life having resulted in a manuscript that didn't interest a soul and two crates full of ridiculous bikinis.

When I got back from Indonesia, I found a job as a film critic. A publisher who'd seen my articles and was launching a series of books on contemporary filmmakers suggested I write one, and I chose Werner Herzog as my subject. I admired his films, which were then at the height of their popularity, but more than that I admired the man. Without wasting time trying to convince anyone of his talents, he'd taken a job in a factory to self-finance ecstatic documentaries about survivors of catastrophe, people who lived on the margins of society, people who were driven by delusions. In *Aguirre, the Wrath of God*, he'd tamed the Amazonian jungle and the madness of his lead actor, Klaus Kinski. He'd crossed Europe on foot in the depths of winter, convinced his trek would prevent the death of an elderly film historian, Lotte Eisner, a contemporary of Fritz Lang and F. W. Murnau and the living memory of German cinema. Strong, physical, intense, totally allergic to the spirit of frivolity and the ironic humor in vogue among us Parisians in the early eighties, Herzog sought out extreme conditions, defying nature, mistreating the natives if need be, refusing to be slowed down by the caution or scruples of those who struggled along behind him. Cinema as he practiced it was radically opposed to the conversations in cafés filmed by young French directors. In short, I considered Herzog a sort of superman, and, per the pattern that should, after the last couple of pages, now be clear, his example made me feel all the more keenly that I was not one myself.

My distress culminated, if I may say so, just after my book came out, when the magazine *Télérama* sent me to the Cannes Film Festival to interview Herzog, who was presenting his latest film, *Fitzcarraldo*. My friends thought I was lucky to go to Cannes. For me it was a disaster, the site of perpetual humiliations. Since then I've returned several times in more satisfying roles—as screenwriter of a film in the official competition, as a director, and even as a jury member—but at the time I was a novice freelancer with no contacts, on the lowest rungs of a ladder that descends from the stars in the firmament to the commoners pressed behind barriers to catch a glimpse of those stars and, with a bit of luck, be photographed with them. Just above the common people, but lacking the naïveté that allows them to be happy with their lot, I had a badge that allowed me to go to only the most inconveniently timed screenings. I was among the lowest of the low. The day *Fitzcarraldo* was screened in competition, the publisher decided to organize a book signing in the Palais des Festivals after the showing. I found myself behind a small table stacked with copies of my book, waiting for customers, as I've often done since at bookstores or book fairs. It can be nerve-wracking under any circumstances, but this was a baptism by fire, and I experienced the ordeal in its cruelest form. The people who leave a screening at Cannes have been bombarded all day long with documents they have no idea what to do with, press kits, photo books, and all kinds of résumés and brochures. For them the idea of *buying* something is completely incongruous. Most of those who paraded past my table completely ignored me, but some, with the weary, mechanical gesture of the buffet parasite who takes a glass of champagne when the tray passes by just because it's free, snatched a copy of my book and walked off. They were already looking around for a garbage can where they could dump it, like a political flyer they'd accepted out of cowardice or politeness, by the time I'd run them down to explain apologetically that the book was in fact *for sale.*

This ordeal, however, was nothing compared with the interview with Herzog. The day before the appointment I'd had my book delivered to him by his press secretary. I knew he couldn't read French and didn't expect him to say much about it, but I thought at the very least he'd greet a young man who'd just spent a year writing a book on his works with a bit more warmth than the string of blasé journalists to whom he'd meted out his time that day in forty-five-minute slots. Herzog himself opened the door of his suite at the Carlton. Dressed in a loose-fitting T-shirt, a pair of work pants, and heavy walking shoes, he looked like he'd just left his tent at the Everest base camp in rough weather, and of course he wasn't smiling: everything was as it should be. I, on the other hand, was smiling way too much. I was afraid his press secretary hadn't let him know, that he wouldn't be able to tell me apart from the other journalists. But when we sat down I saw my book on the coffee table and stuttered something in English like, "Ah, you've got it, I know you can't read it but . . ."

I trailed off, hoping he'd pick up from there. He looked at me for a moment in silence with the air of severe wisdom one imagines emanating from Martin Heidegger or Meister Eckhart, then, in a very low and at the same time very soft voice, an absolutely magnificent voice, he said—I remember his exact words—"I'd rather we not talk about that. I know it's bullshit. Let's work."

Let's work, meaning: let's do the interview, that's what we're here for, it's part of life's unavoidable hassles, like the mosquitoes in the Amazon. I was so timid and so taken aback that instead—instead of what? Of getting up and leaving? Of hitting him? What was the appropriate reaction?—I turned on my tape recorder and asked the first of the questions I'd prepared. He answered it, and the ones that followed, in a very professional way.

One last story, before getting back to Limonov. It takes place in September 1973; the heroes are Sakharov and his wife Yelena Bonner, who are spending a couple of days on the Black Sea. One day a guy comes up to them on the beach. He's an academic, and he tells Sakharov how much he admires him, as a scholar but also as a citizen, that he's the pride of his country, etc. Sakharov is moved, and thanks him. Two days later a long article appears in *Pravda* in which forty academics denounce Sakharov—after which he's exiled to Gorky for fifteen years. Among the signatories is the guy who came up and spoke to them so warmly on the beach. As soon as she finds out, Yelena Bonner curses this two-faced academic, calling him every name in the book. But Sakharov is not infuriated or indignant: he's turning it all over in his head, examining the problem as a scientist. It isn't that the academic's conduct is unpleasant; it's that it's incomprehensible.

I don't know if he found an explanation—or if, as Alexander

Zinoviev would have said, the explanation is Soviet society as a whole. I, on the other hand, do want to know why Herzog acted as he did. What pleasure could he have possibly gleaned from calmly and gratuitously offending a young man who was expressing his admiration? He hadn't read the book, and even if it was bad, that doesn't change anything. I'm sorry to relate so damning an anecdote about a man I, despite everything, still admire. His recent work makes me think he'd no longer say anything of the kind, and would in fact be very surprised if someone reminded him that he had. Nevertheless his comment means something, and it concerns me just as much as it does him.

A friend I told this story to said with a laugh, "That'll teach you to admire fascists." That was terse and, I believe, to the point. Herzog, capable of mustering intense sympathy for deaf and dumb aboriginals or schizophrenic vagabonds, looked on a young film buff with glasses as a bug who deserved to be morally squashed. And I was ideally suited to this treatment. It strikes me that this gets us to something like the roots of fascism.

If you follow these roots, what do you find? Taken to extremes, of course, the result is a clearly scandalous vision of the world: *Übermenschen* and *Untermenschen*, Aryans and Jews. Okay, but that's not what I want to say. I'm not talking about neo-Nazis or the extermination of presumed inferiors, or even about Werner Herzog's frank and robust disdain, but about the way each of us deals with the evident fact that life is unjust and people are unequal: more or less beautiful, more or less talented, more or less prepared for the fight. Nietzsche, Limonov, and this extreme moral stance within us that I'm calling fascist say with one voice: "That's reality, that's the world as it is." What else can you say? What stands against this basic fact?

"Nothing," the fascist will say, "but the pious lie, leftist otherworldliness, and political correctness, which is more common than clear thinking."

I'd offer: Christianity. The idea that, in the Kingdom—which is certainly not the hereafter but the reality of reality—the littlest is the

biggest. Or the idea, as formulated in a Buddhist sutra my friend
Hervé Clerc first told me about, that "a man who judges himself superior, inferior, *or even equal* to another does not understand reality."

Perhaps this idea only makes sense in the context of a doctrine
that considers the "ego" to be an illusion. And unless you yourself
believe it, a thousand counterexamples come to mind. Because our
entire system of thought is based on a hierarchy according to which
Mahatma Gandhi, let's say, is superior to the pedophile and murderer
John Wayne Gacy. Few would contest this example, sure, but there
are any number, the criteria vary. In addition to which, the Buddhists
themselves insist on the necessity of distinguishing, in moral conduct,
the righteous from the depraved. But even if I spend my time estab-
lishing such hierarchies, and even if—like Limonov—I can't meet
one of my own kind without wondering more or less consciously if
I'm above or below them and drawing from that either satisfaction or
mortification, I think that this idea—I repeat, that *a man who judges
himself superior, inferior, or even equal to another does not understand
reality*—is the pinnacle of wisdom, and that one life isn't enough to
adopt it, digest it, and absorb it so that it ceases to be an idea and instead conditions at every moment our way of looking and acting. For
me, writing this book is a strange way of attempting to do just that.

3

IN ADDITION TO writing for *Télérama*, I also hosted a weekly program on a local radio station, and when *Diary of a Loser* came out in
France, I invited Limonov to come on. I drove over to his place to
pick him up on my motorcycle. He lived in a sparely furnished studio
apartment in the Marais district, with weights on the floor and a set
of hand grippers on the table beside the typewriter. Dressed in a tight
black T-shirt that showed off his chest and arm muscles, his hair cut
in a flattop, he looked like a paratrooper, only with big glasses and
something curiously childlike in his profile, his face, and his expres-

sion. The picture illustrating an article I'd written about his book showed him sporting a Mohawk, safety pins, and an outmoded punk outfit; it must have dated back to his arrival in France, and one of the first things he said to me was that we could have found a more recent photo: it really seemed to bother him.

I don't remember much about the show. I took him back to his place and we said goodbye; I didn't ask if he wanted to go out for a drink or meet up again. But in fact, that's how he made his first friends in Paris. A lot of them were freelance journalists like me, or local radio hosts, or publishers just starting out. People in their twenties who'd liked his first book and used the interview as a pretext to meet him, have a drink or dinner, go out with friends, become his friend. New in town, Eduard knew no one and didn't speak good French, which made him especially eager to meet people in just this way. And it's thanks to Thierry Marignac, Fabienne Issartel, Dominique Gaultier, and my friend Olivier Rubinstein that he rapidly joined the small tribe of trendy Parisians: gallery openings, drinks with publishers, evenings out at Le Palace and then the Bain-Douches. I didn't really belong to this little group, which I pretended to disdain and which in fact intimidated me. It's sad to say, but I've never been to Le Palace. After our first encounter, I ran into Limonov from time to time, mostly at parties at Olivier's place. We exchanged vague hellos, traded a few words. He was very much alive for me, while I hardly existed in his mind, or so I thought, which is why I was amazed when I saw him in Moscow twenty-five years later and he remembered the circumstances of our meeting perfectly: the radio program, even my motorcycle. "A red Honda one twenty-five, right?"

Right.

The first years of his stay in Paris were, I think, the happiest of his life. He'd narrowly escaped misery and anonymity. The French publication of *It's Me, Eddie* and then *Diary of a Loser* had turned him into a bit of a star, and among a crowd he liked: less that of serious publishing and the literary presses than of fashionable young people who immediately adored his unusual appearance, his awkward French, and his casually provocative remarks. Cruel jokes about Solzhenitsyn, toasts to Stalin, it was just what we wanted in an era and milieu that, having put both political fervor and the inanity of the pseudohippies behind it, now swore by nothing but cynicism, disillusionment, and a kind of icy good cheer. Even aesthetically, the postpunks favored the Soviet style: big, horn-rimmed, Politburo-style glasses, Komsomol insignia, and photos of Brezhnev kissing Honecker on the mouth. Limonov was at first astounded and then moved to see a hypertrendy young fashion designer wearing a pair of snap-up plastic boots, just like the ones his mother had worn in Kharkov in the early fifties.

The man who had complained so much about only bedding C- or D-class women now had access to A, even A+, lovers, like the famous Parisian beauty he practically felt up during a society dinner—because now he was invited to society dinners. They left together, hit a few bars, and at dawn she took him back to her elegant apartment in Saint-Germain-des-Prés. She had the most beautiful breasts he'd ever seen. But that was just the start of the fairy tale, because it turned out she was a countess—a real countess!—and knew everyone in Paris. To top it off she was funny, drank her booze straight, chain-smoked, swore like a trooper, and, when they met, she was single. Eduard, crowned as that season's must-have lover, made a strong impression on his small entourage of homosexual friends, playing the role of the seductive rogue to general merriment. This flattering liaison lasted several months. A little Rastignac from Balzac's *The Human Comedy* would have known how to take advantage of such a situation. But you've got to hand it to Eduard: he's not a little Rastignac. Even if he wanted to be, he's a genius at doing what you shouldn't do if you want to move up in the world. In the fall of 1982, invited to New York by his American publisher—because now he had an American publisher—he met a twenty-five-year-old Russian girl in the bar where she was singing, brought her back to Paris, and put her up in his studio. If the countess was hurt by their breakup, she didn't let on. They stopped seeing each other—the Russian girl was jealous—but remained good if distant friends.

I only caught a glimpse of Natasha Medvedeva at parties thrown by Olivier Rubinstein, who saw a lot of both of them. She was spectacular: tall, majestic, her powerful thighs wrapped in fishnet stockings, heavily made up, and, even according to Olivier, who liked her a lot, "a real pain in the ass." You may have seen her without knowing it: she's the girl on the cover of The Cars' first album. Eduard was head over heels in love with her—which hadn't at all been the case with the countess. He saw in her an aristocrat after his own heart. A street girl, a delinquent, born like him in the gray Soviet suburbs, who set out to conquer the vast world with nothing more than her raucous beauty, her contralto voice, and her brutal survivor's humor. They were lovers, passionate lovers, but also brother and sister. And even if he liked playing the role of the rube who bags the countess, I think that this particular fantasy had less hold on him than that of the almost incestuous pair of adventurers, who've been through hard times together and are united against the evil world in a life-and-death pact. He was keen to seduce, but at the same time deeply monogamous. He believed that everyone is destined to meet a limited number of people in life, and that once you've blown all your chances you won't have any more. He left Anna because he'd found someone better. Tanya left him because she thought she'd found someone better. Natasha was right for him, he felt, because they were equals: two lost children who'd recognized each other at first glance and would never break up.

In *Book of the Dead*, he tells a lovely story about the couple visiting Sinyavsky. A talented writer and longtime dissident, Andrei Sinyavsky had carried Pasternak's coffin and, after a trial that was almost as famous as Brodsky's, spent several years in Siberia. He was the archetype of the bearded Russian thinker who, after emigrating, spoke nothing but Russian with Russians about Russia—that is, everything Eduard disdained. But Eduard liked Sinyavsky and went to see him from time to time in his book-filled house in Fontenay-aux-Roses, just outside of Paris. He found both Sinyavsky and his wife touching, direct, and hospitable. And although they weren't that much older than him, he thought of them as parents. The wife kept an eye on her husband to make sure he didn't drink, because it was bad for his health. But as soon as Andrei Donatovich had had a swig or two his gravity turned sentimental: he took people in his arms, hugged them, and told them he loved them.

The day Eduard took Natasha to visit them, they drank tea and then vodka, ate herring and pickled cucumbers. It was a warmhearted little Russian island in the Parisian suburbs, and when they asked her to, Natasha started to sing. Romances, ballads from the Great Patriotic War about lost battalions, soldiers who'd died on the front and the fiancées who were waiting for them back home. She had a magnificent voice, deep and throaty. Everyone who knew her says that when she sang you saw her soul, that's all there was to it. When she came to "The Blue Scarf," a song that no one, man or woman, who was born in the Soviet Union after the war can hear without crying, it was so intense, so overwhelming, that the three who sat listening no longer dared look one another in the eye. When they said goodbye Sinyavsky kissed Eduard on the cheek, blinking back a tear. His eyes still red, he said to him softly: "What a woman you've got there, Eduard Venyaminovich! What a woman! How proud you must be!"

She got a job singing in the Russian cabaret Raspoutine. She would get home late after her last set, often drunk. When he discovered that she started throwing them back as soon as she got up in the morning, he had to face the fact that what he'd at first assumed was just a fondness for a good drink was in fact alcoholism. This is always a hard call to make, even more so for Russians; nevertheless, he made it as far as his own drinking was concerned. He could absorb a staggering amount of alcohol over the course of an evening and then drink nothing but water for the next three weeks; even the wildest binge never stopped him from being at his desk at seven o'clock the next morning. He says, and I believe him, that he did all he could to protect Natasha from her demon: keeping an eye on her, hiding the bottles, and telling her over and over that it's a crime when you've got talent to let it go to waste. He gave her the confidence she needed to sober up long enough to write a book about her adolescence in the Leningrad sub-urbs entitled *Ma, I Love a Swindler*, which Olivier published. This respite lasted a couple of months, after which she took another dive; into alcohol, but not just that. She would disappear for two, maybe three days. Beside himself with worry, he wandered all over Paris look-ing for her, telephoned their friends, the hospitals, the police. Finally she returned, haggard, dirty, staggering on her high heels. She crashed onto the bed, and he had to lift her limp, powerless body and undress her. When she came to, forty-eight hours later, he took care of her like a sick child, bringing her broth on a tray, asking her questions. She said she couldn't remember a thing. *Zapoi.*

Friends of theirs told him as delicately as possible that in addition to drinking till she fell down in the street, she slept around, often with guys she didn't know. They had decided to tell him, they said, because it could be dangerous. She confessed tearfully: she'd been doing it since she was fourteen. Every time she'd be embarrassed afterward and would promise herself, never again—and then she'd do it again, she couldn't help it. Before, the word *nymphomania* had aroused pleasantly lewd associations for Eduard: if all girls were nymphos, he said, life on earth would be more fun. In fact, it wasn't fun at all. The superb, flamboyant woman he loved, this woman he was so proud of and whom he had sworn to love and support, was yet another sicko. Violent arguments were followed by passionate rec-onciliations in bed. She cried; he consoled her, held her in his arms, rocked her, and repeated that she could count on him, that he'd always be there for her, that he'd rescue her. Then it started up again: she shook off the security he offered like a drowning man who struggles with his savior and tries to pull him down with him. They separated several times, got back together again, an embodiment of that old saying "Can't live with 'em, can't live without 'em."

His ambition was to go from being a not very well known author to being a truly famous one, and he knew that to do that takes disci-pline. He rarely went to bed after midnight, was up at dawn, and after a session of push-ups and weight lifting sat down at the typewriter for

his five hours of daily work. After that he allowed himself the freedom to wander the streets, preferably the chic neighborhoods, Saint-
Germain-des-Prés or Faubourg Saint-Honoré, proud to have kept his
hatred of them intact: as long as you're mean, you haven't become
anybody's pet. At this rhythm he wrote and published one book a year
for ten years. He had only one subject, his life, which he divvied up
into slices. After the "Eduard in America" trilogy (*It's Me, Eddie,
Diary of a Loser,* and *His Butler's Story*), there was Eduard the juvenile
delinquent in Kharkov (*Memoir of a Russian Punk, The Young Scoundrel*), then Eduard's childhood under Stalin (*Ours Was a Great Epoch*),
mixed in with a couple of collections of short stories, which used
what hadn't been included in the novels. They were very good books:
simple, direct, full of life. Editors were happy to publish them, critics
to receive them, and loyal readers, of which I was one, to read them.
But to his great disappointment, the circle of loyal readers didn't get
any bigger. One of his publishers advised him to write a *real* novel—
preferably a salacious one—for a change; maybe he could win a prize.
He set to it with his habitual seriousness, and pounded out four hundred pages about a Russian émigré who makes a life for himself in
New York high society and introduces women to sadomasochism. But
despite his efforts to make it scandalous, despite the cover of a trendy
magazine showing him in a tuxedo with a perverse look on his face
and two naked girls at his feet, the *real* novel, *Oscar and the Women,*
wasn't a success—in fact it was just plain bad. *It's Me, Eddie* had sold
fifteen thousand copies in France, a big success for a first book. But
this figure didn't double and redouble itself, as he'd expected; instead,
things settled down and print runs stagnated somewhere between
five thousand and ten thousand. In terms of revenue, even with the
proceeds from a few translations and the advance money he charmed
his way into—more than his book would ever recoup—it wasn't El
Dorado: roughly ten thousand to twelve thousand dollars a year, or
what a senior manager made in a month. He was still scouring the
shelves of the local supermarket for the cheapest items, the poor people's fare that he'd been eating all his life: a chicken for a soup that
lasts, noodles, wine in plastic bottles; and when he was short two

francs at the checkout he'd return an item under the contemptuous gaze of the shoppers behind him.

For him, writing had never been a goal in itself; merely the only way he could conceive of attaining his real aim: namely, becoming rich and famous—above all, famous. After five or six years in Paris, he realized it might not happen. He might just grow old as a second-rate writer with a pleasantly fiery reputation, whose colleagues look at him with envy at book fairs because he attracts pretty, somewhat trashy girls who make his life more colorful than theirs. But in fact he lives in a cubbyhole with an alcoholic singer, empties his pockets to buy a slice of ham, and worries over what memories he'll mine for his next book, because the truth is he's running out, he's told practically everything about his past, all that's left is the present, and the present is just that: nothing to get excited about, especially when you consider that that prick Brodsky just won the Nobel Prize.

4

SINCE HE WAS now invited to this kind of event, he found himself one day at an international writers' conference in Budapest. There were big humanists like the Pole Czesław Miłosz and the South African Nadine Gordimer. The French contingent included the young Jean Echenoz, blond, reserved, elegant, and Alain Robbe-Grillet, accompanied by his wife. Robbe-Grillet was sardonic and jovial, spoke with a deep voice and sweeping gestures, and was delighted with his international fame—but in the way that, let's say, a medical student might be delighted by a good joke. His wife was a lively, cheerful little woman who, rumor had it, organized sadomasochistic orgies. In short, both of them were good fun. As for the rest, it was the usual assortment of tweed jackets, half-moon glasses, blue-rinse perms, and tittle-tattle from the world of publishing: all in all not very different from a Soviet Writers' Union delegation on a jaunt to Sochi.

There was a dreary panel discussion with Hungarian writers, and when one of the organizers said how proud he was to welcome such prestigious intellectuals, Eduard declared that he wasn't an intellectual but a worker, and a wary one at that, not progressive, not part of a union, a worker who knows that the workers are always the cuckolds of history. The Robbe-Grillets got a good laugh out of that, Echenoz smiled but as if he were thinking about something else, and the Hungarians were appalled. To finish the job he laid it on thick, saying that he despised laborers because he'd been a laborer himself, that he despised the poor because he'd been poor himself—and still was—and that he never gave them a cent. After that outburst he was left in peace; no one asked him any further questions. Then, that evening at the hotel bar, he slugged a British writer in the face after the writer badmouthed the Soviet Union. Other conference attendees tried to separate them, but instead of letting it drop, Eduard started punching left and right and things degenerated into a Western-style brawl, in the heat of which, Echenoz tells me, the very respectable Nadine Gordimer got hit with a bar stool. But that's not what I wanted to say.

What I wanted to say takes place in a minibus bringing the delegates back to the hotel after one panel discussion or another. A military truck pulls up beside the minibus at a red light, and a muted buzz of fear mixed with delight spreads among the passengers: "The Red Army! The Red Army!" Their noses to the glass, overexcited, the group of bourgeois intellectuals are like kids at a puppet show when the big bad wolf emerges from the wings. Eduard closes his eyes with a smile of satisfaction. His country is still able to frighten these Western wusses: everything's all right.

Solzhenitsyn aside, the Russian émigrés of Eduard's generation were certain they'd never go back, certain that the regime they had fled would last, if not centuries, then at least until after they were dead. As far as events in the USSR were concerned, Eduard followed them from something of a distance. He thought of his homeland as in hibernation, under the ice pack, and although he was better off where he was, he was certain it had remained just as he'd always known it, powerful and morose, and this thought was a source of comfort to him. The television showed the same military parades before a bevy of petrified stiffs, their chests spangled with decorations. It had been ages since Brezhnev had taken more than a step without being propped up. When he finally gave up the ghost after eighteen years of stagnation and innumerable Lenin Prizes for his invaluable theoretical contribution to the understanding of Marxism-Leninism, he was replaced by Andropov, a Chekist who passed in informed circles for a hard-liner but an intelligent one, and who subsequently became the object of a minor cult among conservatives as the man who—if he'd lived—could have reformed communism instead of destroying it. His arrival mostly amused Limonov; he remembered flirting with his daughter fifteen years earlier. But Andropov died after less than a year and was replaced by the doddering Chernenko. I remember the headline of *Libération*: "The USSR Gives You Its Best Whiskers." That made me and my friends laugh, but Eduard didn't crack a smile; he hates it when people make fun of his country. Then Chernenko died as well and was replaced by Gorbachev.

After this procession of mummies who were ceremoniously buried, one after another, Gorbachev was a runaway hit with everyone—I mean everyone *in the West*—because he was young, because he could walk without being propped up, because he had a smiling wife, and because, clearly, he liked the West as well. He was someone you could get along with. At the time the kremlinologists were carefully studying the makeup of the Politburo, distinguishing between liberals and conservatives with varying shades of gray in between. It was clear that with Gorbachev and his advisers Yakovlev and Shevardnadze, the liberals had the wind in their sails, but no one expected more than a limited internal and external détente—decent relations with the United States, a bit of goodwill at international conferences, not quite so many dissidents in psychiatric hospitals—even from the most reformist in this wing. The idea that six years after Gorbachev's arrival as general secretary of the Communist Party of the Soviet Union, neither that party nor the Soviet Union itself would exist could not have occurred to anyone, above all not to Gorbachev himself, the model apparatchik who only wanted—although this "only" was already a lot—to pick up where Khrushchev had left off before being deposed for "voluntarism" twenty years before.

I'm not going to start lecturing about perestroika, but I've got to insist on one point: the extraordinary thing that happened in the Soviet Union during these six years, the thing that swept away everything in its path, was that people were free to write their history as they saw fit.

Many people have studied this unprecedented phenomenon, among them the journalist David Remnick, who covered the period for *The Washington Post*. His book *Lenin's Tomb* is an extraordinarily lively chronicle to which I owe much in this chapter. As for me, in 1986—that is to say right before all this started and without my sensing what was about to unfold—I published a little essay whose title, "The Bering Strait," referred to an anecdote I heard from my mother: after the disgrace and execution of Beria, the head of the NKVD under Stalin, subscribers to the *Great Soviet Encyclopedia* were instructed to cut from their copies of the work the article that sang the praises of this ardent friend of the proletariat, and to replace it with an equally long article on the Bering Strait. Beria, Bering: the alphabetical order was respected, but Beria no longer existed. He never had. In the same way, some fancy scissor work was needed in the libraries after the fall of Khrushchev to remove *One Day in the Life of Ivan Denisovich* from the old copies of *Novy mir.* The Soviet authorities accorded themselves the privilege that Saint Thomas Aquinas denied to God, that is, to make what has happened not have happened, and it's not to George Orwell but to Lenin's companion Pyatakov that we owe this extraordinary sentence: "For the party's sake you can and must at twenty-four hours' notice change all your convictions and force yourself to believe that white is black."

Totalitarianism, which on this decisive point the Soviet Union pushed much further than Nazi Germany, consists of telling people they see black when they see white, and of obliging them not only to repeat it but really to believe it in the long run. It's from this source that Soviet experience draws its fantastical quality, both monstrous and monstrously comical, which all the underground literature, from Zamyatin's *We* to Zinoviev's *Yawning Heights* to Platonov's *Chevengur*, sheds light on. It's this that fascinates the writers like Philip K. Dick, Martin Amis, and me, who are able to absorb entire libraries about what happened to humanity in Russia in the last century, and which is summed up by one of my favorite historians, Martin Malia, as follows: "Socialism leads not to an assault on the specific abuses of 'capitalism' but to an assault on reality *tout court*. It becomes, in effect, an effort to suppress the real world, and this is something that cannot succeed in the long run. But for a protracted period this effort *can* succeed in creating a surreal world, one defined by the paradox that inefficiency, poverty, and brutality can be officially presented as the *summum bonum* of society."

The suppression of the real takes place with the suppression of memory. The collectivization of the land and the millions of kulaks who were killed or deported, the famine organized by Stalin in Ukraine, the purges of the thirties and the additional millions who were killed or deported in a purely arbitrary way: none of that ever happened. Of course, girls and boys who were ten in 1937 knew full well that one night some people came to take their father away and that they never saw him again. But they also knew that you shouldn't talk about it, that being the child of a public enemy was dangerous, that it was better to act as if it had never happened. And so an entire people acted as if it had never happened, and learned history according to the *Short Course* that Comrade Stalin had gone to the trouble of compiling himself.

Solzhenitsyn had predicted it: as soon as people start telling the truth, the whole edifice will collapse. Gorbachev certainly didn't have that in mind—he imagined a localized and controllable set of concessions— when he pronounced the word *glasnost*, meaning "transparency," in an address marking the seventieth anniversary of the October Revolution to the assembled dignitaries of world communism—Honecker, Jaruzelski, Castro, Ceauşescu, Daniel Ortega of Nicaragua (all of whom, with the exception of Castro, would fall in the years to come largely because of this address)—and proclaimed his intention to fill in "the blank pages of history." In this speech he referred to the "hundreds of thousands" of victims of Stalinism. In fact the numbers ran into the tens of millions, but whatever, the green light had been given, Pandora's box had been opened.

Starting in 1988, books which until then only the intellectual elite had had access to—either as *samizdat* or as foreign editions smuggled into the country—became public, and the Russians were seized by a reading frenzy. Each week a new work emerged that had previously been banned. Huge print runs sold out immediately. People stood in line at dawn in front of the kiosks and then, in the subway, the bus, even walking in the street, they read as if possessed by what they'd struggled so hard to get their hands on. For a whole week everyone in Moscow was devouring *Doctor Zhivago* and talking about nothing else; the next week it was *Life and Fate* by Vasily Grossman, and the week after that Orwell's *1984* or the books of the great British pioneer Robert Conquest, who as early as the sixties had written the history of collectivization and the purges, only to be labeled a CIA agent by every fellow traveler in the West. Under Sakharov's patronage a group of dissidents founded the Memorial society, which, a bit like Yad Vashem in Jerusalem, tried to fulfill the wish expressed by Anna Akhmatova in *Requiem*: "I should like to call you all by name." The idea was to name the victims of the repression who'd not only been killed but also erased from memory. Initially, Memorial hesitated to use the word *millions*, but as soon as the group did, it was as if it had been clear all along, as if all people had been waiting for was the right to say it out loud. Parallels between Hitler and Stalin became commonplace. A sure way to score points in a debate was by mentioning the 5 percent theory formulated by the Little Father of the Peoples (in essence: if 5 percent of the people arrested are actually guilty, you're already ahead of the game), or by quoting his commissar for justice, Krylenko: "We must execute not only the guilty. Execution of the innocent will impress the masses even more." Alexander Yakovlev himself, Gorbachev's principal adviser, stressed in a speech that Lenin was the first politician to use the term *concentration camp*. This speech was an official one, given on the occasion of the bicentennial of the French Revolution, less than two years after Gorbachev's address heralded the advent of glasnost, which gives an idea of the distance covered and at what speed. That same year the same Yakovlev explained on television that the decree rehabilitating all those who had been persecuted since 1917 was not at all a measure of clemency, as people in the Party were saying, but of repentance: "We are not pardoning them, we are asking their pardon. The goal of this decree is to rehabilitate us, who by remaining silent and looking away were accomplices to these crimes." In short, there was a sudden consensus that for the last seventy years the country had been in the hands of a gang of criminals.

It was this liberation of history that provoked the collapse of the Communist regimes in Eastern Europe. As soon as the existence of the secret protocol to the Ribbentrop-Molotov Pact—in which in 1939 Nazi Germany ceded the Baltic states to the USSR in a sort of kickback— was recognized, these states had an ironclad case for independence. It was enough to say: "The Soviet occupation was illegal in 1939 and it still is fifty years later. Now scram." Time was the USSR would have responded to this sort of argument by sending in tanks, but those days were over, and so it came to pass that 1989 was Europe's miraculous year. What it took Solidarność ten years to achieve in Poland, the Hungarians did in ten months, the East Germans in ten weeks, and the Czechs in ten days. With the exception of Romania, there wasn't a shred of violence; instead, velvet revolutions brought intellectual heroes like Václav Havel to power amid widespread jubilation. People kissed one another in the streets. Editorials evoked Francis Fukuyama's idea of "the end of history" without a trace of irony. The entire petit bourgeois population of Western Europe, myself included, went to spend New Year's in Prague or Berlin.

———

Two people in Paris didn't share this joy: my mother and Limonov. My mother was happy about the collapse of the Soviet bloc, both because as a child of White Russians she was hostile to it and because she'd said it would happen. But she couldn't bear seeing people give the credit to Gorbachev. In her view (and I think she was right, but that's just what makes him such a fascinating figure), all this was happening in spite of him. He didn't liberate a thing, she thought. All he did was allow people to take him at his word and force his hand, while he pulled the brakes as hard as he could on a process he'd set into motion out of sheer recklessness. He was at once a sorcerer's apprentice, a demagogue, and a complete ninny who—the worst insult, in my mother's eyes—spoke atrocious Russian.

Limonov agreed with all of this. The popularity enjoyed by Gorby, as people were now calling him, had irked him from the start: the leader of the Soviet Union wasn't there to get on the good side of dumb-ass Western journalists, he was supposed to scare them. He didn't like glasnost, or the open repentance of the powers that be, or, especially, their sucking up to the West by abandoning territory they'd paid for with the blood of twenty million Russians. He didn't like seeing Rostropovich scurry over with his cello every time a wall came down to play Bach suites on the debris with an inspired look on his face. He didn't like finding a Red Army jacket in an army surplus store and seeing that the brass buttons of his childhood were now made of plastic. A detail, but for him this detail said it all. What kind of self-esteem can a soldier have if he's reduced to wearing plastic buttons on his uniform? How can he fight? Who can he scare? Who had the bright idea to replace shining brass with this crap? Certainly not the high command, but some civvy dickhead tucked away in his office, charged with cutting costs, and that's how battles are lost and empires crumble. A people whose soldiers are rigged out in discount uniforms is a people that no longer has any confidence in itself, and no longer inspires respect among its neighbors. It's already lost.

5

EDUARD'S FRIEND FABIENNE ISSARTEL, the Parisian nightlife queen, said to him: "You're angry at everyone, you don't agree with anyone. I know just the person you should meet." She set up a lunch at Brasserie Lipp with Jean-Edern Hallier, who'd recently relaunched *L'Idiot international.*

Founded twenty years earlier under the patronage of Jean-Paul Sartre, *L'Idiot* in its first incarnation was a late-sixties polemical weekly; Jean-Edern Hallier, its publisher, was a flamboyant, one-eyed shit-stirrer, and even his own journalists suspected him of being a paid provocateur, in the employ of Georges Pompidou's police. Among this rich boy's exploits—Fabienne had told Eduard the story, guessing he'd appreciate it—had been a trip to Chile to present the anti-Pinochet resistance with funds collected among the French limousine liberals. But the resistance never received a cent, Jean-Edern returned empty-handed, and no one ever found out where the money went. Jean-Edern had cloaked himself in the garb of the great writer, and situated himself somewhere between his friend Philippe Sollers, with whom he'd created the avant-garde literary magazine *Tel Quel* a while back, and the younger Bernard-Henri Lévy, whose good looks and precocious success he envied.

Jean-Edern could have passed as good-looking himself—he was rich, he had a Ferrari and an apartment on Paris's Place des Vosges— but his outward mien concealed a bitter, self-destructive jester who had sabotaged the work of the good fairies bent over his cradle. He revered recluses like Maurice Blanchot and Julien Gracq, who'd been his teacher, but did everything he could to get on TV. Everyone who knew him, and even loved him, can remember, between the bouts of generous affection, other moments when the chasm of his envious soul opened wide. It was as if you sullied yourself just being around him. Brodsky might have said that like our Eduard, Jean-Edern was

less reminiscent of Dostoyevsky than of his dreadful hero Svidrigailov. But he was a Svidrigailov bursting with panache, leaving
broken hearts, bankruptcies, and scandals in his wake; a Svidrigailov
whom François Mitterrand, so proud of his sophistication and his literary taste, made no bones about calling a great writer. Jean-Edern, in
turn, threw his weight behind Mitterrand when he ran for president
in 1981, hoping for a reward—a ministry, a television station—that
never materialized. Overnight, he became the new president's sworn
enemy, spreading rumors about him—which today people are only
too happy to say were open secrets, but I don't think they were, in any
event, they came as news to me—about Mitterrand's friends who'd
collaborated with the Nazis during the war, his cancer, his illegiti-
mate daughter.

Later it came out that the antiterrorism task force at the Elysée
Palace devoted a great deal of its time to listening in on Jean-Edern
Hallier's telephone calls and the calls of his friends; even the pay
phone at the Closerie des Lilas, the restaurant where Hallier spent a
lot of his time, was tapped. Hallier circulated a pamphlet around
Paris called *The Lost Honor of François Mitterrand*. No one dared publish it. He needed a paper. So he relaunched *L'Idiot*, which hadn't
come out in fifteen years, and mobilized a group of brilliant and feisty
writers whose only marching orders were to write whatever was going
through their heads—so long as it was scandalous. Insults were welcome, slander encouraged. If it came to a trial the boss would take
responsibility. Attacks were aimed at all of the president's favorites, at
the most prominent limousine liberals, at everything that would soon
come to be known as "politically correct," at the dominant ideology of
Mitterrand's second term: the antiracist organization SOS Racisme,
human rights, World Music Day. *L'Idiot* was against everyone who was
for something, and for everyone who was against anything. Its sole
credo: we're writers, not journalists; our opinions—forget the facts—
count less than our talent for expressing them. Style versus ideas: the
old antiphony that goes back to Barrès and Céline, found its ideal
apologist in Marc-Édouard Nabe, *L'Idiot*'s chief bad boy, who was
capable of writing and publishing the headline "Abbé Pierre Is a Piece

of Shit." But there's always someone badder out there, and Nabe, who'd written an extremely virulent piece on Serge Gainsbourg, took it very poorly when Hallier republished the "infamous" (Hallier's word) article without his consent the day after the singer died.

(I missed out on this particular adventure—as I missed out on Le Palace discotheque. Since the sad affair of the bathing suits, I'd published several books and found refuge within a very different family, made up of the authors published by P.O.L or Les Editions de Minuit. I'd adopted their values, more aesthetic than political, by virtue of which I didn't feel the slightest curiosity for what—from a distance and without having purchased *L'Idiot* once in its five-year existence— struck me as a clique of loudmouths. They were, in fact, a clique, while my group consisted of people who made a point of not being part of a clique. We saw ourselves as solitary and withdrawn; we didn't care about appearances or making a splash. Our heroes were Flaubert; Melville's Bartleby, who, no matter the question, replies, "I would prefer not to"; and Robert Walser, who died in a psychiatric hospital amid the pristine white snows of Switzerland after twenty years of silence. Many of us were in analysis. I'd become friends with Echenoz—I still am—whose books and impeccable writerly posture I admired: a slightly ironic reserve, a slightly melancholy irony. With him there was no question of wallowing in bombast or in a glut of adjectives. We regarded the guys at *L'Idiot* a bit as you might look on a horde of drunken soccer fans looking for trouble in the Paris metro, and they must have regarded us as a sect of bloodless and pretentious Parnassians. But even that's saying too much: the truth is that we didn't regard each other at all, we didn't even exist for each other.)

But to return to lunch at Brasserie Lipp. Very restless, his hair tousled, his white scarf dangling in his plate, Jean-Edern told Eduard how he'd lost an eye: a Russian bullet had caught him in Berlin where his father, General Hallier, was serving at the end of the war. Pure fiction: there were as many versions of the accident as there were people he told it to. It was part of his dance of seduction, and the two men got along famously. Though each had his own hobbyhorse that the other couldn't have cared less about, Eduard was happy to agree politely that Mitterrand was a lowlife scumbag, while Hallier acknowledged that Gorbachev was too.

"You should write that, you know?" Eduard didn't need to be asked twice; all he needed was a translator. "What do you need a translator for? I can understand you when you talk, I'll understand what you write." That's how Eduard started to write in French and attend the editorial meetings of *L'Idiot*, which were held in the boss's large apartment on the Place des Vosges. Things kicked off with vodka at ten in the morning and finished up around sunrise. When people started getting hungry, Jean-Edern's housekeeper Luisa cooked macaroni. In addition to the staff, who put out the eight pages of *L'Idiot* every week, a wide assortment of people came by uninvited and jumped into arguments. And instead of trying to get them to calm down, the master of the house was delighted, leaping into the fray himself, fanning the flames of controversy that fueled his paper. The first time Eduard came over, Patrick Besson, Marc-Édouard Nabe, Philippe Sollers, Jacques Vergès were all there. They were waiting for Jean-Marie Le Pen to arrive; finally the trade unionist Henri Krasucki came instead, and Sollers sat down at the piano to sing "The Internationale." The libertine dandy Gabriel Matzneff told Limonov he'd been delighted to see his article demanding a court-martial and firing squad for Gorbachev next to his own, which sang the praises of the selfsame "Michel Gorbatcheff," as he insisted on writing, in the traditional style of the White Russians. True to his legend, Matzneff was even polite enough to congratulate his young colleague on his progress in French.

Eduard started coming more and more frequently, since he lived just around the corner. Sometimes he brought Natasha along, and the more often he came, the more comfortable he felt. The extreme right and the extreme left got drunk arm in arm; the most contradictory opinions were encouraged without there ever being a question of having anything so vulgar as a debate. They exchanged tips on how to get paid by Jean-Edern (Sollers's technique: "Hand over the article with one hand, and take the money with the other"), they fought, fell out, and made up with him, and they disconnected their telephone at night because, since he was an insomniac, he was in the habit of calling at five in the morning. The printer wasn't paid, nor were the lawyers; creditors were camped out front, the libel suits rained down, and no one knew how the next issue was going to come out. In the midst of all this at the Place des Vosges, Eduard could believe he was in *The Three Musketeers*, the book he'd so loved as an adolescent: he was the d'Artagnan of the quill pen, inducted into a company of merry drinkers and swashbucklers by this feudal screwball who was like Porthos in his outrageousness, Aramis in his harebrained schemes, and even, on closer inspection, Athos in his profound melancholy—thanks to which all was forgiven. In life, Eduard thought, you've got to have a gang. And there wasn't a livelier one in all of Paris.

V

Moscow, Kharkov, December 1989

☙

I

ON THE ROAD into Moscow from the airport, Eduard thinks back to when he traveled in the opposite direction: he had a massive hangover and lay in the back of the car, his head on Tanya's knees. She stroked his hair as she watched the buildings and woods stream by, sights they were sure they'd never see again. That was February 1974; it was snowing. It's snowing in December 1989. Fifteen years have passed, he's lost Tanya, he's returning to the country alone, and if you don't look too closely you'd say he's coming back a winner. He's been invited back, along with the actress Victoria Fedorova and the singer Willi Tokarev; they traveled business class and were welcomed at the airport like VIPs. The other two are sitting in the back of the minibus with the rather pretty girl charged with public relations, but he prefers to sit next to the driver, a dour fellow with blotches on his face, and now he tries to strike up a conversation. It's important for him to show this simple Russian guy, the first he's had any contact with since setting foot on his native soil, that despite his years abroad and despite his success he's still a man of the people who speaks their language. But the driver remains closed, walled behind a vaguely hostile indifference, and it's the same with the staff at the Hotel Ukrania, where the three visitors are taken.

A cross between a neo-Gothic bank and a Byzantine prison, the Hotel Ukrania is one of the seven Stalinist skyscrapers that make Moscow look like Batman's Gotham. By Moscow standards it's a luxury hotel, reserved for prominent guests and Party dignitaries. Eduard is emotional as he walks through the doors, something he'd never have dared to do back when he was a young underground poet. He's also surprised that in the lobby, which is as vast as a cathedral, he isn't greeted by the solemn silence that befits a seat of power, but by the din of a racetrack or a fair. Sinister-looking types with greasy hair and loud voices hustle back and forth: they even put their muddy shoes on the coffee tables.

His suite, lavish by the spartan Soviet standards he's no longer used to, has ceilings at least twelve feet high. Dimly lit by a very low-watt bulb, it's about as welcoming as a butcher's meat locker. In the old days you could count on the walls and phone being bugged, but you can't count on anything anymore. Back then you could count on the fact that calling Russians when you arrived from abroad was madness, and would get them into serious trouble, but nowadays it seems you can call anyone you want. Eduard's only got one number with him: it's Natasha's mother's number, and he's got to talk to her; she doesn't answer. When he emigrated fifteen years ago he was so sure he'd never be able to call his friends again that he didn't even bother taking down their numbers. But maybe they know he's back? Maybe they'll all be there at Izmailovo to welcome him: Kholin, Sapgir, Voroshilov, and what's left of the Smogists. He doesn't know if that's what he wants, but he does know that an event organized by Semyonov stands little chance of flying under the radar.

He met Yulian Semyonov a couple of months ago, at a party in Paris. Despite knowing nothing about him, he sensed about this brusque and cordial little man an aura of wealth and power. They talked about Gorbachev—Semyonov was for, Eduard against—then about Stalin, where it was the other way around, and despite this they hit it off. "Are you published in Russia?" Semyonov asked when he found out Eduard wrote.

"No, and there's no risk of that happening anytime in the near future."

Semyonov shrugged: "Nowadays you can publish anything."

"Anything, maybe," Eduard answered proudly, "but I'm scandalous."

"Fine," Semyonov said, "I'll publish you."

The next day an employee called Eduard on Semyonov's behalf, picked up some writing samples, and told him that his boss, an author of spy novels that had sold millions of copies in the USSR, had created a weekly newspaper in the fever of perestroika called *Sovershenno sekretno*, which you might translate as *Top Secret*: a tabloid devoted to true crime. *Top Secret* was incredibly successful, and Semyonov had established a publishing house on the side that put out commercial novels as well as the complete works of George Orwell. That's how *Ours Was a Great Epoch*, the book Eduard had just finished writing about his childhood, was published in his home country in a print run of three hundred thousand, and how he himself wound up being invited to Moscow, along with Fedorova and Tokarev.

In the early nineties, I went with my publisher Paul Otchakovsky-Laurens on a trip to Russia organized by the French Cultural Services. While there, I bore witness to those packed auditoriums, wild with enthusiasm for everything foreign, that have completely disappeared today. Paul and I found ourselves in a huge lecture hall at Rostov State University, in front of five hundred people who didn't have the slightest idea what we had written or published, and who gulped down our most anodyne words with stars in their eyes simply because we were French. It was adulation, pure and simple, divorced from any motive or merit, and we still sometimes cheer each other up with the words "Remember Rostov?"

This experience helps me imagine the event organized by Semyonov at the cultural center in Moscow's Izmailovo Park, and the mix of excitement and discomfort that Eduard felt. He's always dreamed of attracting thousands of people, of seducing them and towering above them, but he knows full well that these thousands of people aren't there for him, that they're attracted by everything that comes from the West, no matter what it is—as well as by Semyonov's publicity and the Semyonov trademark: his spy novels and his newspaper full of naked girls and Ukrainian cannibals.

And there he is, Semyonov, standing in the center of the platform: bald and stocky, in a suit and no tie. He introduces his guests, saying that it's important to bring dynamic and creative people like them back to the Soviet Union, people who're ready to roll up their sleeves and rebuild the country. Tokarev beams, Fedorova bats her eyelashes. No one knows anything about them beyond what's been drummed into their heads for the last two weeks by *Top Secret*, which has been billing this starlet and this obscure crooner as huge stars in the West, and the knowledge of this masquerade spoils the pleasure Eduard might otherwise take at seeing himself described in a two-page spread as a kind of literary rock star. When it's his turn to answer questions he does what he can to live up to this portrait. Yes, he was a bum, and then an American multimillionaire's butler. No, his ex-wife was never a streetwalker in New York, but she is now married to a Spanish marquis—that's perfectly true, and seeing that the line about the Spanish marquis goes over well, he makes a mental note to mention it whenever he gets the chance. No questions about homosexuality or black guys, since the article didn't mention them. He thinks about bringing them up himself, just to cast a pall, but judges it wiser to stick with this version of his character: the little ruffian who reached the pinnacle of the jet set but was never impressed by the models, the countesses, the Western depravity; a guy with balls you shouldn't bother trying to bullshit.

He thought he would be the last speaker, but then Semyonov introduces an old guy who was in the Gulag and who launches into a long speech about the need to "fully shed light on the crimes of the Soviet Union." Eduard listens with growing irritation, and when the old geezer explains in a trembling voice that not a single family was spared from the purges, that each and every person can name either an uncle or a cousin who was taken in the night by the NKVD and never seen again, he feels like interrupting and saying that it's time to stop all the brainwashing, that his family was unaffected by the purges, and that's the case for most of the families he knows, but here too he refrains, and to kill time he looks at the audience. They're so poorly dressed! And they all look so provincial, somehow gullible and suspicious at the same time . . . There are some pretty girls, he's got to admit. But not a single familiar face, not a single former friend: they probably don't read Semyonov's papers, or they're dead, of sadness and boredom . . .

The event ends; he signs some autographs but no books. Semyonov reassures him that they printed three hundred thousand copies, but no one seems to have read it and he doesn't once see it for sale. Eduard's surprised, but I can't say there's anything surprising about it at all, bearing in mind the state of book distribution in Russia. When one of my novels was published in Russia, justifying the trip with Paul that I mentioned earlier, the publisher took me to a warehouse where the entire print run was being loaded onto pallets that would soon be shipped off to the city of Omsk. For him it seemed like a top-notch deal: he'd been able to unload, God knows how, all ten thousand copies of my book on a wholesaler in Omsk. He was happy to let me share in his professional satisfaction, which showed that with him I was in good hands, and he raised his eyebrows, struggling to understand, when I commented that still, it was kind of weird: Why Omsk? Why was the *entire run* going to Omsk? Was there any reason to think that the potential readers of *Zymnyi Lager* (*Class Trip*) by an unknown French writer were all gathered in Omsk, an industrial city in Siberia? These questions struck him as absurd. I must have seemed to him like one of those obsessed, permanently dissatisfied authors who go around to all the stores when their book comes out and then call up to complain that they never once saw it displayed as prominently as it deserved to be.

Semyonov takes his group to celebrate the success of the event at a Georgian restaurant that looks, Eduard thinks, like one of the black-market restaurants in French films about the Occupation. Although there's nothing in grocery stores for ordinary people, here the tables are weighed down with all kinds of food and alcohol. Both the other diners and the staff look like extras tasked with creating an especially shady atmosphere. There are rich people, hookers, parasites, heavies, Caucasian gangsters, foreigners taking in the local action—and they're all getting tanked, pawing at one another, blowing massive amounts of cash. Eduard tries to tell himself that places like this must have always existed and that as a penniless poet he just had no access to them before—but no, there's something else about it that thrills his fellow partiers and profoundly disgusts him.

It takes him a while to put his finger on it, but the other thing that struck him, even before he came in the door, was the look of the cop posted on the sidewalk. He wasn't a security guard employed by the restaurant but a real cop, that is, a representative of the state. In the old days a representative of the state, even a junior one, was someone you respected. Someone who inspired fear. But the cop outside the entrance doesn't inspire fear, and he knows it. The customers pass by without even seeing him. If they're afraid of anything, it's not him. They're the ones with the money, they're the ones with the power; the poor guy in the uniform is now at their service.

In addition to his three guests from the West, Semyonov is surrounded by ten or so young guys whose functions within the group are unclear, but who are in any case his yes men. Eduard takes an instinctive dislike to them. He respects Semyonov as he respects Jean-Edern Hallier: because they're gang leaders. But he despises their gangs. He, Eduard, can't be bought, and he can't be domesticated either. He's a highwayman who's happy to deal with the boss one on one, but he doesn't mix with the riffraff—the valets, the informers, the gunslingers. The guy next to him at the table, for instance: a wise-ass punk dressed like Seymonov in a black suit with a white shirt open wide to reveal his chest, who, as he invites Eduard to take spoonfuls from a big bowl of caviar, winks and says, "Mafia." Eduard thinks, You shithead, but he engages him in conversation, and the conversation is instructive. Delighted at his own cynicism, the young man—he's not yet thirty—says that the mafia is good for democracy, good for the market, and there's no doubt in his mind that that's where things are heading: toward the market, toward Western-style capitalism, and nothing could be better. Of course at first things'll be less like Switzerland and more like the Wild West, he says. "The bullets are going to fly," the young man jokes, pretending to slaughter a group of foreigners at the next table with a machine gun as he makes *ta-ta-ta-ta* sounds with his mouth. One of them turns around and his face lights up; he and the machine gunner trade hellos like old buddies. "My American friend," the young man says proudly.

The American is a journalist; the young man works at a security firm employed by Semyonov's group. The two start acting out entire scenes from *Scarface*, which they both know by heart. Eduard drinks too much, goes down to the basement on wobbly feet where he tries to call Natasha's mother again, in vain. Sitting next to the restrooms there's a surly attendant and Eduard wants to take her in his arms precisely because she's surly, because she's Soviet, because she's not like the smart-asses who're busy stuffing themselves just ten or so feet above their heads, but like the poor, honest people he grew up with. He tries to talk to her, to find out what she thinks about what's going on in the country, but, like the minibus driver, she only scowls more deeply. It's terrible: the simple people he'd like to spend time with turn away from him, and the people who are friendly to him, well, all he wants to do is smash their faces in. He starts to go back upstairs, changes his mind, goes back down, reaches for the envelope that he's been given for his incidental expenses. He who prides himself in never giving a thing to the poor takes out a few hundred-ruble bills, at least one month's salary, and puts them in the old lady's saucer, saying, "Pray for us, babushka, pray for us." Avoiding her eyes, he rushes back up the stairs.

The rest of the evening is a blur. An argument breaks out before they leave because a guy who joined Semyonov's table later wants to pay for everyone and Semyonov is offended: these are his friends, he's the one who pays, he has a rule about paying for everyone, when he's around no one touches their wallet. The young man in charge of security suddenly looks so nervous that despite his drunkenness Eduard understands that the new arrival's excessive generosity is in fact a provocation. The diners stand up and noisily push back their chairs, the heavies close in, it looks like things are going to turn out just like in the gangster films whose lines the young man was just reciting— but then the situation defuses as quickly as it escalated.

They all leave and find themselves out on the snowy street and then back at the Hotel Ukrania, where Eduard tries once again to call Natasha's mother, and still there's no answer. He's exhausted but can't get to sleep. He tries to jerk off, thinking about Natasha to turn himself on: her Tartar cheekbones, the yellow glint in her eyes, her shoulders, both frail and abnormally wide, her asshole, stretched from overuse. He imagines her staggering around naked in a sordid apartment in the Moscow suburbs, mean and smelling of alcohol. He imagines her getting fucked by two guys, one in each hole, and, fixing his mind on this image, which he knows from experience will give him an orgasm—or at least make him come—he repeats emphatically to himself that his country's in the process of being screwed by mafiosi, of getting sodomized by real fuckers, and that's the first word that crosses his mind when he wakes up the next morning: the fuckers, the absolute fuckers.

2

A FEW YEARS later the Hotel Ukrania, like all hotels of its elevated class, will serve sumptuous breakfasts with fresh juice, fifteen varieties of tea, and English jam. In December 1989 it's still the Soviet Union, and it's at a Soviet-style buffet run like a factory cafeteria by a fat, bad-tempered woman that Eduard waits in line with a handsome, severe-looking Frenchman. Very courteously, the man introduces himself: his name's Antoine Vitez, he's a theater director and he recognizes Eduard, has read and liked several of his books. The two men sit down together to eat their herring and hard-boiled eggs, whose yolks are almost white.

Vitez has come to the Soviet Union several times and speaks a little Russian, and despite what he calls the "obstacles," each time he feels that here life is real: serious, adult, as weighty as it should be. The faces are real faces, he says, furrowed and strained, whereas all you see in the West are babies' faces. In the West everything is permitted and nothing is important; here it's just the opposite: nothing is permitted and everything is important, and Vitez seems to find that vastly preferable. As a result he only reluctantly approves of the changes under way. Of course, you can't be against freedom or against comfort, but it's important that the country not lose its soul. Eduard thinks that it's a bit too easy, when you yourself live in comfort and freedom, to want to protect others from just that for the good of their souls. Nevertheless he's happy to meet a French intellectual who's not completely infatuated with Gorbachev, and flattered that Vitez knows his books. As he's by that point totally desperate, he confides in him.

"My wife's lost somewhere in Moscow."

Vitez leans closer, attentive. Yes, Eduard explains, they got into a huge fight in Paris, as they often do, and on a whim she left a week before he did. She called him the night she got in, drunk, and kept slurring, "It's awful here, just awful." Since then he's had no news. The only lead he has is her mother's number, and she doesn't answer. He doesn't have her address. Natasha's visa must have expired, but she's not the sort of person to let that bother her. God knows where she is, God knows what she's doing. She's an alcoholic, a nymphomaniac, it's terrible.

"You love her?" Vitez asks with the voice of a priest or a psycho-analyst.

Eduard shrugs: "She's my wife."

Vitez looks at him with sympathy. "That is terrible," he admits. "Still, I envy you. After breakfast I'm going to a boring meeting with some theater bureaucrats, while you're going to plunge into the depths of the city, like Orpheus in search of Eurydice . . ."

Making his way through the horde of thugs that gather in the lobby with the break of day, he goes outside and, since he doesn't know where to start looking, he walks straight ahead, very quickly, because he's freezing in his sailor's jacket and unlined boots. To cross the huge avenues he takes the underground passageways full of dirty water and morose crowds lined up in front of the kiosks that sell cheap items— jars of horseradish, socks, and halved cabbages. No one apologizes, even when they let the swinging doors crash back in your face. He lived here for seven years, but he doesn't remember the city being so gray, so dismal, so inhospitable. Apart from the subway stations, which are veritable palaces, by far the most beautiful things in Mos-cow, there's nowhere you can sit down to rest or catch your breath. No cafés, or if there are they're hidden in basements or back courtyards, and you have to know about them because there are no signs and if you ask someone something they look at you as though you've insulted them. The Russians know how to die, Eduard thinks, but as far as the art of living goes they're still as pathetic as ever. He wanders around Novodevichy Cemetery and other places that served as backdrops to his love affair with Tanya. He passes the building where he slashed his wrists one summer night. He thinks of Tanya's ridiculous poodle, with its white curls that got black with dirt when the thaw started. He feels the urge to call Tanya in Madrid, where she's living with the Spanish marquis. He's got her number in his address book, they talk from time to time, but what would he say? "I'm downstairs, I've come to get you, open up"? That's what he'd have to say, and it's too late, anything else is sentimental claptrap.

That afternoon he's expected at the Central Writers' House, where twenty years ago he had a hell of a time getting in. He accepted the invitation hoping to savor the sweet taste of revenge, but the flavor is anything but. It smells like a cafeteria and is full of third-rate poets dressed like petty bureaucrats. The least unpleasant is the shrew behind the bar who serves him cognac in a coffee cup. She doesn't recognize him, but he recognizes her: she was already there back when Arseny Tarkovsky was doing readings.

He's led into a little room where a sparse audience sits waiting. He was expecting cultural apparatchiks and is stunned to discover that they're all veterans of the underground. No close friends, but he recognizes faces he used to see at parties or poetry readings. Faces of spineless underlings consumed with self-hatred. And how they've aged! Pallid or red-faced, potbellied, beaten. They're no longer members of the underground. No, now that everything is allowed they've surfaced, and the worst thing is that their fatuousness, mercifully veiled in their youth by censorship and secrecy, has come to light. The first to talk—the only one, apparently, to have gotten his hands on one of the three hundred thousand copies of *Ours Was a Great Epoch*—asks harshly what this apology for the KGB is supposed to mean coming from a supposed dissident. Eduard responds curtly that he was never a dissident, just a delinquent. A middle-aged woman with a penetrating, melancholic air says that she knew him a bit in their youth, no matter if he doesn't remember her: she still remembers the young, inspired, long-haired poet who was so full of imagination, and she is shocked to see him now looking like a Komsomol secretary.

What to say? Eduard and his audience are talking past each other. In Eduard's world, an artist can wear a crew cut, horn-rimmed glasses, and tight-fitting black clothes. It's even recommended. He'd rather die than wear the tired old sweater and dandruff-covered jacket that's the last word in underground fashion. In her world, a poet has to look like a derelict; she doubtless would prefer that he look like Venichka Erofeev. Speaking of whom, a third person says that the legendary author of *Moscow to the End of the Line* heard that his former friend Limonov was coming back, but when he found out that he was sponsored by the scandalous media tycoon Yulian Semyonov, he said he wouldn't shake hands with him if Limonov went to see him: What does Eduard think of that? Eduard answers that he doesn't think anything, that he was never friends with Erofeev and it never occurred to him to go visit him. Things continue like that for half an hour, and when the session ends he declines the offer to go have a drink with the young members of the Writers' Union ("the young members of the Writers' Union"!). At four in the afternoon, night has fallen. He leaves, pulling up the collar of his thin *Potemkin* jacket.

This dreadful scene rids him of any desire to go see his old friends. Clearly he was right to give them the slip fifteen years ago! And how they resent him for it! While he was struggling to survive on the Western front, they stayed there and stewed in their uncomfortable comfort, protected by a cloak of silence from the bitter knowledge of their own mediocrity. Failure was noble, anonymity was noble, even decrepitude was noble. They could dream of being free one day, and, when that day came, of being hailed as heroes who had preserved in secret the best of Russian culture for future generations. Only now that freedom has arrived, no one gives a damn about them. Naked, they shiver in the bitter cold of competition; it's the young gangsters like Semyonov's assistants who have the upper hand, and the only place the members of the underground can take refuge is the Writers' Union, where they continue to venerate a pathetic wreck like Venichka Erofeev and distrust someone who's as full of life as the adventurous Limonov.

At one point during that grim evening he goes into a gallery that's exhibiting, almost as objects of kitsch, works by former underground artists, and he's surprised to recognize a canvas that he'd seen his old bohemian friend Igor Voroshilov paint: a portrait of a woman in a red dress in front of a window. The woman was Igor's girlfriend at the time, the window was in an apartment he'd shared with them for a while. The model was pretty, today she must be a big lump of a woman. As for Igor, Eduard learns from the catalog that he died two years ago.

Eduard asks how much the painting costs. Peanuts. And really, he thinks, it's not worth any more. Poor Igor. He wasn't wrong, the night he wanted to kill himself, despairing that he was no more than a third-rate artist. The market decided, the market is right, and this instransigent reasoning means there's no chance for the sweet, spineless souls of the friends of his youth. Suddenly he's gripped by an immense sadness, and something resembling pity. The man who prides himself in despising the weak starts to pity their weakness. He pities the sweet, spineless souls of his friend Igor, of the restroom attendant at the black-market restaurant, of his people as a whole. This strong, mean man suddenly wants to protect all these sweet, spineless souls from the strong and the mean.

He tries to call Natasha's mother from every telephone booth he sees and finally, miracle of miracles, she answers. He introduces himself, asks where Natasha is, and her mother bursts into tears. She's worried sick too: Natasha came, stayed for two days, and left without telling her where she was going. Eduard offers to come over. She lives far away, he takes the subway and calms down a bit: in fact, he feels least anxious inside the subway car. After wandering around for a long time in a Khrushchevian building complex, he finds himself in a tiny studio apartment that betrays an obsessive tidiness, with collections of bound classics behind glass like at his parents' place. Natasha's mother is a tired little woman, consumed by worry, who's wary of him even as she counts on him to find her daughter, because if he doesn't, who will? Her visa must have expired, she fears the worst—and she only knows about the alcohol, which has already killed her husband, Natasha's father. She has no idea about her daughter's nymphomania, or about the bipolar disorder that means she may stay quietly at home writing poems for a while and then disappear without notice for four or five days at a time, screwing anyone who comes along, before coming home haggard and devastated, her underwear brown with blood and shit. Eduard doesn't say anything about that, no point adding fuel to the fire, the mother's fear is already seeping from the narrow walls. But he thinks that he might have an easier time of it if he didn't find Natasha, if she disappeared completely from his life. "You love her?" her mother asks suddenly, just like Vitez, and he gives her the same answer: "She's my wife. I've been taking care of her for seven years and I'm not going to stop now." The mother starts kissing him and blessing him and saying he's a good man. It's not what he's used to hearing, but at least, he thinks, it's true in love.

Natasha's mother gives him the address of one of her daughter's former classmates; she might know something. Three-quarters of an hour on the subway; half an hour's walk in zero degrees Fahrenheit, wearing nothing but a light jacket. It's past midnight when he gets to a sort of artists' squat full of people who look less like artists—even grungy ones—than pickpockets or drug dealers, which they no doubt are. The friend, a shrill, frowzy-looking blonde with dark roots, saw Eduard's photo in *Top Secret*. And Natasha's told her about him as well—certainly nothing positive because from the get-go it's clear she hates him. Still, they sit down and drink vodka in the kitchen, and the friend takes evident pleasure in telling him that yes, his wife came by, with two guys, that she stayed the night under the pretext that it was too far to go back home and walked around stark naked, smoked stark naked on the toilet and gave one of the guys a hand job while the other one tried to fuck her, the blonde, the friend. Eduard thinks that this friend is a mean woman, one of those Russian bitches whose moral code consists in believing that men are the enemy and that making them suffer is a victory in itself. He should go home, but it's late, the subway's closed, he might have to walk for hours before finding a taxi, and as for calling one: let's be real. So he stays, keeps drinking and listening to the friend through a growing stupor. She explains that all this is his fault, that he treats Natasha badly, she knows it because Natasha told her. Other people from the squat come and sit down, including a Chechen guy called Jalal who first of all wants to know if he's Jewish because he's convinced everyone in France is Jewish, starting with Mitterrand, and then, in a joking tone that becomes increasingly menacing, tries to force Eduard to give him his passport. The danger is palpable, things could take a turn for the worse, but Eduard keeps cool—or maybe it's just that the general stupor wins out, because everyone's in the process of getting totally ripped. The last thing he remembers is giving a speech of sorts: "This country is brilliant when it comes to making history, but we'll never lead a normal life. A normal life is not for us . . ." He wakes up at daybreak, his forehead on the kitchen table. Silently he crosses the squat where people are passed out even on the floor, checks that no one has stolen his passport, slips on the shoes he took off when he arrived, as you always do when you come indoors in Russia in the winter. Despite his splitting headache his mind is clear and he's got a plan: go back to the hotel and get his bag, ditch Semyonov and his tour, get dropped off at the station, and take the first train for Kharkov.

3

HE'S SO USED to being poor that he buys a third-class ticket for this eighteen-hour journey without giving it a second thought, and all things considered he doesn't regret it. He's shed his guise as a well-known writer to blend in with the mass of crude, lice-ridden Russians spread out on the benches with their vodka and their foul-smelling food. The car has no compartments, and the bunks stretch out side by side as in a barracks. Some of the passengers look like crooks, others seem so naive and vulnerable that they make you want to cry. Real faces in any case, Vitez wasn't wrong: ruddy or gray or even greenish, but not a single pink American snout. He looks out at the passing countryside through the dirty window: birch trees, white snow, black sky, immense empty stretches punctuated at scattered intervals by small train stations with water towers. On the platforms, when they stop, old women in felt boots vie with one another like fishwives to sell travelers pickles or cranberries. Although he's been around a lot he's never known anything but real cities, and he wonders what it must be like to live way out here in the boonies.

The passenger across from him is reading *Top Secret*. Eduard's photo appeared just last week and he thinks the man might recognize him, but no, in his world you don't cross paths with people who have their picture in the paper. They start talking. The guy tells him the news story he's just read: in a village like the ones they're passing through, a woman punished her daughter by chaining her outside at twenty below, and she got so frostbitten that her arms and legs had to be amputated. As soon as what remained of the girl—no more than a trunk—was sent back home, the mother's boyfriend wasted no time in raping her and she gave birth to a little boy, whom they chained up in turn.

After getting off to that start, the conversation isn't exactly marked by optimism. Not only is everything going to shit—a diagnosis Eduard can agree with—but what's more, according to his traveling companion, nothing ever worked in the country in the first place. This opinion is new. In the past, life was bad and everyone grumbled, but in general people were proud: of Gagarin, of *Sputnik*, of the power of the army, of the size of the empire, of a society that was more equitable than those in the West. For Eduard, the unbridled freedom of expression brought by glasnost has hammered two ideas into the heads of simple, harmless people like this traveler: first, that the people who'd ruled since 1917 were sadists and murderers, and, second, that they'd driven the country into the ground. "The truth," the guy

laments, "is that we're a third-world country: Upper Volta with nuclear missiles." He must have read that expression somewhere, he
clearly likes it, and repeats it with a careworn smugness. For seventy
years people insisted that we were the best, but in fact we're losers.
Vsyo proigrali: we've failed right across the board. Seventy years of
effort and sacrifice have gotten us to where we are today: up to our
necks in shit.

Night falls, Eduard can't get to sleep. He thinks of the couple of letters he's received from his parents during his long absence: whining,
empty phrases, complaints because their only son won't come back to
care for them in their dying days. He skimmed them without really
reading them, refusing to feel sorry for his parents and thanking God
for taking him far from their shriveled, timorous lives. A bad son?
Maybe, but intelligent, and so pitiless. Pity softens, pity debases, and
the terrible thing is that since he arrived he's been seized by pity along
with anger. He gets up, makes his way between the packages stuffed
with all the crumby things poor people burden themselves with when
they travel. In the bathroom the toilet overflows with frozen shit. On
the way back to his seat, he hears the female conductor moaning as two
little punks take turns doing her in her cubbyhole. The idea that he
could suffer for his country would have seemed grotesque to him in
the past; nevertheless, he suffers.

The train gets in at 7:00 a.m., the taxi drops him off in Saltov in front
of the prefab concrete building where he spent his adolescence. His
duffel bag slung over his shoulder, he climbs naked concrete steps that
wouldn't be out of place in a prison. In front of the door he hesitates.
Won't they die of shock? Wouldn't it be better to ask a neighbor to
prepare them? What the hell; he rings. The sound of slippers, probably coming from the kitchen. Without waiting he says through the
door: "Mom, Dad, it's me."

    They must not have heard: "Who is it?" His mother's voice is wary,
frightened; nothing good can come from outside. He suspects that her
eye is glued to the peephole.

"It's me, Mom," he repeats. "Me, Edichka."

She undoes the upper lock, the lower lock, the middle lock, and they're standing face to face. His dad comes up behind her, with the little steps of an old man. They're surprised, but strangely enough not incredibly so: about as surprised as when a cousin living in a nearby city drops by unannounced; not as surprised as they should be when a son who left fifteen years ago and whom they thought they'd never see again knocks at the door. They give him a hug, clasp his face in their hands, but right away his mother holds him at arm's length, looks him up and down, and asks where his coat is. He doesn't have a coat? That's not possible, you can't go out without a coat in this cold. Is he too poor to buy himself one? "No, Mom, trust me, I've got everything I need, really." There's one in the cupboard, a good coat that his father no longer wears, she says, and soon all three of them are standing in front of the closet. He tries on the coat to make them happy, they examine him from every angle, and his father says it's sad, all these good clothes covered and stashed away to protect them from moths, and this apartment no one will inherit when they die. Doesn't he want to move back? It's nice here, comfortable, quiet. Disabusing them of their illusions, Eduard says he's just there for a couple of days. He explains why he came to Moscow: his VIP reading tour, his book and its three-hundred-thousand-copy print run. He wants his parents to understand that he's made it, he wants them to be proud, but nothing he says seems to interest them. It's too far from their world; they don't even ask if he's got a copy of his book for them. And a good thing too, because he doesn't, and if he did, they wouldn't be happy with the portrait he's painted of them. The only thing they want to know is if he has a wife and if they can look forward to having grandchildren one day. "Yes, I have a wife," he says without going into detail, "but no kids, not yet."

"Not yet? At forty-six?" Raya shakes her head in dismay.

Their curiosity quickly satisfied, daily routine takes over. Venyamin, who's become a real old man, clutches the furniture as he makes his way back to the bedroom to lie down, and Raya, over a cup of tea in the kitchen, explains that he suffered a heart attack a year ago and hasn't felt like doing anything since. She has to dress and undress him, he practically never leaves the apartment anymore, and apart from going out to do the shopping neither does she. Anyway, where would she go? Downtown scares her, she's happy she doesn't live there. "Here it's calm," she repeats, as if in time she were hoping to persuade him to move in, to slip into his father's old coat now and then into the new one when he dies, to don his sheepskin *chapka* hat. To prove that they lack for nothing, she opens the cupboards and proudly shows him the food they've got stored up in case of a shortage. Sixty pounds of sugar, bags of buckwheat, and there are just as many more in the cellar.

The blue flame of the gas burning nonstop on the stove gets on Eduard's nerves. He wants to turn it off but she protests: it keeps them warm, and aside from that it keeps them company, like having someone with you in the room. "If I did that in Paris it'd cost me thousands of francs," he says, and of the few things he's said about his life abroad it's this detail that strikes her the most.

"You mean over there the state's so cheap it makes you *pay for gas?*" She can't believe it but adds pensively: "Come to think of it, they say Gorbachev and his toadies want to do the same here . . ."

Outside the big cities and the more or less intellectual milieus, discussing Gorbachev is harmony itself: there's no risk of getting into an argument, everyone hates him. This thought comforts Eduard somewhat.

His inner voice tells him to take the train back to Moscow that very evening, but that would be too cruel. It's the first time he's seen his parents in years and will no doubt be the last, so he decides to spend a week with them, sitting the stay out like a convict, marking the days off on the calendar. He's found his old weights and exercises for an hour each morning. Lying on his childhood bed he rereads his old copies of Jules Verne and Alexandre Dumas, eats three heavy meals a day, and forces himself to have prickly conversations with his mother— his father doesn't say a thing. She tells him all the tiny things that make up her day in almost hallucinatory detail. The idea of leaving anything out is completely foreign to her. To say she got a letter, she describes the walk to the post office, the line in front of the counter, her exchange with the clerk, the bus stops on the way back. It's a way to pass the time.

He asks what's become of his boyhood friends. Kostya, alias the Cat, who was sentenced to twelve years in a prison camp, was stabbed in a fight a couple of days after he got out. He's dead, his parents are slowly dying of grief. As for Kadik, Kadik the dandy who dreamed of becoming a saxophonist, he still works at the Hammer and Sickle. His Lydia left him, he went back to live at his mother's place, where he raised his little daughter. The little daughter grew up, she left, Kadik stayed with his mother. He drinks too much. "He'd be happy to see you," Raya ventures. Eduard declines.

And Anna? "Anna? My God you didn't hear? She hanged herself in the hovel where she lived alone between stints in the mental institution." She tried to paint and became extremely fat. Raya went to see her sometimes. One day Anna asked her for Eduard's address in Paris: "I couldn't say no. Did she write?" Eduard nods. He received five or six letters oozing a sordid madness, which he didn't answer.

The television is on all the time: Soviet television, the most masochistic in the world according to Eduard, which drowns its litany of catastrophes and lamentations in an endless flood of syrupy music. His old nemesis Sakharov has just died and, according to the journalists, the entire country is weeping as one. "They've gone nuts," says Raya, who hardly knows who Sakharov was. "You'd think they were burying Stalin." One speaker compares yesterday's exile with Gandhi, another with Einstein, a third with Martin Luther King, and one little joker with Obi-Wan Kenobi in *Star Wars*, the wise old mentor of the weak-willed and undecided Jedi knight, whom Gorbachev is increasingly starting to resemble. "And who's Darth Vader?" the interviewer asks.

The inescapable Yevtushenko pushes himself in front of the cameras to recite a poem in which the deceased is described as "the era's trembling wick"—a metaphor that makes Eduard snicker and will become a private joke only he understands in his articles for *L'Idiot*, where he will refer to Sakharov as "the wick." Suspense: Will Gorbachev declare a national day of mourning? No, because it's not the custom, he says: three days of mourning are prescribed for the general secretary of the Party, one for a member of the Politburo, none for a simple academic. Commentators see this coolness as presaging a shift to the right, an impression that's confirmed the day of the funeral. Gorbachev puts in a hasty moment of contemplation in front of the coffin but doesn't lead the funeral procession that several hundred thousand people follow through Moscow—follow spontaneously, an unprecedented event in the country's history. A deputy whose frank and likably oafish mug Eduard has already noticed, Boris Yeltsin, seizes the moment. He's already installed himself as head of the democrats by noisily resigning from the Politburo, now he's the one walking behind the coffin with Sakharov's wife, Yelena Bonner. Each time the camera films her, the old crow is invariably smoking a cigarette, stubbing one out or lighting another. Noticing that the people around Yeltsin and Bonner are carrying signs with a crossed-out 6, Raya asks: "What do all those sixes mean?"

"That they want to delete Article 6 of the constitution, the single-party rule," her son explains.

"What do they want then?"

"Well, for there to be multiple parties, like in France."

Raya looks at him in horror. Having multiple parties seems as barbarous to her as making people pay for their gas.

VI

Vukovar, Sarajevo,

1991–1992

෩

I

THEY'RE SITTING IN chairs placed in the right angle formed by two brown Formica tables, their backs to a blank wall. Nothing more of their surroundings is visible; they could be in a classroom, a mess hall, an administrative office. She's wearing a light-colored coat and a peasant's shawl; he's in a dark overcoat and a scarf, and he's put his sheepskin *chapka* in front of him on the table. They look like a retired couple. Though the camera jumps around without rhyme or reason, panning in and out, they remain the focus; there are no reverse shots. You can't see the men sitting or standing across from them. You can't see the face of the person offscreen who accuses the two old people in an angry monotone of living in unbridled luxury, of causing children to starve to death, of committing genocide in Timişoara. After each salvo of accusations the invisible prosecutor invites them to answer, and what the man says while fingering his *chapka* is that he does not recognize the legitimacy of the tribunal. Every now and then his wife loses her temper and starts to argue, until he puts his hand on hers to calm her with a familiar, touching gesture. And every now and then he looks at his watch, which led people to believe that he was waiting for troops to come and rescue them. But no troops arrive and after half an hour the scene cuts. There's a break. The next shot is of their bloody corpses lying on the pavement of a street or a courtyard, there's no telling where.

The scene has all the strangeness of a nightmare. Filmed by Romanian television, it was broadcast across France on the evening of December 26, 1989. I saw it, aghast, before leaving for Prague for New Year's, and Limonov saw it on his return from Moscow. He'd found and brought back Natasha, who was meek and gentle as she always was after running away. Perhaps he was thinking of their marriage, of his dream of growing old with her and dying by her side. In any event I'm sure he was thinking of his parents when he wrote the following lines as soon as the program ended:

> The videotape that was meant to justify the murder of the Romanian head of state bears glaring and terrible witness to the love of an elderly couple, the love expressed by the touch of a hand or a simple look. Of course the two were guilty of something. It's impossible for the leader of a nation not to be. Even the most innocent among them will have signed a shameful decree, failed to pardon someone. That goes with the job. But hunted and cornered in an anonymous room, underslept, helping each other face death, they've given us, unrehearsed, a scene worthy of the tragedies of Aeschylus and Sophocles. Journeying together toward eternity, simple and majestic, Elena and Nicolae Ceaușescu have joined the immortal lovers of world history.

I wouldn't have put it so lyrically, and I didn't think these grotesque tyrants were guilty only of the unavoidable mistakes you make when you're in power. Still, I too remember feeling terribly uncomfortable witnessing this parody of justice, this summary execution, right up to and including the supposedly exemplary staging that missed its mark completely; dignity in this case was on the side of the accused, no matter how criminal. I felt the same thing later when Saddam Hussein was flushed out and hanged. The enchanted year that had seen nonviolent revolutions sweep humanists like Václav Havel to power was ending on a sour note.

Other bizarre signals sounded from Romania in the months that followed. The revolution that had slaughtered the Ceaușescus claimed that thousands of martyrs had been massacred in a last spasm by the dying regime. The mass graves discovered at Timișoara were the source of particular emotion. The figure generally advanced was four thousand dead. *Libération* was more precise: 4,630. Then the television station TF1 boldly raised the stakes by upping the count to seventy thousand. As holiday festivities approached, the news on TV showed skeletal corpses exhumed from hastily dug graves, clothed in striped pajamas and covered in mud. Europe trembled. There was talk of sending international brigades to stop the genocide that the desperate killers of Ceaușescu's political police, the Securitate, were perpetrating. Then it emerged that the bodies, a few dozen at most, had been dug up for the cameras at Timișoara Cemetery where they'd been buried after dying natural deaths, and that the killers of the Securitate, far from carrying out a suicidal genocide, had shown their shrewdness and become officials of the National Salvation Front, the party of the new president Ion Iliescu. Banned entirely, charged with every crime imaginable, the Communist Party had simply changed its name and leader; in fact it was still alive and well. And the elections of March 1990, in which it won a sizable majority, proved that indeed the Romanians are the only people in history to have freely elected Communists. This all intrigued me enough that I took an assignment reporting in Romania that spring.

Freud developed the notion of the *Unheimlich*, or the "uncanny": that feeling you can have in dreams and sometimes in reality that the familiar object before you is in fact profoundly alien. Postrevolutionary Romania struck me as a veritable Disneyland of the *Unheimlich*. A twilight zone which, according to disturbing rumors, was mined like Swiss cheese with a network of underground passageways dug by the secret police, into which people disappeared. A perpetual and insidious shadowland frozen between light and darkness. Even the tens of thousands of stray dogs that ran wild in Bucharest, competing for scraps with tens of thousands of children—also stray—seemed less frightening than the men, who had become not dogs but wolves. Hatred, suspicion, and slander were like a toxic gas, making it impossible to breathe. Just one example among many: a writer who'd been showered with prizes and official appointments for the last twenty years went on and on to me about his "inner resistance" to the reviled regime. I asked him if, all the same—while of course I wasn't blaming him, while of course I understood very well that such an attitude was virtually impossible—it wasn't true that others had resisted a little less inwardly than him, and would he mind mentioning some names (I was thinking of a few opposition figures with untarnished reputations, Romania's Sakharovs). He looked at me gravely before answering that he preferred not to, out of discretion and mercy, as it was no secret that the Securitate recruited its most zealous informers among these supposed opposition figures. Okay. Which is only the first convoluted twist. The second, which complicates things even more, is that all the subtle minds I talked to about this exchange said that of course the guy was right. Everyone knew that, it was an open secret.

The time has come to talk of subtle minds. It was in Romania that I first encountered them; they thrived in the wreckage of communism. Diplomats, journalists, observers who'd long been stationed in the country, they've made it their specialty to systematically contradict the official discourse, the media clichés and the well-intentioned illusions. Sworn enemies of "political correctness," the subtle minds delight in insisting that the KGB or the Securitate, denounced by the naive as dens of death and darkness, were in fact no more than the Russian or Romanian equivalents of the elitist École nationale d'administration in France, or that, like the poems of Radovan Karadžić, who will soon make his appearance in this book, the scientific work thanks to which Elena Ceaușescu was awarded honorary doctorates from every university in her country wasn't as bad as people said. The subtle minds had the ear of our President Mitterrand; they made their mark on his foreign policy—and Romania, where everything was two-faced, where everything was rigged and deceitful, where the mass graves that excited indignant compassion in the West really *were* sinister masquerades, was their El Dorado.

After two weeks in over my head in this pit of lies and slander, I was ready to hear the impressions of an old Romanian who'd been exiled in France for thirty years and who'd returned to his country not long ago. He told me something that wasn't especially subtle, but it wasn't especially politically correct either: "Have you seen their faces, in the street? Have you seen their faces? The poverty, the dirt, okay—but the bitter suspicion, the depravity, the malicious fear written all over their features? My people were not like that, trust me. These are not my people. I don't understand. *Who are these people?*" The trembling in his voice recalled the horror of the hero in *Invasion of the Body Snatchers*, when he discovers that one by one, everyone around him has been replaced by extraterrestrials, and that the people he knows, even if they look unchanged, are really dangerous mutants.

Near the end of my stay, President Iliescu and his prime minister, Petre Roman, called on the workers to defend "democracy" (I use quotation marks here; in fact you'd need them around almost every word) against a neofascist plot no less imaginary than the genocide perpetrated at Timișoara by the Securitate. What wasn't imaginary at all, however, were the logistics set in motion: buses and trains chartered specially by the National Salvation Front to bring twenty thousand miners to Bucharest on June 14, 1990, all galvanized by frenetic brainwashing and armed with iron bars. They terrorized the city for two days, at first beating up anyone suspected of belonging to the opposition and then, since that didn't include many people, pretty much anyone at all, indiscriminately, to show they weren't kidding around. I was just finishing up my reporting in the Carpathian Mountains and only made it back to Bucharest in time for the end of the spectacle. Congratulated by President Iliescu, the miners started to leave as the journalists flocked in and overran the Hotel Intercontinental, where, delaying my departure, I spent three days waiting for something to happen, looking for signs of mobs that dissipated as quickly as they gathered, listening to the rumors pooling at the hotel and wondering if it would be better to leave and risk missing out yet again on what was going on, or to hang around and risk running out of good reasons to leave.

During these three days I talked a lot with an American journalist who'd had his face bashed in pretty badly and who moreover shared my passion for the kind of paranoid science fiction tales among which *Invasion of the Body Snatchers* is paradigmatic. We outdid ourselves naming films and books and authors, and when we got to Philip K. Dick we were in complete agreement: his novels, which paint with terrifying sharpness the breakdown of reality and of the minds that perceive it, were the only reliable guide for a voyage to the Romanian twilight zone.

One of them, *The Penultimate Truth*, tells the story of humanity after a biological war. Taking refuge in underground tanks, the people have led an atrocious existence for years. They know from television that war is raging on the surface, that cities are destroyed each week, and that the atmosphere is increasingly toxic. But one day a rumor starts circulating: the fighting ended long ago; a handful of the powerful control the TV networks and are conspiring to keep the masses underground so they can live in peace alone under the starry firmament. The rumor spreads—the worst, of course, is that it's true—and you can imagine the abject, righteous hatred that drives the masses when they launch an attack on the surface. This is the sort of hatred that the American journalist and I saw blazing in the eyes of the miners who'd descended on Bucharest to "save democracy." And I'll admit that we made an impious wish, there at the bar of the Intercontinental: that this hatred would one day turn against those who'd fanned it.

2

I RETURNED FROM Romania disturbed, and persuaded that the best way to give an account of my disturbance was to write Philip K. Dick's biography. This work kept me busy for two years, during which time I followed what was going on in the world, and particularly in what people had started calling the former Yugoslavia, only from afar. From my perspective, at least initially, when only the Serbs and the Croats were involved, it was like the Syldavians and Bordurians in *The Adventures of Tintin*: mustachioed villagers wearing embroidered vests and caps, and inclined, after a good drink or two, to get out their rifles and kill one another in the name of ancient feuds. One such feud was over who owned a field that the Serbs, for reasons that are difficult for anyone else to understand, consider the most sacred place in their history because it was the scene of their bitterest defeat. From afar, the situation seemed as discouraging as the one in Romania; there was reason to believe that the euphoria of 1989 had waned considerably. But I didn't have a firm opinion, so I listened to the discussions without taking part.

At the time, most of my friends championed Croatian independence in the name of the right of peoples to self-determination. The argument seemed indisputable: if you want to go, you go. You can't imprison a nation by force. But some were of another mind. First of all, they said, by that token you'd have to grant the same right to anyone that claims it: Corsicans, Basques, the Flemish, Italian supporters of the Northern League—we'd never see the end of it. Second, France was historically a friend to the Serbs, who'd resisted Nazi Germany while the Croats had not only supported the Nazis but had done so in a particularly zealous and bloodthirsty way. Those who advanced this argument were fond of bringing up the memorable scene in Malaparte's book *Kaputt*: the author, visiting the Croatian leader Ante Pavelić, sees a wicker basket full of slimy gray objects and asks if it contains Dalmatian oysters. No, Pavelić tells him, it's forty pounds of Serbs' eyes, a present from his loyal Ustashis—that's what the Croatian partisans were called; on the Serbian side it was the Chetniks.

The last argument, finally, which seemed to me the most convincing: even if you viewed Croatian aspirations for independence as legitimate, the fate of the Serbs who'd been living among them for so long wasn't exactly enviable. After so long in the majority and dominant in Yugoslavia, they would find themselves in the minority and dominated in Croatia. Their fears were understandable when you considered the Croatian government's first acts under President Franjo Tudjman: banning signs in Cyrillic script; dismissing the Serbs in the civil service; replacing the red-starred flag of the Yugoslav Federation with the red-and-white checkerboard of the independent state of Croatia. The flag had been created in 1941 by the Germans, and for those who lived through the Second World War, it evoked pretty much the same associations as the swastika did. I say all this to stress that in the first months after Yugoslavia imploded, you couldn't just divide people up into good and bad, and that even if there was a healthy dose of propaganda in the mix, it wasn't entirely crazy to view the Serbs of Croatia sort of like Jews fated to be persecuted. Things only started to clear up with the spectacular destruction of Vukovar, and that's precisely where we catch up with Limonov.

In November 1991 he's invited to Belgrade for the launch of one of his books, and during a signing some uniformed men come up and ask him what he knows about the Serbian Republic of Slavonia. Not too much in fact. Well, he's told, it's an enclave inhabited by Serbs in the easternmost tip of Croatia. Not wanting to go along with the Croatian secession, these Serbs went ahead and seceded themselves, the Croats objected, and so it's war. And a key city in this war, Vukovar, has just fallen: would he care to come and see for himself?

Eduard had other plans; what's happening in his own country interests him more than these disputes between Balkan peasants, but he thinks that he'll soon be fifty and he's never been to war, which is an experience a man's got to have sooner or later, so he says yes. He's so excited he doesn't sleep a wink that night. At dawn two officers come pick him up at his hotel. They take the highway connecting Belgrade, the capital of Serbia, with Zagreb, the capital of Croatia. Although it hasn't seen a private vehicle since the start of the hostilities, the highway is dotted with roadblocks and checkpoints. While soldiers check the travelers' ID, others keep their rifles trained on them. Suspicion mounts when they find out that although he's Russian and so presumably Orthodox and pro-Serbian, Eduard has a French passport, meaning Catholic and so presumably pro-Croatian. Things cool down after a couple of heartfelt jabs at Tudjman and Hans-Dietrich Genscher, the German foreign minister who encouraged his European colleagues to recognize independent Croatia, and who's seen in Belgrade as a theoretician of the Fourth Reich. Promising to hang the one with the intestines of the other, they have a drink to seal the deal and they're off again.

One detail in the version of things he's presented should arouse Eduard's suspicion: all of these soldiers who back the Serbian cause are wearing the uniform of the Yugoslav People's Army, which still exists, and which in theory cannot take part in the conflict but which in practice, since it's majority Serb, has just conscientiously shelled Vukovar and all the surrounding Croatian positions. This detail compromises the comparison I've just sketched, and which the officer charged with accompanying Eduard complacently develops, between the fate of the Serbs now and that of the Jews during the Second World War. The Jews didn't exactly have the steadfast support of the Wehrmacht to defend themselves against the Nazis. But Eduard couldn't care less about that. What he likes are the armed soldiers, the tanks, the sandbags, the gray-green uniforms that stand out against the snow, the mortar fire that they start to hear from a distance. It's crossing villages whose ruins are still smoking. It's being able to think, in this frozen corner of the Balkans, that it's 1941 instead of 1991. It's war, real war, the kind his father missed out on, and he's in it.

Vukovar was liberated by the Serbian troops two days earlier. The fact that what everyone around him is calling a "liberation" without a hint of irony is in fact a total devastation doesn't make him suspicious either. Berlin was also in ruins when the Red Army liberated it, and it's Berlin, only smaller, that this once-pretty Habsburg city looks like now. When he gets back to Belgrade he'll tell a writer about his escapade and the writer will ask him naively what hotel he stayed at. Eduard, grasping all that separates a man like himself, who's seen war close up, from a civilian like the guy he's talking to, doesn't even bother explaining that there are no longer any hotels in Vukovar, that very few houses are still standing and that none of them is habitable. Just a wasteland of rubble, twisted metal, and heaps of glass that bulldozers are starting to clear away. Even taking a piss alongside the path is forbidden because of the mines. Not a bird in the sky. Not many corpses, they've already been evacuated, but he sees his fill when he's taken to visit the body identification center.

Tortured, purple, charred bodies. Slit throats. The smell of decomposing flesh. Bags of human remains that soldiers unload from trucks. Who were these men? Serbs? Croats? "Serbs, of course," answers the officer who acts as his guide. He seems shocked by the question: for him casualties of war are Serbs by definition; their torturers are Croats. That may be true thirty miles away, but it's a more difficult claim to make on the outskirts of a Croatian city that's literally been annihilated by Serbian (or rather, federal) artillery and a quarter of whose population is missing. Whatever. Eduard doesn't doubt that there have been just as many innocent victims, just as many valorous warriors and just as many peasants unjustly uprooted and displaced on both sides. He doesn't believe one camp is entirely right and the other entirely wrong. But he doesn't believe in neutrality either. Being neutral means being a coward. Eduard isn't a coward and he feels fate has put him on the side of the Serbs.

He feels good here. He feels good in the evening around the fires where the unshaven men warm their swollen, black-fingernailed hands. He feels good in the camp at night, surrounded by the heavy odor of charcoal stoves, prune schnapps, and feet. As a child he dreamed of just this sort of encampment, this military brotherhood. Fate denied them to him and then without warning, at a bend in the path, it dropped everything he was born for right in his lap. You learn more about life and people in two hours of war than in four decades of peace, he thinks. War is dirty, sure, war is senseless, but come on! Civilian life is also senseless, in its sameness and its reasonableness and because it dulls the instincts. The truth that no one dares speak aloud is that war is a pleasure, the greatest pleasure there is, otherwise it would stop immediately. Once you've tasted it, it's like heroin: you want more. We're talking about real war, of course, not "surgical strikes" or the other bullshit that's good enough for the Americans who want to play good cop in foreign countries without risking their precious privates in ground combat. The taste for war, real war, is as natural to man as the taste for peace, it's idiotic to want to eliminate it by repeating virtuously that peace is good and war is evil. In fact it's like men and women, yin and yang: you need both.

———

The wars in the former Yugoslavia were not—or were almost entirely not—fought by regular armies, but by militias. And now that we've come this far I'd like to call two witnesses to the stand, who followed the wars on the ground and wrote books about them: Jean Rolin and Jean Hatzfeld. The first is a friend of mine, I know the second a little, and I admire them both. They themselves are closely acquainted and their accounts overlap. Jean Rolin's book is called *Campagnes*, Jean Hatzfeld's *L'Air de la guerre*.

On the first page of *Campagnes*, Jean Rolin describes "a roadblock manned by militiamen whose affiliations it wasn't easy to gauge. It was the start of the war, the weather was nice, the losses hadn't been too high on either side, and everyone was just getting used to the pleasure of carrying arms and using them to have their way, to terrorize civilians, to abuse girls, and all in all to enjoy for free everything you can only get in times of peace by working your fingers to the bone, if at all." These packs of young peasants were thrilled to get trashed and shoot off their weapons, and were soon joined by all manner of soccer hooligans, small- and big-time delinquents, authentic psychopaths, foreign mercenaries, Russian Slavophiles who'd come to defend Orthodoxy (with the Serbs), neo-Nazis nostalgic for the Ustashis (with the Croats), and jihadists (with the Bosnian Muslims, who will soon make their appearance). This small world shared a paramilitary culture consisting, again in Jean Rolin's words, of

> camouflage uniforms, green berets, and Ray-Bans; Kalashnikovs, pump-action shotguns, and Uzi submachine guns decorated with reams of Smurf stickers; ferocious alcoholism, four-by-fours without license plates overloaded with guffawing, tattooed Chetniks, whose long hair and beards fly in the wind, and who, coming back from the "front" or some other cleansing operation, shout, blast their sound systems, screech their wheels, and, best-case scenario, shoot their weapons off into the air, or else at anyone they can find; sluts giggling in the kitchen while in the bathroom someone's getting his ribs split open with a hacksaw; and graffiti on a wall: WE WANT WAR, PEACE IS DEATH.

Jean Hatzfeld, for his part, describes the most famous of these Serbian militias at work. It's the "Tigers," whose leader, a certain Željko
Ražnatović, popular among Belgrade's pimps, earned his stripes as a
war criminal under the name of Arkan. The scene, which Eduard
could have witnessed, takes place the day after the surrender at Vukovar, in a warehouse where Croatian prisoners are assembled after
being flushed out of their cellars during the final attacks. In principle
they're under the protection of the People's Army, but the People's
Army obligingly steps aside to let Arkan's militiamen decide their
fate. Most often this is done with an eye to personal grievances, because the victors and the vanquished know each other well from the
days not so long ago when no one cared who was Serb and who was
Croat. They lived in the same villages, the same neighborhoods. Just
yesterday these pale, terrified captives lived, worked, and drank at the
bar beside the people who now use the butts of their rifles to force
them onto military trucks headed for unknown destinations.

Hatzfeld describes Arkan, who presides over the operation, as a
sort of Rambo. As for Arkan's men, the day after the scene described
above, Hatzfeld happens to pick one of them up hitchhiking. He's a
nice, athletic young guy on leave and on his way see his mother, who
cheerfully tells Hatzfeld what he and his buddies do to the Ustashis—
the Croats, that is—who fall into their hands: "Initiation consists of
slowly slitting the throat of a kneeling prisoner. The boy explains that
those who are too nervous have to start over, that not many refused
and that those who did left the patrol. Of course it's a little weird the
first time, he says, but afterward you're happy to go out and celebrate."

I wanted to quote this account before giving Eduard's version.
When they met at Arkan's headquarters in Erdut, near Vukovar,
Eduard found Arkan "astute and circumspect," and he was flattered
to have been singled out from the ordinary run of journalists by this
military man. They drank slivovitz together, and there wasn't a thing
they didn't agree on: Gorbachev and Yeltsin deserved to be shot
alongside Tudjman and Genscher; what Russia needed was a revolution; the French intellectuals who supported the Croats were irre-

sponsible, and so on. Eduard asked Arkan if he'd accept him as a Russian volunteer. "Everyone's welcome," Arkan answered with a sweeping gesture. A fast friendship was born that day, and when he read in *Le Monde* several months later that a clash between Serbs and Muslims in Bosnia had ended in a victory for Arkan's militiamen, tears even came to Eduard's eyes. He got out the photo that showed him and Arkan posing with the little tiger that was the group's mascot, and, looking at it, he felt taken by a radiant nostalgia. "My brother Arkan, how I'd love to be back at your side! How I long to return to the war in the Balkan mountains!"

3

WHEN THE FIGHTING between Serbs and Croats came to a provisional halt and shifted to Bosnia in the spring of 1992, things became clearer, at least in the circles I frequented. The Serbs, roused to fanaticism in Belgrade by the ghastly President Milošević and on the battlefield by the shifty Radovan Karadžić, were clearly the villains of the whole thing, while the Bosnian Muslims, represented by Alija Izetbegović, an elderly man with a handsome, humanist's face, were obviously being subjected to heinous aggression—a term that was soon considered too weak and dropped in favor of *genocide*. These blond, blue-eyed men and women who listened to classical music in book-filled apartments were ideal Muslims, just the kind we wanted in France, and it was they above all who were credited with creating the harmonious, multiethnic society that had made Sarajevo the symbol of the Europe we all wanted. Anxious to defend this Europe and impassioned by the memory of the Spanish Civil War, several people I knew started taking regular trips to the besieged Sarajevo, sleeping in bombarded buildings where it was impossible to bathe, zigzagging across shattered streets under sniper fire, getting drunk with the thought that this day could be their last and often—the surroundings lent themselves to it—falling in love.

Retrospectively, I wonder why I denied myself so romantic and status-enhancing an experience. A little because I was chicken: I probably would have gone if I hadn't found out, right when I was asked if I wanted to, that Jean Hatzfeld had just had a leg amputated after taking fire from a Kalashnikov. But I don't want to make my case worse than it is: it was also out of wariness. I was on my guard, and still am, against sacred missions—especially those that attract people in my own circle of friends. As much as I sincerely believe I'm incapable of gratuitous violence, I can also imagine, perhaps too readily, the reasons or circumstances that might have pushed me in other times toward Nazi collaboration, Stalinism, or the Chinese Cultural Revolution. Maybe on top of that I also tend to wonder too much if, among the values that are taken for granted in my surroundings, and which the people of my era, country, and social class believe unsurpassable, eternal, and universal, there aren't some that will one day appear grotesque, scandalous, or just plain wrong. When unsavory characters like Limonov and his kin say that our faith in human rights and democracy is the modern equivalent of Catholic colonialism— the same good intentions, the same good faith, the same absolute certitude in bringing truth, goodness, and beauty to the savages—I may not be pleased by this relativist argument, but I've got nothing solid enough to counter it with. And because when it comes to politics I'm too easily of the same mind as the last person who's spoken, I lent an attentive ear to the subtle minds who explained that Izetbegović, widely touted as an apostle of tolerance, was in fact a Muslim fundamentalist surrounded by mujahideen, determined to install an Islamic republic in Sarajevo, and, unlike Milošević, strongly interested in having the siege and the war last as long as possible; that the Serbs had been subjected to the Ottoman yoke long enough in their history for it to be clear that they didn't want yet another helping; and finally that of all the photos published in the press showing victims *of the Serbs*, one in two, if you looked closely, actually showed a *Serb* victim. I nodded: yes, things were more complicated than they seemed.

With this in mind I listened to Bernard-Henri Lévy object to precisely this expression, saying that it justified every act of resignation,

procrastination, and diplomatic cowardice. Answering those who denounce the ethnic cleansing of Milošević and his gang with the words
"Things are more complicated than they seem" is exactly like saying
that yes, there's no doubt about it, the Nazis exterminated the Jews
of Europe, but if you look closely things are more complicated than
they seem. No, things are not more complicated than they seem,
Lévy raged. On the contrary they're tragically simple—and I nodded
my head as well.

I remember, around this time, flipping through a little book with the
unambiguous title *With the Serbs*, authored by ten or so French writers
including Patrick Besson, Gabriel Matzneff, Jean Dutourd, and a lot
of people from *L'Idiot* in reaction to the demonization of an entire
people "used as scapegoats by the masters of the new world order
[meaning the Americans] to establish their terrorist domination." The
undertaking had struck me as courageous if nothing else, because
there was nothing the authors could gain from it. Such courage has
nothing to do with wisdom and I think it's stupid, but it's courage all
the same. Finding it difficult to start this part of my book, sifting
through as much material as I could to put it off, I even went back and
reread this lampoon, which made the same impression on me this
time around as it had fifteen years ago. It contains a good dose of traditional French Serbophilia (Jean Dutourd: "What advantage will
France gain from running afoul of its old comrades—the Serbs—to
the benefit of people who mean nothing to it and will show no
gratitude—Bosnians, Kosovars?"), while the arguments of the younger
writers came down to: I was in Belgrade, the women are beautiful,
the slivovitz flows like water, they sing late into the night, the people
aren't barbarians at all but proud, modest, and pained by the knowledge that everyone thinks ill of them, starting with the French, whom
they've always considered their friends. Okay, I'd thought, but that's
not the issue. And if I'm going to be impressed by the argument "I
was there," I—who wasn't—find it more convincing when it comes
from people who were at the front, on both or even all three sides, not
just behind the lines of one, and who spent a couple of years there, not

just a couple of days. Deep down, the eyewitnesses whom I trusted, and whom I think I was right to trust even when I reread them today, are Jean Rolin and Jean Hatzfeld.

I'd bet neither of them is keen to play the role of the hero in these pages. Too bad. I admire their courage, their talent, and above all the fact that, like George Orwell, after whom they've modeled themselves, they prefer the truth as it is to the truth as they would like it to be. They don't pretend to ignore how exciting war can be any more than Limonov does, and they acknowledge that when you've got the choice you don't go to war out of a sense of virtue but because you want to. They like the adrenaline and the crackpots you meet on all front lines. They're touched by the suffering of the victims regardless of which side they're on, and to a certain extent they can even understand the motivations that drive the torturers. Filled with curiosity for the complexity of the world, they make sure to put a fact that contradicts their opinion front and center instead of hiding it. In this way Hatzfeld, whose first instinct was to believe he'd been caught in an ambush by Serbian snipers determined to do in a journalist, came back to Sarajevo after a year in the hospital to investigate and reached the conclusion that as luck would have it, the shots that cost him his leg were fired by Bosnian militiamen. I'm all the more impressed when such honesty doesn't lead to that old saw "one side's just as bad as the other," as the subtle minds are so fond of concluding. Because the moment comes where you've got to choose a side, or, in any event, the side from which you're going to observe the goings-on. During the siege of Sarajevo, after the first days when you could still hightail it from one side to the other with your foot on the accelerator at the price of a good scare, the choice was between following things from inside the besieged city or from the besieging positions. Even for men as reticent as Hatzfeld and Rolin to rally noble-minded followers the choice was natural: when one side is weaker and the other stronger, even if you make it a point of honor to note that those on the weaker side aren't all angels and those on the stronger side aren't all devils, you side with the weaker. You go where the shells are falling, not where they're being fired from. Of course when the situation shifts there's a moment when you're surprised to feel, like Jean Rolin, "an undeniable satisfaction at the idea that for once the Serbs were the ones taking it on the head." But this moment doesn't last, the wheel turns once more, and, if you're that sort of person, you find yourself denouncing the partiality of the International Tribunal in The Hague, which steadfastly prosecutes Serbian war criminals while leaving their Croatian and Bosnian counterparts to the predictable leniency of their own courts. Or you write reports on the horrible conditions faced today by the vanquished Serbs in their enclaves in Kosovo. It's a sinister but rarely contradicted rule that the torturer easily becomes the victim, and vice versa. You've got to have a strong stomach and be quick to adapt to make sure you always end up on the side of the victim.

4

PAWEŁ PAWLIKOWSKI IS a Polish-born British filmmaker with whom I share many interests, and whom I've run into several times while writing this book. He made a moving documentary about the last months of Venichka Erofeev's life—remember, the author of *Moscow to the End of the Line* and hero of the Brezhnevian underground. Poverty-stricken, destitute, alcoholic, and ravaged by cancer, Erofeev cuts a figure that Limonov would probably judge without pity but which had me almost in tears. In 1992 Paweł was disturbed by the prevailing rhetoric—in London as in Paris—that presented the Serbs as heirs to the Nazis. Like me, he knew many journalists, writers, and filmmakers who'd set up shop in the besieged Sarajevo, and he decided to go see what people were thinking on the other side.

He wound up filming musicians playing the hurdy-gurdy in front of soldiers' tents, singing monotonous chants almost as ancient as the *Song of Roland* about defeat on earth, victory in heaven, and burning down Turkish houses. He traced the echo of these songs through country weddings and children's ditties—ditties sung, it must be said, by children slinging Kalashnikovs. The names of valiant forefathers from six centuries ago were replaced by those of today's valiant heroes: Radovan (Karadžić) and Ratko (Mladić, the Serbian military leader). He filmed a council of war where you see them, Radovan and Ratko, bending over maps that they mark up, moving borders and with them populations, trying to agree on what can be conceded and what must never be, not at any price. It's the same exercise armies of diplomats were toiling away at in Lisbon, Geneva, and Dayton, except that here it's basically just the two of them and it's fascinating to observe. And he filmed Pale, the ski resort built in 1980 for the Sarajevo Olympics, which served as the capital of the "Bosnian Serb Republic"—a sort of Balkan Vichy with ski chalets and bobsled tracks instead of spas.

It's at the officers' mess at Pale that Paweł noticed a bit of an odd character with big glasses and a crew cut, who wore a People's Army overcoat over his leather jacket and seemed to be on very good terms with a particularly off-putting group of Chetniks, though he clearly wasn't one of them. The 7.65 pistol at his side looked, on him, like part of a disguise, Paweł thought. He wore it the way tourists in Tahiti wear the flower garlands offered as a token of welcome when they get off the plane.

A team from the TV station Antenne 2 was just having lunch. Hearing them speaking in French, the guy went over to their table and introduced himself in the direct fashion customary during wartime: Eduard Limonov, writer, interested in the planet's hot spots. Present at Vukovar in December, Transnistria in July. "A sort of Bernard-Henri Lévy," he added with a chuckle, "but not exactly on the same side." The TV crew sized him up, at first perplexed and then disgusted. "You think it's normal for a journalist to walk around carrying a gun?" one asked. Another even called him an asshole. No doubt the Russian wasn't expecting this reaction, but he didn't lose his cool. "I could gun you all down," he said, adding, with a nod over to the Chetniks, "my friends wouldn't be too thrilled, but I think they'd cover for me. Let me just say that I'm not a journalist. I'm a soldier. A group of Muslim intellectuals is brutally pursuing their dream of setting up a Muslim state here, and the Serbs don't want that. I'm on the Serbs' side and you can go to hell with your neutrality, which is nothing but cowardice. Enjoy your meal."

With these words he turned on his heels and went back to his table of Chetniks. A deathly silence hung over what remained of lunch. As they were leaving the mess tent, Paweł's soundman said he knew who this Limonov guy was. He'd read one of his books: terrific, incidentally, about his years living hand to mouth in New York and how he got screwed by black guys. Paweł burst out laughing. "Screwed by black guys? You think his Chetnik buddies know about that?"

Foreign writers were a dime a dozen in the other camp, but here they were much rarer. Paweł hit on the idea of asking the Russian asshole if he'd agree to interview Karadžić for his film. This tactic suited his own purposes because he didn't want anyone talking from offscreen or holding a mike in his film; he considered these techniques the scourges of lazy documentaries. This is how *Serbian Epics*, a BBC production that was subsequently showered in prizes and screened all over the place, ends up showing "the famous Russian writer Eduard Limonov" talking with "Dr. Radovan Karadžić, psychiatrist and poet, leader of the Bosnian Serbs."

The scene takes place on the heights from which the Serb batteries bombard Sarajevo; located at the bottom of a basin, the city lends itself ideally to this kind of attack. The rumble of mortar fire is almost incessant. Soldiers surround the two men. With his tall build, his large overcoat, the shock of salt-and-pepper hair blowing in the wind like the leaves of an oak tree, Karadžić cuts an imposing figure, and I regret to say that Limonov, puny in comparison in his little black leather jacket, seems like a pallid, two-bit thug trying to impress the godfather. He nods respectfully when Karadžić explains that he and his people are not the aggressors, but simply want to retake territory that has belonged to them since time immemorial. With a sincerity that I don't doubt in the least but that doesn't stop him from looking like a brownnoser, Limonov answers that, on behalf of his Russian compatriots and all the free men of the world, he admires the heroism of the Serbs in gallantly standing up to the fifteen countries all in league against them. Then, as they're both poets, the talk comes around to verse. Karadžić pensively recites several stanzas of an ode he composed twenty years ago describing Sarajevo engulfed in flames. A moment of silence follows, imbued with a sense of portentous fore-shadowings, interrupted when the president is called to the phone. It's his wife. He takes the call in the burned-out shell of a ski gondola where a field telephone has been installed. "Yes, yes," he says; you can sense he's annoyed. In the meantime a soldier plays with a little dog (I'm describing scenes from the film), and Limonov, left to himself, walks over to another soldier who's busy greasing his machine gun. Seeing that he's fascinated and no doubt eager to honor a distin-guished guest, the soldier offers to let him try it out if he wants. Like a child, Eduard takes his place behind the gun and dutifully obeys as the soldier shows him the right position. Finally, still like a child en-couraged by the adults' laughter and by their slaps on the back, he abandons all his inhibitions and empties a magazine in the direction of the besieged city.

Ta-ta-ta-ta-ta.

I didn't see the film when it was shown on French TV, but the rumor quickly got around that it showed Limonov shooting people on the streets of Sarajevo. When he's asked about it fifteen years later, he shrugs his shoulders and says no, he wasn't aiming at people. In the direction of the city, yes. But at nothing in particular, or at the sky.

Examined closely, the images tend to prove him right. A wide shot at the start shows that the scene takes place on the heights quite a distance from the city, from where mortars fire on the buildings, and not lower down from where the snipers pick people off in the street. But the scene in which Limonov gets his kicks with the machine gun is followed by a shot of the city much closer up, and this change of perspective presented as a reverse angle is somewhat misleading. Whether Limonov would have been troubled by really shooting at people, and whether he's actually done it in other circumstances, remain open questions. What is certain is that these images and the stories that circulated about them made the people he knew in Paris stop thinking of him as a charming adventurer and start thinking of him as more or less a war criminal. What's also certain is that when I contacted Paweł Pawlikowski and arranged for him to send me a DVD, *Serbian Epics* so chilled me that I stopped working on this book for over a year. Not so much because it shows my hero committing a crime—it's true, it doesn't—but because it makes him look ridiculous. A little boy playing the tough guy at the amusement park. What Jean Hatzfeld, in his typology of fanatics attracted by war, calls a "mickey."

Another unpleasant story circulates about Limonov's time at Sarajevo. In a restaurant in Pale called Kon-Tiki, he attends a banquet thrown by officers who drink and toast like Lermontov's hussars. A violinist warms up the crowd from a small stage: he's a Muslim prisoner. At one point the Serbs have a laugh forcing him to accompany one of the Chetnik songs you hear in Paweł's film, about setting Muslim houses on fire. Limonov—at least according to his version—doesn't find it particularly funny and offers him a glass of *rakia*, the local rotgut, to console him. The violinist answers curtly that his religion doesn't allow him to drink alcohol. Embarrassed by his blunder, Limonov attempts to beat a hasty retreat, but a Serb who's overheard the exchange feels the need to butt in with his own two cents: "Just do what my Russian friend's asking you to do! Drink! Are you going to drink, you Turkish mongrel?"

You can imagine the scene: horrible.

The rest of the evening Limonov feels the violinist glowering at him. The latter interpreted his well-intentioned gaffe as a deliberate attempt at humiliation. And while he might be able to understand something like that coming from the Serbs—who are his enemies and whom he'd treat just as cruelly if the roles were reversed—coming from a foreigner it seems far less pardonable. Eduard feels so bad that he goes over to him later in the evening to justify his behavior, but the violinist answers coldly, "I hate you. You understand? I hate you." To which Eduard responds: "Okay. You're a prisoner, I'm free. I can't fight you, all I can do is put up with it. You win."

What to make of this story? At first glance it must be true, and true exactly as Limonov recounts it because nothing obliged him to tell it in the first place. But things are more complicated than they seem. In fact, it was first reported by an eyewitness, a Hungarian photographer, as an example of despicable cruelty on Limonov's part. And it gets around. When you type "Limonov" into Google you end up running across it. So he was pretty much obliged to give his version, and it could be that this story about a gaffe that sparked a horrible misunderstanding is the most plausible he could think of to cover up truly disgraceful behavior, committed in the heat of his Chetnik fervor and which he himself is rightly embarrassed about. Personally, I don't think that's the case, because I don't think Eduard is either vile or a liar. But who's to say?

VII

Moscow, Paris,
Republic of Serbian Krajina,
1990–1993

∽

I

IN THE LAST months of his life, the exhausted Sakharov never stopped repeating to Gorbachev: "The choice is simple, Mikhail Sergeyevich. Either you side with the democrats, who you know are right, or you side with the conservatives, who you know are not only wrong but also certain to betray you. There's no point in procrastinating."

"I know, Andrei Dmitrievich, I know," Gorbachev sighed, a little annoyed and having a hard time digesting the fact that according to the opinion polls, Sakharov was the most popular man in the country. "That's all well and good; but in the meantime the thing is to reform the Party."

"Absolutely not," Andrei Dmitrievich answered in his clear voice. "The thing is absolutely not to reform the Party, but to abolish it. That's the first condition for a normal political system."

When people started saying things like that to him, Gorbachev simply couldn't keep up. The Party? Now wait a second . . . He fell back into the typical hedging of a politician who tries to make everyone happy, taking himself for the pope one day and Luther the next, and so wound up equally hated by the democrats and the conservatives.

Western political references are quite difficult to transpose onto Russia, where right and left don't mean much; nevertheless the words *democrat* and *conservative* don't strike me as all that inappropriate. After all, the democrats wanted democracy and the conservatives wanted to conserve power. The first group—for the most part urban, young, and intellectual—adored Gorbachev at first. But when he no longer dared to push ahead, their disappointment spread. At the May Day parade on Red Square in 1990, they even jeered at him in a public display of anger. That was now allowed—and it's poignant to think that the man to whom despite everything the people owed their freedom had to suffer the insults that in former times people only dreamed of saying to Brezhnev because no one had the guts: scrap the Party, and Gorbachev with it!

And these whiners weren't even the worst. At Sakharov's funeral, when a young man compared the deceased with Obi-Wan Kenobi and Gorbachev with an awkward Jedi, the journalist asked him whom he saw as Darth Vader. Unfortunately, the young man answered, there was no shortage of candidates. In fact the Politburo and the military-industrial complex harbored plenty of hard-liners. But, in the grand Soviet tradition, they were unimaginably gray and uncharismatic, which assured the media success of a second-stringer who's all but forgotten today: Colonel Viktor Alksnis.

Eduard met him in a television studio during a brief trip to Moscow. Both had been invited to take the anti-Gorbachev side in a conversation with democrats, former dissidents, and people from the Memorial society. Dressed in black leather and sporting a savage grin, Alksnis resembled a mediocre actor auditioning for the role of the bad guy who throws his enemies to the alligators. A parliamentary representative for Soviet military personnel in Latvia, he denounced the Baltic separatists, recommended martial law, and called for a sacred union of "Marxist-Leninists, Stalinists, neofascists, Orthodox believers, monarchists, and pagans" to save the country from disintegration at the hands of people who didn't love it and wanted to subjugate it to foreign powers. Familiar as we're starting to become with the political leanings of our hero, it will come as no surprise that he and Alksnis were soon as thick as thieves. After the show, the "Black Colonel," as he was known, introduced Eduard to his comrades in arms, whose names I will spare the reader; suffice it to say they were an appealing little group of soldiers and Chekists, readers of *Mein Kampf* and *The Protocols of the Elders of Zion*, publishers of ultranationalist rags like *Dyen* (The Day), a self-proclaimed "newspaper of the intellectual opposition" which the democrats nicknamed "The Herald of the General Staff" and in which Eduard made his debut as a Russian journalist. The two stayed in contact after Eduard went back to Paris, exchanging telephone calls and faxes, and hyping each other up for what seemed like an imminent coup d'état.

In an increasingly tight spot, Gorbachev was also, it must be said, increasingly blind. In January 1991, taking advantage of the fact that the entire world was watching the First Gulf War on television, Russian tanks entered Vilnius. After encountering major resistance they retreated, leaving around fifteen dead. This "Black Sunday" completely discredited Gorbachev in the eyes of the democrats: who, after that, was going to listen to talk of socialism with a human face? To shift responsibility for both the intervention and its failure, Gorbachev claimed he hadn't been informed, and people wondered what was worse, for him to be a liar or completely in the dark. The army increased its troop movements and border clashes without telling him, preferably during international summits to embarrass him in the eyes of his beloved West. Curiously, however, the provocations produced the opposite result: photos showed him smiling all the more. As general secretary of the Party, his mandate was from the Party alone, and he treated with disdain the "so-called democrat" Boris Yeltsin who'd just been elected president of Russia by direct suffrage. That of course only enhanced Yeltsin's stature—but Gorbachev couldn't seem to grasp that fact. The loyal Shevardnadze resigned from his post as minister of foreign affairs, publicly declaring that a dictatorship was in the offing, and Gorbachev ignored the warning. The even more loyal Yakovlev didn't resign, but each time he bid farewell to a journalist he said, "Goodbye, see you soon—if I'm not sent to Siberia, that is." Fueled by despair, he tried to warn his boss about the increasingly overt sedition in the Politburo, but Gorbachev shrugged and answered: "There you go exaggerating again. I know them, they're a little stubborn but they're good guys. Everything's under control."

It's in this confident frame of mind that he leaves on a well-deserved vacation to the sumptuous villa that he's had built in Crimea. And it's there that all of a sudden his telephone is cut, the house isolated, and the perimeter cordoned off. During this time, the group of generals whose names I'll give now because despite everything they belong to history—Kryuchkov, Yazov, Pugo, and Yanayev—declare a state of emergency and waste no time messing up their coup completely by putting the most pathetic of their number, Vice President Yanayev, in charge. The poor fellow will spend the next four days in a state of panic: he shuts himself away in his office and has to be forcibly removed before he's willing to hold a televised press conference. Despite the old-style attempt to clamp down on the press, on TV his hands tremble and he has a lost look on his face; he's presented as triumphant and yet he's already defeated. This farcical impression is the strangest thing about the coup of August 1991. It all comes back to the characters of the conspirators, who were mediocre men and above all real boozers. They got drunk very quickly. Not on power, no: drunk on booze. Wasted. Plastered out of their minds. And very quickly, being maudlin drunks, they sensed that it wasn't going to work, that they were in the midst of making an enormous mistake, but by then it was too late to turn back. The order had been given, the tanks were entering Moscow, they were obliged to go on—but their hearts weren't in it. They'd have rather gone to bed with some aspirin and a jar of pickles, pulled the covers over their heads, and waited for it all to blow over.

This all emerges in retrospect. At the time, the democrats believed what they hadn't believed in several years: that after a second thaw the ice was forming again, that they'd been foolish and overconfident, that they should have fled while the time was ripe. And in fact the coup might have succeeded. Everything depended on the army. The young conscripts who received the order to march on Moscow were terribly afraid they'd have to do what their fathers had done in Prague in 1968, and it took a great deal of courage on their part to obey not their superiors but Yeltsin, who urged them to stay on the side of the law and the state.

Keenly aware of the symbolism of his actions, Yeltsin organized the resistance from the seat of parliament, which is known in Moscow as the White House. And so during these historic days on the world stage there was a second White House, far from the one in Washington. This White House became the scene of Russia's fight for democracy. The glorious imagery of August 1991, every bit as stirring as the Tennis Court Oath in the French Revolution or George Washington's crossing of the Delaware, is exemplified by the photo of Yeltsin perched on a tank in front of that White House. It's Rostropovich, who rushed to guard the door of Yeltsin's office in that White House. It's the crowds of Muscovites who came to defend that White House, erecting barricades, protecting their fledgling freedom with their bodies. It's the tanks backing up, the girls kissing the soldiers as they slip flowers into the barrels of the soldiers' rifles. And it's the immense sigh of relief, on the fourth day, because the nightmare had not come to pass and the people would continue to live in freedom.

Twenty years later, the young people in the cities, those who made *Star Wars* comparisons when recounting the history of their country, remember August 1991 as one of the most intense moments of their lives, like a terrifying horror film with a thrilling climax. First the USSR returns and they have the scare of their lives. Then it collapses in ridicule and they have the time of their lives. Because it was also beautiful, beautiful and just, that the last heirs of seventy years of oppression should depart not in a Wagnerian twilight of the gods, but as objects of ridicule. As buffoons who are definitely not scary anymore. Whose only supporters in the world are Castro, Gaddafi, and Saddam Hussein, the last survivors of the dead poets' society—and also our president, François Mitterrand, the prince of the subtle minds, who pushed Machiavellianism to the point of stupidity and who, when he was criticized for having so hurriedly congratulated the people he believed were the new masters of the USSR, answered loftily that they should be judged by their actions—as if a coup wasn't itself an action, and a significant one at that.

The story ends like this: Gorbachev returns from Crimea absurdly tan, without a clue about what's happened; in fact the affair only registers because of the inconveniences he and his family suffered as a result, cut off from the world in a villa fit for an oil sheikh. Three of the putschists commit suicide, and luckily Eduard's still there to mourn them—because, regardless of what one may think of his choices, he at least remains loyal and honors the vanquished. Then on

August 23, there's the tremendously theatrical moment, rebroadcast by television stations around the world: the parliamentary session when Yeltsin, after forcing Gorbachev to read with an unsteady voice the minutes of the council meeting during which the ministers he had named resolved to betray him, leans over, milking the moment for all it's worth, and says, "Oh, I almost forgot, there's a little decree to be signed . . ."

"A little decree?" Gorbachev says with a haggard look on his face.

"Yes, suspending the activities of the Communist Party of Russia."

"Wh-wh-what?" Gorbachev stutters. "But I haven't read it . . . we haven't discussed it . . ."

"No matter," Yeltsin says. "Go on, Mikhail Sergeyevich, sign it."

And Gorbachev signs it.

And then, immediately afterward, the statue of Dzerzhinsky on the square in front of the Lubyanka, the headquarters of the KGB, is toppled. The red flag is replaced by the tricolor flag of the 1917 provisional government. And finally, a few months later, there's another historic drinking binge, bringing together in utmost secrecy the Russian president Yeltsin, the Ukrainian president Kravchuk, and the Belarusian president Shushkevich at a hunting lodge in Belovezhskaya Forest. Yeltsin leaves Moscow without saying a word to Gorbachev about what he's going to do; nothing's been prepared, none of the three conspirators has the slightest idea what a federation or a confederation might be. All they repeat to one another while downing huge quantities of vodka in the sauna is that their three republics created the Soviet Union in 1922, so that gives them the right to dissolve it. Yeltsin gets so drunk that the two others have to carry him off to bed, and just before conking out completely he calls George Bush (senior) so he'll be the first to know: "George, the guys and I have worked something out. The Soviet Union no longer exists." To make the humiliation complete, it's the least important of the troika, Shushkevich, who's given the task of telling Gorbachev, and Shushkevich affirms that Gorbachev, aghast, answers, "But then what will become of me?"

What will become of him? A well-off retiree who'll be granted a dacha, a foundation, and the right to give exceedingly well-paid lectures until the end of his days. Bearing in mind Russian history since the Middle Ages, it's an exceptionally lenient fate for a deposed czar.

2

IN THE EPIC clash between Gorbachev and Yeltsin, the French sided with the former from the start, and I find their sentimental loyalty to him somewhat surprising. Yeltsin was considered a brutal, ill-mannered ruffian who'd been playing an ambiguous role since the putsch of 1991, and that impression didn't improve over the course of his time in power. Gorbachev was our hero; those who wanted to depose him were monsters. Sure, Yeltsin had saved Gorbachev's skin, but then he wouldn't stop rubbing it in, so in the end, no one really knew if he was good or bad. His words smacked of populism; some people even thought he had the makings of a dictator.

Alone in France but in agreement with the immense majority of Russians, my mother spoke of Gorbachev as an apparatchik who'd been overwhelmed by the forces he'd unwillingly set in motion, and of Yeltsin as the man who embodied his people's wish for freedom. Shaped by communism, he'd had the courage to break with it. He'd followed Sakharov's coffin at Yelena Bonner's side. He was Russia's first elected president. He'd defended the White House as Lafayette had taken the Bastille. He'd outlawed the Party that had stifled its people's consciences and liquidated the Union that had imprisoned its nations. In two years he'd become a major historic figure. Building on this momentum, would he succeed in creating a democracy, a market economy, a new society in a country hitherto condemned to backwardness and misfortune?

Aware of his ignorance in economic matters, Yeltsin pulled a young prodigy named Yegor Gaidar out of his hat. A descendant of the high

Communist *nomenklatura*, Gaidar professed an absolute faith in lib-
eralism. As David Remnick nicely sums up in *Resurrection*, the book
that follows his memorable *Lenin's Tomb*, and to which I also owe
many insights into this era, no theoretician of the Chicago School, no
adviser to Ronald Reagan or Margaret Thatcher believed in the vir-
tues of the market as fervently as Yegor Gaidar. Russia had never had
anything remotely like a market; the challenge was enormous. Yeltsin
and Gaidar thought it was essential to act quickly, very quickly, to
force their ideas through and catch the reactionary forces that had
gotten the better of all Russian reformers since Peter the Great off
guard. They baptized their remedy "shock therapy," and as far as shocks
go, this one was quite a jolt.

First of all, prices were liberalized, which provoked inflation of
2,600 percent and rendered completely useless the parallel "voucher
privatization" initiative. On September 1, 1992, vouchers valued at ten
thousand rubles were sent by mail to all Russian citizens over a year
old; these vouchers represented each citizen's share in the national
wealth. After seventy years during which in theory no one was allowed to work for him- or herself but only for the collectivity, the idea
was to involve people as investors and foster the development of busi-
nesses and private property—in short, of the free market. Because of
inflation, unfortunately, by the time these vouchers arrived, they were
already worthless. Their beneficiaries discovered that, at most, they
could purchase a bottle of vodka with them. So they resold them en
masse to some cunning individuals who offered them, let's say, the
value of a bottle and a half.

These cunning individuals, who would become multibillionaires
in just a few months, were named Boris Berezovsky, Vladimir Gusinsky, and Mikhail Khodorkovsky. There were others, but to go easy on
my readers I'll just ask them to remember these three names: Berezovsky, Gusinsky, Khodorkovsky. Three little pigs who, as in those
penniless theater troupes with more roles than actors to play them,
will represent for the purposes of this book all those known as the
oligarchs. They were young, intelligent, energetic, and not dishonest
by nature; but they had grown up in a world where it was forbidden to

do the very thing they were gifted at—business—and then overnight they were told, "All right, go to it." With no rules, no laws, no banking system, no taxation. As Yulian Semyonov's young bodyguard had predicted with delight, it was the Wild West.

For someone who returned every two or three months as Eduard did between trips to the Balkans, the speed with which Moscow changed was hallucinating. The drab Soviet monotony had been thought eternal, and now, on streets that had been named after great Bolsheviks and once again went by the names they'd had before the Revolution, the neon signs were as densely packed as in Las Vegas. There were traffic jams and, beside the old Ladas, black Mercedes with tinted windows. Everything foreign visitors used to cram their suitcases with to please their deprived Russian friends—jeans, CDs, cosmetics, toilet paper—was now readily available. No sooner had people gotten used to the appearance of a McDonald's on Pushkinskaya Square than a trendy disco opened next door. Before, restaurants had been immense, dismal places. Headwaiters who looked like surly clerks brought you fifteen-page menus, and no matter what you ordered there wasn't any more of it—in fact there was only one dish, usually revolting. Now the lights were subdued, the waitresses pretty and smiling, you could get Kobe beef and oysters flown in that day from the coast of Brittany. The "new Russian" entered contemporary mythology, with his bags full of cash, his harems of gorgeous girls, his brutality, and his boorishness. A joke from those days runs: two young businessmen notice they're wearing the same suit. "I paid five thousand dollars for it in Paris," one says. "Is that a fact," the other trumps: "I got mine for ten thousand!"

While a million crafty people started to enrich themselves frenetically thanks to the "shock therapy," 150 million less quick off the mark were plunged into misery. Prices kept climbing, while salaries stayed put. An ex-KGB officer like Limonov's father could hardly buy two pounds of sausage with his monthly pension. A higher-ranked officer who'd started his career in the intelligence service in Dresden, East

Germany, and who'd been hastily repatriated because East Germany no longer existed, found himself without a job or a place to live. Reduced to working as a black-market cab driver in his hometown of Leningrad, he cursed the "new Russians" as bitterly as Limonov. This particular officer isn't a statistical abstraction. His name is Vladimir Putin, he's forty years old, like Limonov he thinks that the end of the Soviet empire is the worst catastrophe of the twentieth century, and he will be called upon to play a role of no small importance in the last part of this book.

The life expectancy for a Russian man dropped from sixty-five in 1987 to fifty-eight in 1993. The lines of desolate people waiting in front of empty shops were replaced by old people walking up and down in underground passageways trying to hawk the few possessions they had. Anything they could sell to survive, they sold. If you were a poor retiree, it was two pounds of pickles, a tea cozy, or old issues of *Krokodil*, the pathetic "satirical" magazine of the Brezhnev years. If you were an army general, it might be tanks or planes; some fraudulently set up private companies that sold military aircraft and pocketed the profits themselves. If you were a judge, you sold your verdicts. A police officer, your tolerance. A bureaucrat, your stamp of approval. A veteran of the Afghan wars, your ability to kill. A murder contract was negotiated at between ten thousand and fifteen thousand dollars. Fifty bankers were shot dead in Moscow in 1994. As for the wheeler-dealer Semyonov, by that time barely half of his gang were still alive and he himself was dead and buried.

My cousin Paul Klebnikov arrived right around then. His grandparents, like mine, had fled the Revolution of 1917. But they'd gone to the United States, so that Paul was as American as I am French—only he spoke better Russian. He was my age, and despite being separated by the Atlantic, we'd known each other since we were kids. I liked him a lot, and my sons adored him. He was their hero—the very picture of a great reporter to a little boy. Handsome, strong, with an honest smile and a firm handshake: Mel Gibson in *The Year of Living Dangerously*. He worked for *Forbes* magazine, which sent him to investigate economic crime in Moscow in 1994. When he got there he filled his date book with appointments, but more than one of his contacts were killed before he ever had a chance to meet them. That affected him so profoundly that he stayed. Appointed *Forbes*'s permanent correspondent in Moscow, this great investigative journalist continued his research. He wrote a book on the subject in which, using Boris Berezovsky as an example, he explains in detail how the largest Russian fortunes were created under Yeltsin. And he was assassinated in turn, gunned down at the entrance to his building much as Anna Politkovskaya would be. And like Politkovskaya's, the inquiry into his murder has, to this day, failed to turn up anything.

The big players slaughtered one another for control of industrial combines or mineral deposits, the small fry for kiosks or market stalls, and even the smallest kiosk or stall needed a "roof": that's what the countless security providers—all more or less protection rackets because they shot you if you refused their services—were called. The holding companies of oligarchs like Gusinsky or Berezovsky employed veritable armies, commanded by high-level KGB officers who'd privatized their talents. Moving down a rung, the protection services no businessperson could do without recruited from the Georgian, Chechen, or Azeri mafias, and from among the police, which had become just one mafia among many.

I've got a good story on that subject. Its hero is my friend Jean-Michel, a French guy who, after his wife died in the crash of TWA flight 800 in 1995, went to Moscow to start a new life, the way other people might join the Foreign Legion. There he opened restaurants, bars, and nightclubs that were actually brothels for new Russians and rich expats. You can think what you like about that on a moral level, but building up such an empire from scratch, with only a smattering of Russian, at a time when a misplaced word could send you to the bottom of the Moskva River in cement shoes, calls for nerves even our very demanding Eduard might envy. It would take a Scorsese to do the whole of it justice. I don't propose to attempt that, but just to tell the following story: one night, elite troops in combat uniform, their faces masked by balaclavas, invaded one of Jean-Michel's clubs. There they terrorized the girls, the personnel, and the customers, making everyone lie on the ground at the point of their Kalashnikovs. Once the mood had been set, the boss took off his balaclava, sat down, ordered a drink, and explained calmly to Jean-Michel that his roof wasn't trustworthy and that he needed to make a change. And from now on the police—because this commando unit was in fact the police—would take care of everything. It'd be a bit more expensive but safer, and the transfer of authority would be painless. The boss would take care of explaining the situation to the previous guardians, and he guaranteed that there would be no trouble. When he left he gave Jean-Michel a CD of the rock band a few of his men had started. Everything happened as promised. Jean-Michel had no complaints about his new roof, and likes to amuse his friends by playing them the CD. He was lucky: this sort of incident all too often turned into a Saint Valentine's Day Massacre.

Before he died not long ago, the former prime minister Yegor Gaidar confided to a journalist: "What you've got to understand is that we didn't have a choice between an ideal transition to a market economy and a criminalized transition. Our choice was between a criminalized transition and civil war."

3

TO JUSTIFY THE collectivization, the famine, the purges, and, in a general way, the unassailable fact that the "enemies of the people" were the people themselves, the Bolsheviks liked to say that when you chop wood, chips fly, the Russian version of saying you can't make an omelet without breaking a few eggs. The free market replaced the dictatorship of the proletariat as the horizon of a radiant future, but the same proverb still served the chefs of "shock therapy" and all those close enough to power to get a bite of the omelet. The difference now is that those who see themselves as broken eggs are no longer afraid of being sent to Siberia, and they speak out. Moscow is the scene of numerous demonstrations by retirees reduced to begging on the street, unpaid soldiers, nationalists maddened by the liquidation of the empire, Communists who mourn the days when everyone was poor but equal, and people who are disoriented because they no longer understand their own history. And it's understandable: how to know what's right or wrong, who are the heroes and who the traitors, when you keep celebrating the October Revolution year after year, repeating all the while that this revolution was both a crime and a catastrophe?

Eduard doesn't miss a single one of these demonstrations when he's in Moscow. Recognized by the people who read his articles in *Dyen*, he's often congratulated, kissed, and blessed: with people like him, Russia is not lost. Once, invited by his comrade Alksnis, he gets up on the platform where the leaders of the opposition are speaking one after the other, and takes the megaphone. He says that the supposed "democrats" are profiteers who've betrayed the blood shed by their fathers during the Great Patriotic War. That the people have suffered more in one year of supposed "democracy" than in seventy years of communism. That anger is brewing and people should prepare for civil war. This speech differs little from the others, but after each sentence the immense crowd applauds. The words come naturally to him, and they express what everyone feels. Waves of approval, gratitude, and love wash over him. It's what he dreamed of when he was poor and desperately alone in his room at the Embassy Hotel in New York, and his dream has come true. As when he was mixed up in war in the Balkans, he feels good. Calm, powerful, borne aloft by like-minded individuals: right where he belongs.

"I'm Looking for a Gang" is the title of one of his articles. He didn't form his own right away, first he tried to join up with others. I'm guessing the name Vladimir Zhirinovsky is vaguely familiar to readers. He was—and still is—regarded as the Russian Jean-Marie Le Pen, and the comparison isn't misleading. He's as loudmouthed as Le Pen, with the same audacity and a similarly direct way of speaking.

No doubt he's crazier, but there you go, he's Russian. I've already said a few words about Alksnis, who cuts a picturesque background figure. As for the others—Zyuganov, Anpilov, Makashov, Prokhanov—I get the impression that because I'm writing this book and immersing myself in this era, I'm the only one who's still familiar with their convoluted paths, simple ideas, hazy programs, fleeting alliances, and poisonous clashes. Anyhow, it's this mixed bag of nostalgic Communists and farouche nationalists that Eduard hangs around with in Moscow, trying to persuade himself that they're the locus of the nation's vital forces. And it's during a banquet organized by Prokhanov, editor in chief of *Dyen*, that he meets Aleksandr Dugin.

Eduard is sad that night. And he's got every reason to be: he's just learned that the sawed-off torso of a friend has been found in the trunk of a car, beside his half-charred head. He'd met the friend, the battalion leader Kostenko, in Transnistria on a reporting mission for *Dyen*.

Just a quick word about the Moldovan Republic of Transnistria: it's the same situation there as in the diverse Serb republics of the former Yugoslavia. Moldova was a part of eastern Romania, annexed by the Soviet Union. The Moldovans are so impoverished that they dream of rejoining Romania, just to give you some idea. When the Soviet Union collapsed, they declared their independence, much to the displeasure of the Russians living on their territory. These Russians were settlers of a sort, and had lorded it over the local population, composed for the most part of Romanians. Now, subject to harassment and reprisals by the new state, they in turn created an autonomous republic (Transnistria), and took up arms to defend it. Eduard, who is unreservedly sympathetic to their cause and didn't want to miss a single one of the wars breaking out one after the other in the ruins of the empire, just loved it down there. He participated in a punitive raid against the Romanians, crossed a block of bombed-out buildings under sniper fire, and ran between fields strewn with mines. And there he met battalion leader Kostenko, whose story he now tells to the person sitting next to him, a bearded fellow introduced to him as Aleksandr Dugin.

Formerly the commander of a paramilitary unit in Afghanistan, Kostenko had opened a garage in Moldova. Subsequently he became a warlord and absolute master of his town as it fell into chaos around him. A Ukrainian like Eduard but born in the Far East, where his father had been garrisoned, he had Asian features and a reputation for old-school cruelty. An aura of fear surrounded him. He dispensed justice in his garage, surrounded by bodyguards armed to the teeth and a blonde in a miniskirt and dark glasses. Eduard saw him condemn to death a fat, sweaty guy suspected of being a traitor paid by the Romanians. He approved of such firmness, and Dugin, his table companion, does as well.

Kostenko and Eduard had spent several nights talking. The battalion leader told him about his adventurous life and predicted his imminent death: his enemies would get him sooner or later, he had nowhere to run and at any rate, why bother? You don't go back to being a mechanic once you've ruled a city. Dugin listens, more and more interested as the story takes a dark turn. "If he told you all that it's because he knew he was going to die," Dugin says. "He wanted some trace of his obscure and violent fate to survive."

Maybe he's right; after all, Dugin seems to know everything. He's a philosopher, the author of half a dozen books, although he's only thirty-five, and it's a real pleasure to talk with him. He and Eduard understand each other intuitively; when one starts a sentence the other can finish it. They drink solemnly to the memory of Kostenko, and for the next round Dugin proposes they drink to the memory of Baron von Ungern-Sternberg. Eduard's got no problem with that—only he doesn't know who that is. "You don't know who he is?" Dugin feigns astonishment—in fact he's happy for Eduard, the way you're happy for someone who hasn't yet read *War and Peace*. He's also happy because it's his turn to talk and because while Kostenko makes for a good yarn, he's got a super-Kostenko up his sleeve, a story for a special occasion whose success he knows is guaranteed.

In 1918, Baron von Ungern-Sternberg, a virulently anti-Bolshevik Latvian aristocrat, went with his division as far as Mongolia to fight alongside the White armies. He distinguished himself by his ability to wield authority over his men, by his bravery, and by his cruelty. He professed a sort of Buddhism that included a taste for the most refined forms of torture. He had a gaunt face, a long, thin mustache, and very pale eyes. The Mongol horsemen believed he was a supernatural being, and even his White allies became afraid of him. He grew distant from them, making his way deep into the steppes at the head of his cavalry unit, which, completely isolated, became a sect of visionaries, obeying only his command. Drunk on power and violence, he finally fell into the hands of the Red Army, who hanged him. I'm giving the short version here, but Dugin gives it all he's got, bringing this figure, comparable to Werner Herzog's Aguirre or to Kurtz, the hero of Joseph Conrad's *Heart of Darkness*, to life with consummate perfection. It's one of his showpieces, and he takes his time teasing it out, building the suspense, making full use of his cellolike voice. Because this academic, this man so at home in his den with his books and theories, is also a storyteller capable of bewitching his audience, and Eduard, who normally has nothing but disdain for intellectuals, is in fact bewitched. He'd love someone to tell his life story like that one day.

For the next few days they're inseparable; they talk nonstop. Dugin makes no bones about calling himself a fascist, but he's different from the fascists Eduard's met. The fascists of his acquaintance are either Parisian dandies who, having read a bit of Drieu La Rochelle, think being fascist is chic and decadent, or brutes like their host Prokhanov, whose conversation—a jumble of paranoia and anti-Semitic jokes— you really have to force yourself to follow. He had no idea that between the stupid little poseurs and the stupid fat pigs there was a third kind, a genre of fascist I met several examples of in my youth: the intellectual fascists, who were generally feverish, wan, awkward, but ultimately very well-read young men, who lugged around big schoolbags and hung out in small esoteric bookstores, developing nebulous theories on the Templars, Eurasia, or the Rosicrucians. Often they wound up converting to Islam. Dugin is this kind of fascist, except that he's not an awkward, sickly young man but an ogre. Large, bearded, hairy, he walks with the light steps of a dancer and has a funny way of balancing on one leg while lifting the other behind him. He speaks fifteen languages, he's read everything, he drinks his alcohol straight up, has a frank laugh, and is a mountain of knowledge and charm. God knows, Eduard's not quick to admire anyone, but he admires this man who's fifteen years his junior, and he resolves to learn from him.

In the past his political thinking was confused and sketchy. Under Dugin's influence it becomes even more confused but a little less sketchy, embellishing itself with allusions. Far from opposing fascism and communism, Dugin reveres both equally. He welcomes pell-mell into his pantheon Lenin, Mussolini, Hitler, Leni Riefenstahl, Mayakovsky, Julius Evola, Jung, Mishima, Groddeck, Jünger, Meister Eckhart, Andreas Baader, Wagner, Lao-tzu, Che Guevara, Sri Aurobindo, Rosa Luxemburg, Georges Dumézil, and Guy Debord. If Eduard wants to test the limits and include Charles Manson, well then, no problem, we'll make room. A friend of yours is a friend of mine. Red, white, brown, no matter: Nietzsche was right, all that counts is the vital impetus. Quite quickly, Eduard and Dugin agree that their comrades in the opposition haven't really got what it takes. Alksnis, maybe, they can get along with, but the others . . . Above all, they discover that they complement each other. The man of thought and the man of action. The Brahmin and the warrior. Merlin the wizard and King Arthur. Together they'll do great things.

Which of them came up with the name National Bolshevik Party? Later, when they separate, each will claim it for his own. Still later, when they're each vying for respectability, each will say it was the other's idea. Meanwhile, they're both delighted with it. And they're delighted with the name that Eduard thinks up—this, no one disputes—for their future newspaper: *Limonka*, the Grenade. And, finally, they're delighted with the flag that a painter friend of theirs, a guy as meek as a lamb and specializing in Umbrian and Tuscan landscapes, draws on a kitchen table. A white circle on a red background, it brings to mind the Nazi flag, except that instead of a swastika, the circle contains a black hammer and sickle.

4

THEY HAVE A flag, a title for their newspaper, and a party name. And they've got a member: a Ukrainian student named Taras Rabko. It's a start. Their models—the Bolsheviks, the fascists, and the Nazis— had no more auspicious beginnings on the road to power. What's missing is money. Eduard goes back to Paris hoping to raise some.

This is in 1993, and he spends the whole summer there; it's a strange visit. For almost two years, between politics in Moscow and war wherever it breaks out, he's only been back to his apartment on the way to someplace else. He feels like a stranger in the studio he shares with Natasha. He's not used to living there anymore, and she's gotten used to living there without him, and certainly also to sleeping with other men. The friends he'd made in the small world of Paris, put off by his Bosnian exploits, turn their backs on him. A press campaign denounces the collusion between the extreme right and the extreme left, and in fact, if you were to do a facial composite of this mix that people are starting to call "brown-red," it would be his portrait. His popularity is at an all-time low, his usual publishers won't take his calls. No matter: he no longer considers himself a writer but a fighter and a professional revolutionary, and the fact that he's scorned in this fainthearted, petty bourgeois milieu doesn't bother him in the least. The problem is that literature is his only source of income, and he is barely managing to sell his pieces on the war to a small publishing house run by a Serbian patriot; his attempts at fund-raising come to nothing. Dugin, who has ties with all the players in the European extreme right, was full of optimism when he referred him to his contacts. But Eduard does the round of confidential magazines and bleak little offices without obtaining anything from the timid fascists who run them but statements of goodwill; they all have enough trouble sustaining their own little boutiques. As far as his contacts go, he knows that even if all doors are closed to him, one will always be open, because he has an old friend nothing can shock and no bad reputation can scare. Unfortunately, Jean-Edern Hallier no longer lives on the Place des Vosges. Sentenced to pay four million francs in damages for having written that the businessman and politician Bernard Tapie was dishonest, which was common knowledge, he was forced to sell the big apartment where *L'Idiot* held its meetings on the cheap. Burdened by other suits, crippled with debts, his newspaper on the verge of collapse, Jean-Edern doesn't have a cent for Eduard. But he does invite him to come visit him in his manor in Brittany.

Eduard goes there with Natasha. It's been several years since either of them has taken what normal people would call a vacation. The manor impresses them in its fallen grandeur and its lack of amenities. It rains into the rooms, and the master of the house isn't in such great shape either. Almost blind, he uses a magnifying glass to read the numbers on the telephone, not that his failing eyesight prevents him from putting pedal to the metal in his old VW Rabbit on the narrow country roads while the handbrake's still engaged. The first day they go shopping in anticipation of a visit by Jean-Marie Le Pen, who'll be coming over for a neighborly dinner. Jean-Edern loves to shock people by telling them that Le Pen's coming over; he's already done it once to Eduard, who's not shocked at all, and this time as well they wait in vain. Dockside, Jean-Edern pitches a fit because he's not allowed to park his car in a spot reserved for the fishermen. He gesticulates, shouts that it's an insult to French literature, the French Republic, Victor Hugo—and Eduard has the rather sad impression that he's forcing himself to rise to his own reputation. If he stops making a scene for just one minute, he'll die. Over dinner, however, he really is in fine fettle, and has his guests, all pickled on mead, in fits of laughter over how he appeared on the television program *Thirty Million Friends*. It's all about animals, and he got a spot on the show by pretending he had a dog, that he simply adored it, that he wrote all his books with this dog lying at his feet. It's not true, he's never had a dog, but he'll do anything to get on television, so he borrowed one. He held it on his knees, petted it, played the affectionate master, but the dog didn't know who he was and panicked, and the more Jean-Edern gushed on about his faithful four-legged friend, the more the dog growled, struggled, wriggled to escape, and finally bit him. Jean-Edern plays himself and the dog, mimes the fight; he's got the act down to a T.

The next day there's a sunny spell and they go to the beach, where Eduard takes a dip. Despite his less than poor vision, Jean-Edern says to Natasha in admiration, "Wow, your guy's got quite the body." And when Eduard joins them after his swim, he asks, "So what is it you do in Russia?"

"In Russia?" Eduard answers, shaking the sand from his beach towel. "I'm getting ready to seize power. I think the time is right."

5

WHEN THEY SAY you can find everything in Moscow now, it's not true. You can find foie gras, yes, as much as you want, and Château d'Yquem to wash it down with. But no one's thought of importing bouillon cubes or baker's chocolate, staples that don't interest the new Russians but form the basis of Eduard's diet. Each time he goes abroad he stocks up, and he's sitting down in front of the television with a bowl of broth on the September day in 1993 when Yeltsin announces to the country with a grave face that he's dissolving the Duma and calling for new elections.

You could see it coming. If the parliament's hostile to you, as it is to Yeltsin, dissolving it is a classic move in politics. Either it works or it doesn't. If it doesn't, you kick yourself, but there you go, you've got to resign yourself to your fate in a democracy. What isn't certain is that the democrat Yeltsin will see things the same way and resign himself to his fate if the new elections don't result in a more submissive parliament. In any case he's still talking when the phone rings at the place where Eduard's staying. It's Alksnis, the "Black Colonel," who tells him that things are heating up. The patriots are meeting at the White House. Eduard empties his bowl of broth and heads off.

When he gets there, several thousand patriots are already gathered in front of the building that two years earlier was a symbol the world over for the triumph of Yeltsin and the "democrats." Who are these "patriots"? Broadly speaking, the people we saw protesting on the streets of Moscow a few pages back. Some, not all, are what we'd call fascists. But today these fascists are posing as the guardians of the constitutional order, and when they accuse the democrats of being ready to install a dictatorship to defend a democracy that nobody wants, you can't say they're entirely wrong. Compounding the confusion, the two men heading the rebellion against Yeltsin were in the very same place, only at his side, two years ago: the Chechen Khasbulatov, president of the Duma; and General Rutskoy, vice president of the Russian Republic and a former military leader in Afghanistan, who, although he's part of Gaidar's team, won't stop lashing out at the "little boy in pink shorts"—his nickname for the prime minister ever since he was gauche enough to have himself photographed playing golf in just such a getup.

That very evening, Rutskoy and Khasbulatov convene an extraordinary session of the dissolved parliament. This assembly then declares its own dissolution unconstitutional, deposes Yeltsin, names Rutskoy president in his place, and ultimately occupies the White House. The assembly announces that it is there by the will of the people and that it will only come out if forced at the end of a bayonet. In addition to the rebel members of parliament, a crowd of patriots is also there, dead set on supporting them and defending the building. Among them is Eduard, who spends the night there hopping around as excitedly as a flea, going from one meeting to the next in a thick cloud of cigarette smoke. They pass the time discussing, shouting, drinking, writing communiqués, and forming the new government. All this talk makes Eduard impatient: there'll always be time to divvy up the ministries, he thinks. Now the key thing is to prepare for the impending siege.

He manages to reach the office on the highest floor where Rutskoy has locked himself away. Soldiers are stationed in front of the door, but Eduard insists and manages to obtain an audience. The general receives him dressed in army fatigues, with a feverish air. He doesn't quite know who his visitor is, but it's three in the morning and there's so much pressure on him that he'd talk to pretty much anyone. It doesn't hurt that Eduard starts by addressing him as "Comrade President": he's not used to that, and he likes it.

The whole evening the comrade president has been calling all the military bases in Russia to get the lay of the land. "And how do things look?" Eduard asks. The general pulls a face: "*Normalno,*" an expression that could mean anything from "Very well, thank you," to "Could be better." The crux of the matter is: whose side will the army take in this showdown? Supposing it remains on the side of the law, as it did two years ago—well then, which side is that? Who's the legitimate president, Yeltsin or Rutskoy? The United States, Britain, Germany, and France have just declared their support for Yeltsin against the new putschists, and this news seems to have shaken the general.

To cheer him up, Eduard stresses that there's nothing surprising about the attitudes of the Western countries. "They only want one thing: a Russia that's on its knees. That's why they'll always back traitors like Gorbachev and Yeltsin. But what's happening this time isn't a coup. It's a democratically elected parliament saying no to dictatorship, and the West will be forced to accept that in the name of its own values."

"That's true," the general says, frowning as if the argument was new to him and he was trying to remember it for a future speech.

"What counts," Eduard goes on, exploiting his advantage, "isn't what happens between the diplomats. It's not even what happens on the army bases. It's what happens here, in the White House. Everything played out here last time, and everything will play out here this time too. Yeltsin's not going to back down, neither are we. So we'll have to fight. Do we have weapons?"

"Yes," the general says, as if hypnotized.

"Enough?"

"Yes, enough."

"Well then, what are you waiting for to hand them out?"

"Not now," the general says. "It's premature."

Eduard frowns: "Premature? That's what the social democrats said in 1917. That the moment wasn't ripe for revolution, that there was no working class in Russia, et cetera . . . Luckily, Lenin thought different. A great man senses when the moment is right. What the Greeks called *kairos.*" (Dugin taught him this word and he loves it.) "We're in that kind of moment right now. The bravest men in Russia are here, ready to fight. It's up to you to decide, Comrade President. Do you want to go down in history as a great man or as a coward?"

He's gone too far, Rutskoy gets angry: "Just who are you, anyway? A writer, right? An intellectual? Leave military decisions to the specialists."

Eduard chokes: him, an intellectual? Rutskoy's had enough, and dismisses him.

The next day Eduard makes a mistake: he leaves. Access to the White House is pretty much unfettered, he intends to be back in a flash, so he goes over to some friends' place to take a shower and change, then to see Dugin, whom he urges to join the patriots. But Dugin prefers to watch events unfold on TV, and for the first time Eduard suspects him of being a bit of a chickenshit. When he gets back, the siege has started. Yeltsin has had the electricity and the telephones cut off and he's deployed detachments of OMON riot police; of course there's no getting through. Nevertheless he tries all night. Slipping between the military trucks and the lines of soldiers with machine guns at their hips, he feels like a French partisan during the Nazi occupation. Loudspeakers are blaring government propaganda nonstop, calling on the insurgents to surrender. From the outside you can see flickering lights and ghostly shadows in the windows: the place is now lit with candles.

The siege lasts ten days, which will count among the cruelest in Eduard's life. He'd give ten years, an arm, anything, not to have left so foolishly, to be inside with these brave men who, he's certain, will soon pay dearly for their acts. What's better? To wait around behind the police barricades in case a gap opens or go back home and watch the news? Wherever he is he feels bad, he feels like he's not where he should be. The television drives him into a fury. God knows that the press was free under Yeltsin, but even so, now, with the siege underway, there's no more kidding around. Twenty-four/seven, journalists and commentators take turns presenting the "constitutionalists," as the insurgents call themselves, as fascists and madmen. The pro-Yeltsin demonstration is shown nonstop, as is the concert in support of Yeltsin given by the inevitable Rostropovich. No word, on the other hand, of what's happening inside the besieged White House. There are no cameras in there; you have to imagine the scene.

Everyone who was there and came out alive describes the same thing: the *Titanic*. No lights, no telephones, no water or heat. It's freezing, everyone stinks, all they have to eat or drink is what they can find in the cafeteria, and that runs out. They burn the office furniture and gather around the makeshift fires to sing Orthodox hymns and songs of the Great Patriotic War, and urge one another on to martyrdom. "They" are Cossacks with long mustaches, old Stalinists, young neo-Nazis, legalist members of parliament, priests with thick beards. Given the gravity of the situation, the priests have their hands full: the parliamentarians' offices are transformed into confessionals and baptisteries, in front of which lines form. The little water that remains is blessed. Icons and posters of the Sainted Virgin vie with portraits of Lenin and Nicholas II, red flags with swastika armbands. Cell phones didn't exist yet, so the only contact with the outside comes via an English journalist's radio telephone, a huge trunk that looks like a wartime radio transmitter. Rumors circulate, some completely crazy: the American Congress has had Clinton arrested for betraying democracy by supporting Yeltsin. Others are dangerously plausible: the army is going to attack. Everyone knows it, in fact: the army is going to attack, and the whole thing is going to end in a bloodbath, unless they agree to a capitulation, which everyone rejects out of hand as the adrenaline mounts. The two leaders, Rutskoy in his military fatigues and Khasbulatov in a black shirt and a bullet-proof vest, start to talk of mass suicide. No one sleeps.

————

Eduard's missing out on all this and he's inconsolable. But he doesn't miss out on the huge demonstration that gathers in front of the White House on October 3: several hundred thousand people waving red flags in support of the insurgents. He came with young Rabko, the Ukrainian student who is, after him and Dugin, the third member of the National Bolshevik Party. Around them people are shouting, "So-vi-et U-nion! So-vi-et U-nion! Yeltsin fascist!" And "Death to the Jews! Death to the black asses!" (the term *black asses* refers to natives of the Caucasus region), which Eduard doesn't approve of: first of all it's stupid, second of all it's the only thing the Western media will pick up on. They provoke the OMON. Dare they fire on the Russian people? They dare. First blood, first casualties. The crowd roars, resists, pushes its way through a barricade. The OMON panic, redouble their fire, pull the demonstrators into their trucks and beat the hell out of them. Some young people recognize Eduard, surround him and protect him with their bodies. Rutskoy appears on a balcony of the White House and harangues the crowd with a megaphone. "We're coming out! March to the Kremlin! Arrest Yeltsin! Take Ostankino!"

Ostankino is the television tower, and so of vital strategic importance. If the insurgents take control of the news, everything can turn around. Buses and cars start filling with armed men shouting, "To Ostankino! To Ostankino!" Eduard and the young Rabko jump on one of these buses. They cross the deserted city: no one dares to go outside. The occasional bystander, seeing the procession pass by, makes the V for victory sign. In the bus, Eduard gives an interview to an Irish journalist. It's not over by a long shot, he says, but his people are beginning to hold their heads high.

"Do you happen to like the term 'civil war'?" he wrote fifteen years earlier in *Diary of a Loser*. "I love it."

There were several hundred of them when they left the White House, and now several thousand arrive on the hill at Ostankino. But barely one in ten is armed, and OMON squadrons are ready and waiting. No sooner have the buses arrived than they open fire and charge, batons raised. On they rush, swinging and firing at the same time: it's a massacre. Eduard, who luckily finds himself a bit to one side of their onslaught, throws himself on the ground. Another body falls on top of him. It's the Irish journalist. He's not moving. A trickle of blood runs from his mouth. Eduard touches him, looks into his glassy eyes, feels his pulse. He's dead. I'm the last person he filmed, Eduard thinks fleetingly: will anyone see that video one day?

Machine gun fire crackles all around him. He gets up, staggers under the impact of a bullet, puts his hand to his shoulder. Young Rabko manages to get him to some trees in the park, which offer cover, and tears his own shirt to dress Eduard's wound. It's bleeding profusely but it's not deep, and anyway a shoulder wound is good: in films the hero's always hit in the shoulder. The fighting continues a couple of hundred yards away, they can hear the shouting and gunfire. Then things grow calm. Night falls. The OMON flush out the demonstrators who've taken refuge in the park, shoving them roughly into their vans, but Eduard and Rabko escape. Since the entrances are being watched, they spend the entire night hidden in the bushes, freezing. Eduard repeats to himself that next time he'll be the one in charge instead of those cowardly, prattling generals who call him an intellectual.

At dawn, he and Rabko venture out of the park and make their way to a subway station, where they learn that tanks have surrounded the White House. Just a few hours ago they believed victory was within their grasp; now it's clear that all is lost. The Orthodox litanies and patriotic songs grow all the more fervent during the attack. General Rutskoy repeats that he's going to commit suicide, like Hitler in his bunker. In fact he surrenders, but only in the afternoon: time enough for 150 casualties, people who would still be alive today if he'd been less keen on playing the tough guy. Shots are fired all afternoon: in front of the White House, where thousands of curious onlookers have gathered to watch the assault like a sporting event; and inside the building, where, as soon as they manage to get inside, the OMON hunt the besieged down in the halls, in the offices, in the toilets. At the very least they work them over; at most they kill them. It's a bloodbath. The hundreds of dead and thousands of injured that make it onto the official register include not only insurgents but also fanatics, passersby, old people, and curious kids, lots of kids. Fearing a wave of arrests in the nationalist refuges, Eduard and Rabko decide to lie low.

They take the train to Tver, a hundred miles from Moscow, where Rabko's mother lives. There they spend two weeks watching television, holed up in her little apartment. Cracks have appeared in the official version of events that was imposed on the media during the crisis. Democracy may have been saved, but now no one uses the word without quotation marks. The recent events are compared to the Paris Commune, except that the fascists take the place of the Communards and the democrats that of the Versaillais. No one knows who's good and who's bad anymore, who's progressive and who's reactionary. A journalist interviews Andrei Sinyavsky, the émigré intellectual who was moved almost to tears when Natasha sang "The Blue Scarf" at his house in the Paris suburbs. And this historic dissident, a democrat through and through, an honest and upstanding man, is again not far from tears—this time out of anger and despair. "The terrible thing now," he says, "is that the truth seems to be on the side of people I've always thought of as my enemies."

6

SINCE THE DUMA has not only been dissolved but bathed in blood, elections are essential, and Eduard decides to run. Young Rabko, a law student, helps him register as a candidate in the Tver region. It's easy: the Yeltsin years are marked by chaos but also by freedom, which will soon be sorely missed. Anyone can run for any position and express any opinion. Dugin promised to help out but won't leave his well-heated office in Moscow, and so the National Bolshevik Party's campaign staff is limited to Eduard and the loyal Rabko, who together crisscross the district all through December at the wheel of an old clunker with Moldavian plates, lent to them by an officer they know, and then, when the officer wants it back, by bus and train—third class, of course.

Coming from a big city and having lived abroad for many years, Eduard regretted not being more familiar with the Russian hinterland, what's known as the *glubinka*. He discovers Rzhev, Staritsa, Demidovo, and a host of other godforsaken backwaters, devastated by the "shock therapy" and, if you scratch beneath the layer of contemporary affliction, unchanged since Chekhov described them so depressingly. I'm very familiar with one such village, Kotelnich, where I spent several months shooting a documentary, and have no trouble imagining in all the others the lone, run-down hotel without running water because the pipes burst in the frost, the scuzzy restaurants, the small abandoned factories, the empty square decorated with a bust of Lenin, where, since they have no money for posters, Rabko accosts the passersby like a fairground crier to get them to come to Eduard's rally. There are seven hundred thousand voters to win over in the region; he gathers them in groups of fifteen to twenty, mostly old people, poverty-stricken, fainthearted retirees who listen as he recites his Russian nationalist catechism, nod their heads, and ask at the end, "Fine, but who're you for? Yeltsin or Zhirinovsky?"

He sighs in despair. Not for Yeltsin, that's for sure. "Did you see the ad on TV for his party, the one that knucklehead Gaidar thought up?" The ad is really something. You see a prosperous family, with a kid and a dog, in a residential suburban house that exists only on American TV shows. All smiles, the parents go to the polling station to vote for Gaidar. When they come out, the kid concludes with a wink, "Too bad we can't vote too, huh doggy?" This propaganda, addressed to a totally imaginary middle class, is an insult to 99 percent of Russians, Eduard says. His listeners agree, though that won't stop them from voting for the party in power, because when you have the right to vote in Russia, you vote for the party in power: that's the way things are.

A few rebels support Zhirinovsky. Paweł Pawlikowski, the director we've already crossed paths with in Sarajevo, shot a documentary for the BBC about Zhirinovsky's campaign. It shows the candidate mouthing off, promising all kinds of things to those who've been swindled by the reforms: that he'll make vodka free, reconquer the empire, give full support to the Serbs, drop bombs on Germany, Japan, and the United States, reopen the Gulag, and lock up the new Russians, the people from Memorial and other traitors paid by the CIA. His stock-in-trade is not very far removed from Eduard's own; meanwhile Eduard is having a lot of trouble explaining the advantage of voting for him. When he says he's independent, no one understands.

Yeltsin and Gaidar win the elections, but Zhirinovsky nevertheless gets a quarter of the vote. If Eduard had run alongside him, he'd be a member of parliament. And he could have; Zhirinovsky was all for it. Eduard's the one who didn't want to, for the same old reason: he prefers to be the head of a party with three members than beneath someone who has millions of supporters. There's so little doubt about the outcome that he doesn't even wait for the results to be announced before returning to Paris, furious and humiliated.

He wants to tell Natasha but there's no answer when he calls. He arrives early in the morning, knocks, waits a minute—he's well mannered in his own way—then opens the door with his key. He finds her sprawled across the bed surrounded by empty bottles and full ashtrays. She snores heavily, dead drunk. The room must not have been aired for several days: it smells awful. He puts down his bag and starts silently cleaning. Natasha opens one eye, props herself up on an elbow and watches him work. In a slurred voice she says, "You can yell at me later, right now I need you to fuck me." He joins her on the bed, rams into her. They clutch at each other like castaways. When it's over she tells him that she's spent three days without leaving the room, getting banged by two strangers. If he'd come back a bit earlier he'd have met them, they could have played cards. She lets out a shrill laugh. He puts his clothes back on without even bothering to change, picks up his bag without a word, closes the door behind him without slamming it, and takes the metro then the commuter train to Roissy Airport, where he buys a ticket for Budapest.

7

FROM BUDAPEST, THE practically empty bus takes all night to reach Belgrade. It's the only way to get there now. Since the embargo was put in place, there's been no air traffic into or out of the Serbian capital. The airport is closed. Ostracized by Europe, the country sinks into isolation and paranoia. The reasonable Serbs despair at the insane crusade that Milošević is leading them on, and do their best to resist the brainwashing. But Eduard doesn't know any reasonable Serbs and doesn't want to, either. What he wants is war. He needs to throw himself into it, and he's ready to lose himself in the process. At this moment in his life it strikes him as his only salvation. He's got a plan: drop off his bag at the Hotel Majestic, where he's stayed already, and go to the ad hoc embassy set up by the Republic of Serbian Krajina.

The conflict that continues to rage between the Serbs and the Bosnians has now also reignited between the Serbs and the Croats, who are battling for control of this other Serbian enclave, situated not far from the Adriatic. Now three parties are involved, not counting everyone who's trying to separate them, and it's like during the Thirty Years' War: at any moment your worst enemy can become your ally because he's another enemy's enemy. Diplomats and journalists are at their wits' end. This time Eduard no longer wants to be a journalist, but a soldier. A simple soldier, yes, he explains to the Belgrade representatives of the Republic of Serbian Krajina—a self-proclaimed entity that, of course, only the Serbs recognize. His behavior is the source of some surprise because there hasn't exactly been a deluge of foreign volunteers. He's told that it's difficult to get to Krajina, that he has to wait, he will be contacted. He goes back to the Hotel Majestic.

Going by his description, I imagine the place a bit like the Hotel Lutetia in Paris under the German occupation. There's a piano bar, people trafficking in foreign currencies, hookers, gangsters, shady journalists, and politicians trying to best one another in their nationalist intransigence. Many of these people, like Vojislav Šešelj, who is in favor of "cutting the throats of the Croats and Muslims, not with a knife but with a rusty spoon," will soon die violent deaths or be condemned for war crimes. Eduard likes the place. A very pretty seventeen-year-old girl comes up to him; not a hooker but a fan. She's read all his books, all his articles in the Serbian press, and her mother's read them as well. Basking in the glow of these two groupies, Eduard inscribes a few books for the mother, who then complacently turns a blind eye when he sleeps with the daughter. He's not used to having sex with very young girls, and he discovers that he likes it. Plus, he's seriously considering getting himself killed, and the thought that it may be the last time intoxicates him. His hard-on lasts for hours.

Three days pass like this, at the end of which the barman serving his vodka tells him that Arkan has been informed of his presence and is waiting to see him. Arkan! His dear friend Arkan! He takes the elevator to the top floor, which no one but the warlord's guests can access. A couple of heavies do a body search, and he enters the suite where Arkan, dressed in a khaki uniform and a green beret, is feasting with a dozen of his henchmen.

"So, Limonov, still haven't made a revolution in Russia?"

Caught off guard, Eduard stutters that he's been giving it his best shot. He was among the heroes who defended the White House against Yeltsin's tanks. He was wounded trying to take Ostankino. And what he wants now is to go to war in Krajina. Not easy, Arkan confirms. The access corridor connecting Krajina and Belgrade is constantly being cut off, one day by the Croats, the next by the Muslims, not to mention the UN peacekeeping force. But a group's heading out tomorrow. "You in?"

"You bet I am!"

Five in the morning. A minibus with muddy windows waits on the snow-covered lot in front of the hotel. Eduard's the first one on board. Slowly they make the rounds of the outlying districts, where, like a school bus, the vehicle picks up sleepy-eyed men who look like peasants. They leave Belgrade as the sun comes up. Drinking coffee from thermoses and slivovitz from the bottle, they drive all day long on roads lined by the remains of trucks and burned-out villages. They cross Herzegovina, a dry, rocky, wind-swept plateau where a lot of spaghetti westerns were shot and where the only things that grow, they say, are stones, snakes, and Ustashis. In theory, you know whether you're on Serbian, Croatian, or Bosnian territory. On the ground it's more complicated. The front lines cut villages in two; alphabets, official languages, monetary systems, religions, and national fanaticisms change from one stretch of road to the next. It's also difficult for anyone who's not directly implicated to say whether the roadblocks are manned by Serbian, Croatian, or Bosnian militias, but strangely the minibus passes without a hitch. I say strangely because Eduard's traveling companions, disguised as peasants going to a livestock market, are actually Arkan's militiamen returning to the front after a leave in Belgrade, and the cargo space is loaded with weapons.

Three-quarters of the way there, the radio announces a disturbing piece of news: during the night there was a sort of coup in the Republic of Serbian Krajina, and it seems that the defense minister to whom Arkan recommended Eduard has been put in prison. Soon posters appear, freshly glued to the tree trunks, showing pictures of Arkan with a price on his head. It's like San Theorodos in *Tintin and the Picaros*: you can never be sure whether General Alcazar is in a position to have General Tapioca shot or the other way around. What's happening, which Eduard starts to guess and events will confirm, is that Milošević, likened by an American diplomat to "a Mafia boss who's tired of dealing drugs in the Bronx and wants to set himself up in the casinos of Miami," is starting to shuffle the deck for upcoming negotiations. In collusion with his best enemy Tudjman, he prepares to abandon Krajina to the Croats in exchange for Serbian territories in Bosnia and an end to the embargo. In this new phase of the game, a diehard like Arkan becomes a nuisance. He's got to be eliminated, and you'd think the dozen makeshift soldiers being jostled up and down in the minibus were headed for a trap. That would be logical, but the Balkans have a strange logic of their own. There are short circuits and information delays, and in the end Eduard, left on his own in town to present himself to the authorities, isn't given a particularly unpleasant welcome, just shunted from one office to the next and finally dispatched to an Austro-Hungarian garrison somewhere out in the sticks.

There he's given a uniform—though the elements are so disparate that it's impossible to tell for which side—the rank of captain, and a room of his own. The rank goes with the room: the previous tenant was a captain, he got blown up by a land mine; the next tenant will be a captain as well; it's simpler that way. The next morning they finish equipping him: he's issued a Kalashnikov and a guardian angel, a brutal and irascible Serb officer who, visiting one of his subordinates, starts insulting then menacing his wife because she's a Croat. Eduard's shocked, but he's told he's got to understand: the officer's entire family had their throats slit the year before. A couple of days later it'll be the subordinate's turn to slit the officer's throat.

This is really one of the war's dead ends. No one goes there, no one leaves, no one really understands who's fighting whom. There are many losses on both sides, and the Serbian peasants are all the more wary because they feel they've been betrayed by everyone: not just the West but even their homeland, which is getting ready to abandon them. And in fact one year later the Republic of Serbian Krajina will no longer exist; its inhabitants will be dead, in prison, or—if they're very lucky—refugees in Serbia.

Eduard remains in this wild, mountainous region for two months. He participates—he says this himself and I believe him—in a number of guerrilla actions: raids on villages, ambushes, skirmishes. He risks his life. One thing I've often wondered while writing this book is whether he killed anyone. For a long time I didn't dare ask, and when I finally did he shrugged and said that was a typical civvy question. "I've shot, often. I've seen men fall. Did I hit them? Hard to say. War's not cut and dried." I rarely suspect him of lying; here I do a bit. He knows I'm writing a book about him, for a French readership—that is to say, righteous and quick to take offense—and perhaps he didn't want to pat himself on the back for an experience he himself must consider enriching. I think that in his philosophy, killing a man in hand-to-hand combat is like getting screwed from behind: something to try at least once. If he did, which I don't know, the chances are good that he did it during these two months in Krajina, where there are practically no witnesses.

Finally, he gets a ride back to Belgrade with a Japanese journalist. At each roadblock he swears he doesn't have a weapon, although he's kept his 7.65 as a souvenir of his Balkan escapades: he knows this will be the last. The whole time he's been there he hasn't stopped brooding over Arkan's quip: "So, Limonov, still haven't made a revolution in Russia?" He's understood that the time for peripheral struggles is over for him. The hour has come to fight on the true front, to return to Moscow and there be victorious or die.

VIII

Moscow, Altai,

1994–2001

෨෨

I

PARALLEL LIVES OF illustrious men, continued: Eduard and Solzhenitsyn left their homeland at the same time, in the spring of 1974,
and they return at the same time, exactly twenty years later. Solzhenitsyn has spent these twenty years behind the barbed wire that
fenced in his property in Vermont to discourage curious onlookers,
venturing out only to lambaste the West—which earns him a solid
reputation as an irascible old man—and writing, sixteen hours a day,
365 days a year, a cycle of novels on the origins of the 1917 Revolution
compared to which *War and Peace* is a slender psychological tale in the
style of Benjamin Constant's *Adolphe*. He never doubted that he
would live to see the day when he would return home, never doubted
that everything would have changed there. And sure enough, the
Soviet Union no longer exists, he's finished *The Red Wheel*: the time
has come.

Fully aware of the historic dimension of the event, he doesn't want
to return like just another émigré. No: he flies to Vladivostok, and
from there he journeys to Moscow by rail. One month of travel in a
special train, with stops in the villages where he listens to the people's
grievances, all filmed by the BBC. It's like Victor Hugo returning to
France from his exile in Guernsey after the death of Napoleon III. It's
also, it must be said, as if he's come out of twenty years of hibernation,
and this spectacle of a return is met with nothing but indifference and
irony in Moscow: the eternal, inevitable irony that results when the
mediocre is confronted by genius. But it's also the irony of a new Russia being faced with the anachronism that Solzhenitsyn has become.
Five years earlier, crowds would have gotten down on their hands and
knees. *The Gulag Archipelago* had just been published and people
couldn't believe they had the right to read it. But he comes back to a

world where, after a few years of compulsive reading, people couldn't care less about real books, especially his literature. They've had enough of concentration camps; the bookstores only want international best-sellers and how-to guides: how to lose weight, get rich, exploit your potential. Gone are the days of yakking in kitchens, venerating poets, and proudly declaring yourself a conscientious objector. Those nostalgic for communism—and Solzhenitsyn has no idea how large their numbers are—think he's a criminal, the democrats think he's an ayatollah; literary types have nothing but snide smirks for *The Red Wheel* (they haven't read it, no one's read it), and young people all but confuse him with Brezhnev in the graveyard of Soviet icons.

The more people make fun of Solzhenitsyn, the higher Eduard's star rises. The Captain Levitins who poisoned his youth are hardly players anymore: the bearded old man buried beneath his sermons, Brodsky, venerated by academics and blathering odes to Venice. Eduard almost pities him: Venice! An old fart's topic if ever there was one! Their glory days are over. His, he thinks, are dawning. And in fact, when he wound up his life in France and moved back to Moscow for good, he discovered he was famous. Some of his other books have come out since Semyonov published *Ours Was a Great Epoch*, the most scandalous ones: *It's Me, Eddie*; *His Butler's Story*; *Diary of a Loser*. It was the right choice. No one's ever read anything like them in Russia, the books sell hundreds of thousands of copies. Thrilled with their own audacity, the newspapers print story after story about him, and he doesn't let them down. He lives with Natasha in a sort of squat in an abandoned building that hasn't yet been renovated, with no lights in the shared rooms or railings in the staircases. Photographers love the grunge environment and the two pose wearing leather and black glasses. In France it would be hard for an ultranationalist political agitator to enjoy this kind of rock star status, but not in Russia: you can write for a paper that serializes *The Protocols of the Elders of Zion* and be a teen idol at the same time. Another difference is that you can sell two hundred thousand or three hundred thousand copies of a book and still be poor. The "shock therapy" and the chaos of distribution reduce the value of copyrights to a minimum, but deep down he doesn't really care. If he has to choose between money and fame he'll choose fame every time, and even if he dreamed of having both when he was younger he knows now that it wasn't meant to be. He's frugal, spartan, disdains all forms of comfort. Far from being humiliated by the poverty that's dogged him his whole life, he now draws from it an aristocratic pride. And in the end, without any other revenue streams at his disposal, it's with his meager royalties that he publishes the first issue of the newspaper of his dreams.

In a totally megalomaniacal text written several years later, he imagines how future historians will view this crucial moment in Russian history: the creation of *Limonka* in the fall of 1994. Everyone, he says, will want to have taken part in the venture, but in fact the only people in Dugin's little office at the newspaper *Sovietskaya Rossiya* were "the greatest Russian writer and the greatest Russian philosopher of the second half of the twentieth century" (meaning himself and Dugin); Natasha, who wrote articles under the pseudonym Margot Führer; a couple of Siberian punks and some of Dugin's students, who argued endlessly about Orthodoxy; plus the loyal Rabko, who was in charge of logistics. They found a printer in Tver, Rabko's hometown. He and Eduard drove there in the old Moldavian clunker to pick up the five thousand copies of the first edition which they hurried to distribute—though "distribution" in this case meant selling it on the roadside and doing a tour of the Moscow train stations, where they put copies in trains headed for the large provincial cities. They didn't really hope people would buy it, but maybe a few would open it, as you'd open a bottle that's washed up on shore. In Eduard's recounting, the beginnings of *Limonka* and the National Bolshevik Party sound like an exhilarating epic; in the second act they're all forced to move to a sordid basement after being kicked out of *Sovietskaya Rossiya*. They pull up their sleeves ("they" being the half-dozen historic founders minus Dugin as usual, who merely encourages them and inspects the finished work), shovel out mountains of rubble, plaster the walls, and fix the leaks. Despite their efforts, the place is still humid and rat-infested, but soon this will become their party headquarters, which they call the bunker.

The bunker, Margot Führer . . . At this point I'm not sure my readers really want to hear any more of the exhilarating epic about the beginnings of a neofascist party and its official rag. And I'm not sure I want to tell it, either.

Nevertheless, things are more complicated than they seem.

I'm sorry. I don't like that sentence. I don't like the way the subtle minds use it. The problem is that it's often true. Here, for example. Things are more complicated than they seem.

2

TODAY ZAKHAR PRILEPIN is pushing forty. He lives with his wife and kids in Nizhny Novgorod, where he's editor in chief of the local edition of *Novaya gazeta*, the independent newspaper that Anna Politkovskaya wrote for. The author of three novels, he's maturing from a promising young writer into a confirmed talent, both at home and abroad. The first of these novels deals with Chechnya, where he served as a soldier; the second with the doubts and wanderings of a young guy from the provinces who believes that by becoming a *nazbol*—a militant of the National Bolshevik Party—he's giving meaning to the swampy mess of his life. The book is based on his own experiences as well as those of friends his age, because Zakhar Prilepin has been a committed *nazbol* for the last fifteen years. He looks every bit the part: stocky, shaved head, black clothes, Doc Martens, and to top it all off he's as sweet as a lamb. I know, you've got to be careful, but after spending several hours with him I'm ready to swear that Zakhar Prilepin is a terrific guy. Honest, courageous, tolerant—the sort of person who looks at life the way he looks at you: straight in the eyes, and not because he wants to be confrontational but because he wants to be understanding, because he tries to love life as much as possible.

The very opposite of the fascist brute or the decadent dandy who finds Nazi or Stalinist aesthetics sexy. In his books, which are beginning to be translated and which I heartily recommend, he tells of his daily life in the Russian provinces, odd jobs, drinking binges with his buddies, the breasts of the woman he adores, and his worried and wondrous love for his children. He describes the cruelty of the times but also the moments of pure grace each day reveals when you're attentive. He's an excellent writer, serious and tender.

And this is the story Zakhar Prilepin tells.

He was twenty and bored out of his mind in his little town in the region of Ryazan, when one of his buddies gave him a weird newspaper that had come in on the train from Moscow. Neither Zakhar nor his friend had ever seen anything like it. No one in Russia knew *L'Idiot international* or the American underground press—both of which Eduard acknowledges as influences—and so there was every reason to be blown away by its gaudy layout, vulgar drawings, and provocative headlines. Although it was the organ of a political party, *Limonka* dealt less with politics than with rock and roll, literature, and above all style. What style? Fuck you, bullshit, up yours style. Majestic punk.

Now, says Zakhar Prilepin, you have to imagine what a provincial Russian city is like. The sinister life the young people lead there, their lack of a future, and—if they're at all sensitive or ambitious—their despair. All it took was for a single issue of *Limonka* to arrive in a city like that and fall into the hands of one of these idle, morose, tattooed youths who played the guitar and drank beer under his precious posters of The Cure or Che Guevara, and it was a done deal. Very quickly there were ten or twenty of them, a whole threatening gang of good-for-nothings with pale complexions and ripped black jeans who hung out in the squares: the usual suspects, regular visitors to the local cop shop. They had a new watchword and it was *Limonka*, copies of which they passed around. It was their thing, the thing that spoke to them. And behind every single one of these articles was this Limonov guy, whose books Zakhar and his buddies started to read fervently and who became both their favorite author and their real-life hero. He was old enough to be their father, but he wasn't like any of their fathers. He was afraid of nothing, he'd led the adventurous life that all twenty-year-olds dream of, and he said to them, "You're young. You don't like living in this shitty country. You don't want to be an ordinary Popov, or a shithead who only thinks about money, or a Chekist. You're a rebel. Your heroes are Jim Morrison, Lenin, Mishima, Baader. Well there you go: you're a *nazbol* already."

What you have to understand, Zakhar Prilepin goes on, is that *Limonka* and the *nazbols* were the Russian counterculture. The only one: everything else was bogus, indoctrination and so on. So of course the party had its share of brutes, guys recovering from military service, skinheads with German shepherds who got their kicks from pissing off the *prilitchnyi*—the upstanding citizens—by giving the Nazi salute. But the party also included all the frozen backwaters of Russia had to offer in terms of self-taught cartoonists, bass players looking for people to start a rock band, amateur video freaks, and timid guys who wrote poetry in private while pining after girls who were too beautiful for them and nursing dark dreams of wasting everyone at school and then blowing themselves up, like they do in America. Plus the Satanists from Irkutsk, the Hell's Angels from Kirov, the Sandinistas from Magadan. "My buddies," Zakhar Prilepin says softly, and you get the feeling he could have all the success in the world—all the literary prizes, all the foreign editions, all the book tours to the States; but what's important to him is to remain loyal to his friends, the lost youths of the Russian provinces.

These guys—at first there were only guys—were poor. If they worked at all it was loading and unloading crates, sweeping courtyards, plastering walls, or watching over parking lots where SUVs that cost what it would take their mothers half a century to earn spattered them with slush; their drivers, men not much older but more cunning than they, got out, still shouting into their mobile phones. They despised these privileged men with all their hearts. Zakhar and his buddies were around fifteen when communism collapsed. They spent their childhood in the Soviet Union, and they remembered that time as better than their adolescence and young adulthood. They looked back with tenderness and nostalgia at those days when things made sense, when you didn't have much money, but there wasn't much to buy either, when the houses were well kept and a little boy could admire his grandfather because he'd been the best tractor driver in his kolkhoz. They'd witnessed the defeat and humiliation of their parents, people who were modest but proud to be who they were and who had now been plunged into poverty and, worst of all, had lost their pride. I think that's what they couldn't stand the most.

Soon branches of the National Bolshevik Party sprang up in Krasnoyarsk, in Ufa, in Nizhny Novgorod. One day Limonov visited Zakhar's city, accompanied by three or four of his men, and the whole gang showed up to meet them at the station. Those who needed a place to stay were put up here and there, and they spent entire nights talking—well, mostly listening to Limonov talk. He expressed himself in a simple, colorful way, with the authority of someone who knows he won't be interrupted. He displayed a predilection for the words *magnificent* and *monstrous*—for him everything was either magnificent or monstrous, there was nothing in between, and the first time he saw him, Zakhar thought to himself, He's a magnificent man capable of monstrous deeds.

He'd read everything Eduard had written, even the youthful poems that express, Zakhar says, the fresh and primitive vision of a little child. But Limonov was no longer at all like a little child, he'd lost all his illusions on his long journey through the world. "You've got to plan your life around the presumption of other people's hostility," he said. The only realistic approach to and the best protection against that hostility is to be courageous, to be always on your guard, and to be ready to kill. One only had to spend a few minutes in a room with him and feel the energy diffused by his compact, alert, muscular body to be convinced that he possessed all of these qualities. And, in contrast, there wasn't the slightest trace of kindness in him. Interest in others, yes, and a lively curiosity, but no kindness, no softness, no serenity. That's why Zakhar, who admired him and wouldn't have traded his place in Limonov's circle for anything in the world, didn't feel totally comfortable in his presence, though he was completely at ease among the other *nazbols*. He had absolute faith in them. These guys with nicknames like Negative, Shaman, Soldering Iron, or Cosmonaut were the best people in the world as far as he was concerned: as loyal and stalwart as they were insolent and violent. Capable of giving their lives to save a comrade or going to prison for their ideas. Their sense of right and wrong was diametrically opposed to what prevailed in the corrupt, disoriented world that had succeeded the Soviet Union of their childhood. No sooner did he meet them than Zakhar stopped hanging out with anyone else. Everyone else just seemed empty and boring.

"I was lucky," he thought. "I met people it would be an honor to die with. I might have gone my whole life without meeting them, but I did. That's good."

He started going to Moscow, which after all is just 250 miles from Nizhny Novgorod. The first few times he wasn't particularly cautious, but as the years passed and the crackdowns became more frequent, the *nazbols* from the provinces were told to avoid the express trains because you've got to show your ID at the ticket counter and you risk ending up in the database of the FSB—as the KGB is now called. The solution was to take the slow suburban trains, the local lines that let you break the trip up between cities and avoid detection. That took two days, two days which they would spend getting drunk and sleeping. They traveled in threes and fours, acned boys with pale skin and red hands, in jeans, black shirts, and berets, types the other travelers viewed with suspicion. Moscow frightened them. They felt poor and provincial. They were scared of being arrested by the police in the subway, scared of the pretty, well-dressed girls they didn't dare approach. So as soon as they arrived they hustled over to Frunzenskaya subway station, and from there to the bunker. They rang at the armored door that had been replaced over and over because the special

forces had cut it open with a blowtorch numerous times before ran-
sacking the place and hauling everyone in. They were let in, and went
downstairs into the basement. There they could finally breathe. They
were at home.

Zakhar describes the bunker as a mix between a workshop where an
artists' collective is squatting, a home for young delinquents, a martial arts *dojo*, and an improvised dorm set up to shelter people at a
rock festival. The walls were corroded by humidity and the posters
and paintings that covered them showed Stalin, Bruce Lee, the Velvet
Underground and Nico, and Limonov in a Red Army officer's uniform. There was a large table where they ate and did the layout for
Limonka, a sound system for concerts, and frayed carpets on the floor
where the young people who had come in from the provinces could
unroll their sleeping bags and crash pell-mell between the full ashtrays and empty bottles, amid the strong odor of men and dogs.
Eventually girls started to come, who, according to Zakhar, were either very ugly or very pretty. Most of them cultivated a goth or punk
look. A lot of the boys had shaved heads, but some had long hair,
others wore sideburns, and a few even had impeccable haircuts of the
kind favored by household appliance salesmen. No one was surprised
by anything. Everyone was admitted, accepted as they were; the
only requirement was not being afraid of taking a punch or landing
in prison.

At the back of the big room were two offices. Dugin's was comfortable, equipped with an electric heater and filled to the ceiling with
bookshelves, carpets, even a samovar, though he was only there for a
couple of hours a day at most. Eduard's was far more spartan, even
though sometimes he practically lived there. A famous writer and cult
figure in the trendy circles of Moscow and St. Petersburg, he knew a
lot of artists and fashionable people who would drop by the bunker
the way they would have dropped by Andy Warhol's Factory in New
York. The grassroots *nazbols* were a bit intimidated to see famous rock-
ers, singers, and models pick their way between their sleeping bags
and German shepherds over to the big table, where my friend the

publisher Sasha Ivanov remembers spending the most exhilarating evenings of the decade. You met people there whom you never met anywhere else, he says: young, original, uncynical, their eyes bright with enthusiasm. The place was terrifically alive.

Dugin's followers—fascist students with big schoolbags or anti-Semitic Orthodox priests—weren't as glamorous by a long shot. But when he was in good form and had a feel for the crowd, "the greatest Russian philosopher of the second half of the twentieth century" would join the group and captivate the fashionable artists and crude provincial adolescents with some of the amazing stories he had up his sleeve: the heroic sacrifices of the Japanese kamikazes, Mishima's suicide, the paramilitary Buddhist sect created in Mongolia by Baron von Ungern-Sternberg. With his black beard, his bushy eyebrows, and his warm voice, he once more became the magus who had seduced Eduard. Unfortunately, as a writer, he possessed none of the persuasive charm he had as a storyteller. Eduard, who put out *Limonka* almost on his own, didn't dare refuse the dry, abstract, tedious articles that the party's cofounder and theoretician submitted to him each month with the solemnity one would accord the Holy Grail. Dugin seemed honestly convinced that these doctrinal elaborations were the backbone of the newspaper, the reason why its readers rushed to snatch it up when it came out. He liked neither the tone nor the look of *Limonka*. He would have preferred it to resemble one of those gray, confidential journals he subscribed to: the parish bulletins of the European extreme right.

The more time passed, the more the gulf widened between the followers of the two offices. Like Brahmins looking down on the pariahs, Dugin's disciples had nothing but scorn for the horde of commoners recruited by Eduard, fans of rock music and slugfests who cared little for the glorious history of fascism and were even—the most sensitive among them at least—put off by it. That was the case with Zakhar, who hated all these references to the Freikorps and other paramilitary units. He wasn't particularly amused by the fact that Eduard affectionately called Dugin "Dr. Goebbels," and was relieved when the latter, as the quarrels became increasingly poisonous, ultimately left the party to found a center for geostrategic studies which today is prosperous and in part Kremlin-funded. No more Brahmins: the pariahs were left to themselves. Zakhar liked it better that way.

3

IN *SANKYA*, his novel on the *nazbols*, Zakhar relates a conversation between his hero and one of his former teachers, who's fond of him and does his best to understand him. The teacher has flipped inquisitively through a couple of issues of *Limonka*. The party's name, its flag, and its slogans make him uncomfortable, but he's willing to see them as deliberate provocations, like those of the French Surrealists, whom he reveres. The actions of its militants—tagging trains, unfurling banners on hard-to-access monuments, throwing tomatoes at the governor during official events—seem to him immature, condonable, and courageous. Condonable because they are courageous: in Russia disturbing the peace is a serious offense, and these schoolboy pranks that would get you a fine in Western Europe earn their perpetrators prison sentences that they serve with pride. With a feverish and rather touchy solemnity, Zakhar's hero (and, I suppose, Zakhar himself ten years ago) speaks of the fatherland, the suffering of the fatherland, the essence of the fatherland, and all this talk worries the teacher. Trouble is never far away, he tells his former pupil, when the Russians start going on about their fatherland, the greatness of their empire, or the sanctity of their cause, or saying things like "The point isn't to understand Russia, but to believe in it." "It'd be much better," the teacher goes on, "to let the Russians lead, or at least try to lead, a normal life for once. It's hard right now, but it'll happen. Right now there are a few rich people and a lot of poor, but a middle class will spring up wanting nothing more than comfort and protection from the spasms of history. And that's the best thing that can happen to this country."

No, Zakhar's hero doesn't think that's the best thing that can happen to it. He wants more, he wants something else. "But what? More what?" the teacher demands. "More order? More disorder? Reading your newspaper there's no telling. You bellow: Soviet Union! Soviet Union! Is that really what you want? To go back in time? To restore communism?"

The question is not rhetorical: it comes up in the 1996 presidential elections. Saying that things don't look good for Yeltsin and the democrats is putting it mildly. The disastrous effects of the "shock therapy" and the first wave of privatizations plunged the country into chaos, and for the majority of the population it's absolutely clear that what's happened since 1989 is a historic calamity. Yeltsin, in whom so many hopes had been placed, seems to have completely lost control. Holed up in the Kremlin with no one to talk to but his family and his security chief, a sort of paramilitary boss named Korzhakov, he copes with what he calls his black moods—which are plainly serious depressive episodes—by drinking beyond reason. As much as the Russians are willing to indulge alcoholics, they no longer find it so funny when their president gets plastered every time he represents them at an international summit. During the solemn celebrations in Berlin commemorating the victory of 1945, they're downright embarrassed to see him nodding his head on the grandstand, then beating time with an increasingly tickled look on his face, and finally, lurching to his feet and pretending to conduct the military fanfare under the appalled eyes of the other heads of state. Just as with Tintin's friend Captain Haddock, these swings between depressive lows and drunken euphoria are conducive to bursts of belligerence. With the venal Korzhakov nearby to tell them when the right psychological moment was at hand, the hawks on the general staff had no trouble persuading Yeltsin that a nice little war carried off with aplomb against the "black asses" would pull the rug out from under the nationalists and boost his waning popularity.

Before he was murdered, my cousin Paul Klebnikov—who, trust me, was not at all an adept of conspiracy theories—had the following theory concerning the hawks' motives: Chechnya, which had been independent since 1991 and governed by a former Soviet apparatchik who'd hastily converted to Islam, was without the shadow of a doubt a free zone for organized crime, a hub for drug trafficking and counterfeiting. But even if its piece of the illegal but lucrative pie was shrinking, Russia continued to benefit from the situation and didn't see any great need for intervention. What was necessary, however, was to conceal the massive corruption rampant in the military high command. The generals had sold huge amounts of weapons, ammunition, and above all tanks on the black market, and what they needed was a major conflict for this material to be officially considered destroyed.

Whether or not this was as decisive a factor as Paul thought it was, the Russian army didn't cut corners. There were 3,500 detonations per day at the height of the siege of Sarajevo; at the beginning of the siege of Grozny in December 1994, there were 4,000 per hour. The city was laid waste as completely as Vukovar had been. But true to the reputation for bravery and cruelty that Russian literature has given them for the past two centuries, the Chechens replied with a merciless guerrilla war: they grilled the Russian soldiers in their tanks and staged bloody terrorist actions on Russian territory. And the forty thousand young conscripts, among them Zakhar Prilepin, who'd been promised a victorious lightning strike and a triumphant return, found themselves bogged down in a conflict as horrible as Afghanistan had been for their fathers and older brothers. After Gorbachev withdrew his troops from Afghanistan in 1988, there were only six years of peace; only six years between these two dirty wars from which young Russians returned—if they returned—crippled, humiliated, and suffering from hallucinations. Yeltsin, so loved at first, is now even more hated than his predecessor, and the presidential elections seem to be off to such a bad start that he seriously considers canceling them. As Korzhakov repeats to him in the sauna, "Boris Nicolayevich, democracy is good, but without elections it's more of a sure thing."

This time the alternative isn't a buffoon like Zhirinovsky, but the Communists, of all people. Five years earlier Yeltsin declared the party illegal. The grand and gruesome experiment that had been carried out on the human race in the Soviet Union seemed over for good. But after five short years of the democratic experiment, all the polls agree. There's no choice but to face up to this troubling fact: the people are so fed up with democracy, the market, and the injustice that goes along with it that they're ready to vote massively in favor of the Communist Party.

The party's leader, Gennady Zyuganov, doesn't propose reopening the Gulag or rebuilding the Berlin Wall. Under the label "Communist," this drab and cautious politician sells less the dictatorship of the proletariat than the fight against corruption, a bit of national pride, and the spiritual mission of Russian Orthodoxy faced with the new world order. He says that Jesus was the first Communist. He promises that if you vote for him the rich will get less rich and the poor less poor. Everyone should agree with at least the second part of this program: Who really wants old people to die of hunger and cold?

Nevertheless the oligarchs are spooked by the idea that someone wants to make them less rich, especially since they've just cooked up and sold to Yeltsin a marvelous scheme for getting even richer: "loans for shares." The idea is simple: their banks lend money to the state, whose coffers are empty, and the collateral for these loans is shares in the as yet unprivatized jewels of the Russian economy: natural gas, petroleum—the country's true riches. And if the state hasn't repaid them after a year, they'll proceed to checkout and serve themselves. The deadline falls after the presidential elections, so for the oligarchs it's essential that Yeltsin—and not someone like Zyuganov, who might repudiate the agreement to show his virtue—stay in power.

Word has it that they became aware of the danger at the Davos World Economic Forum, where the superrich and superpowerful of the planet meet. Because not only does Zyuganov—whom they consider a ridiculous little politician—have the nerve to come to Davos in 1995, but a swarm of journalists and advisers of heads of state is constantly buzzing around him, writing down all his comments—which are, incidentally, moderate—with the deference due to a future Russian ruler. Oh shit, Berezovsky says to himself. This man, the most

representative of the oligarchs, is the one—Jewish, brilliant, unscru-
pulous—everyone loves to hate. He goes out for a drink with George
Soros, the prominent American financier who's setting up an array
of foundations and philanthropic programs in Russia. "Well," Soros
says, "looks like you're in for some choppy waters ahead."

"So it seems," Berezovsky sighs.

"Maybe you'll even be sent to Siberia," Soros adds with a look of
commiseration. "If I were you, I'd watch out."

This conversation electrifies Berezovsky, who immediately calls
the six most powerful Russian oligarchs on their cell phones. He suggests they put their differences (the biggest being the one between
himself and Gusinsky: their goon squads are slaughtering each other
in a big way) behind them for the moment and join forces to get the
old czar reelected. Together, the seven of them pour all their financial
and media clout into the campaign—and their media clout means *all*
the media. All the newspapers, all the radio stations, all the television
channels hammer home the message: either Yeltsin or chaos. Either
Yeltsin or the great leap backward. And just so that no one forgets or
starts idealizing communism, terrifying documentaries about the
Gulag, the famine organized by Stalin in Ukraine, and the Katyn
Massacre are broadcast around the clock. Grand fictional films on
the purges, like *Burnt by the Sun* by Nikita Mikhalkov, are commis-
sioned. Personally I like this film a lot, but I can just imagine how
furious it would make Limonov if he saw it. He's always had a chip on
his shoulder as far as Mikhalkov—the scion of a great family of the
cultural *nomenklatura*, friend of dissidents as long as there are no
risks involved, in favor under every regime, and now very logically
the official eulogist of the counterrevolution—is concerned. The dachas under the summer sun; the big, happy families enjoying peace
and quiet; the deceitful political commissar who destroys all this hap-
piness as much out of envy as out of fanaticism: it's an anti-Stalinist
film in the Stalinist style, and if he's got to choose, Eduard prefers
the vintage Stalinist films. They were less duplicitous, more honest
about what things were like in his childhood.

———

The *nazbols* Zakhar's age are also disgusted by this barrage of propaganda that repudiates everything they were taught to love and puts the ideals their parents fought for on a par with Nazism. What to do with this disgust, what political form to give it? They'd like their leader to tell them, but for Eduard choosing between Yeltsin and Zyuganov is like choosing between cholera and the plague, and he can't find anything better to do than link up with the "Stalin Bloc," a little group even more marginal than his own, only to have himself supplanted as the candidate of this absurd coalition by a certain Yevgeny Dzhugashvili, who is not only Stalin's grandson but also a dead ringer for the dictator, right down to the mustache and pipe.

When it's time for the runoff vote (between the two rounds Yeltsin suffered a heart attack, which was hidden from the public as best as possible), the *nazbols* have to be told whom they should vote for, and Limonov surprises everyone with the theory that the more chaos there is, the better it will be for the revolution, so Yeltsin it is. This reasoning will be held against him, and it's at the basis of a rumor according to which, under all the apparent rabble-rousing, he's a paid agent of the Kremlin. He concludes from the episode that you've got to be careful of paradoxes in politics. The masses understand nothing about them; *Mein Kampf* is very clear on this point.

In fact, the general impression at the moment is that he's losing his mind. And it's true, he is losing his mind: Natasha has just left him.

I don't know much about the reasons or circumstances surrounding her departure, as his writings at this time are far less personal than those of his youth, but his reaction seems to have been just as convulsive as when Tanya left him. A borderline delirious text written on the spur of the moment gives a "philosophical and mystical" interpretation of the end of their thirteen-year relationship. Clearly influenced by Dugin, who hasn't yet jumped ship, Eduard tells of disturbing coincidences, prophetic dreams, hallucinated wanderings, and even, coming from such a prosaic, unappreciative reader of Bulgakov's *The Master and Margarita*, a very unconvincing encounter with the devil in the streets of Moscow. He consults a psychic, who tells him that in a past

life he was a Teutonic Knight and Natasha a prostitute under his protection. This interpretation strikes him as very telling. He protected
her, yes, like a valiant knight. He was faithful, as he was to Tanya, and
like Tanya she betrayed him. He tries to persuade himself that she isn't
worthy of him, does his best to look down on her, but, walking until
he all but drops in the stifling Moscow summer, he can't stop himself
from chanting over and over in his head, like a litany, a catalog of the
most glorious parts of her body: her large hands, so supple that they're
double-jointed; her white, somewhat sagging breasts; her pussy, always
wet, always ready for his cock and, alas, for those of other men. She
turned him on like no other woman in his life, except Tanya. He
thinks of how she masturbated dreamily, still smoking, sitting naked
on the toilet in their studio apartment in Paris. Lying on the mattress,
he'd watch her through the open door. He thinks back on the day when
he found her drunk and sprawled across the bed when he returned
from his catastrophic electoral campaign, and how, when she realized
he was there, she said, "You can yell at me later, now I need you to fuck
me." No matter how often Dugin repeats the Nietzsche quote that
sophisticated friends always trot out in these situations—"What
doesn't kill me makes me stronger"—he's in hideous pain. He'd give
his life to thrust his cock one more time into that sublime washout of a
singer, that alcoholic, that nymphomaniac, that creature of depths and
excesses who, he thinks, was once lucky enough to be Eduard Limonov's wife, and who now has had the even more incredible nerve to
turn that honor down.

This period of quasi delirium ends just after the elections, which,
largely rigged, proclaim Yeltsin the winner. One night, Eduard is
coming home alone when he's attacked by three guys in a deserted
street. They knock him down and kick him in the ribs and face. They
don't want to kill him—if they had they would have—but the damage
they inflict is serious: he spends eight days in the hospital and almost
loses an eye.

He wonders a lot about who was warning him, and about what.
His most persistent suspicions center on General Lebed. This former

parachutist, a hero of the war in Afghanistan who looks like a plumper version of Arnold Schwarzenegger and has a reputation for rough-and-ready honesty, came in third in the presidential elections. Many people, not only in Russia but also in the West, consider him a sort of Siberian Charles de Gaulle. Alain Delon, showing an unexpected interest in Russian domestic affairs, gives him his support in *Paris Match*. Eduard, on the other hand, hates him, first of all because even more than his natural enemies he hates people who occupy the same niche he does but more successfully—and in the "real man" category that's just what Lebed does—and second because although he's a general he courageously opposes the war in Chechnya and spares no effort in trying to bring it to an honorable conclusion. *Limonka* lambastes him violently, and even if *Limonka* is just a fanzine with a circulation of five thousand read by provincial punks, it's not entirely impossible that the honest general or one of his entourage could have vented his irritation the way it's commonly vented in his country, even in the best of circles.

In any event, Eduard no longer sets foot outside without three tough-looking *nazbols* at his side. He's not the only one: a huge number of people in Russia have bodyguards. Once, in Moscow, I flirted with a girl who had one. I could see him over her shoulder while I was turning on the charm in a restaurant. He ate at the next table, with absolutely no expression on his face. Later in the evening he stood guard on the other side of the door. It's unsettling at first, but after that you get used to it.

4

THE FOREIGNERS WHO came to try their luck in Russia, business-men, journalists, adventurers, speak with nostalgia of the second Yel-tsin term, 1996 to 2000, as the most rock-and-roll years of their lives. During these years Moscow is the center of the world. Nowhere else are the nights so crazy, the girls so beautiful, the checks so exorbitant.

That is, of course, for those who can afford to pay them. But you don't hear from those who can't anymore. Even when the crash of 1998 eradicates their meager savings for the second time in a single decade, they don't take to the streets. They remain stunned, sitting in the back of their sordid coffee shops, hypnotized by televisions that show nothing but the magical world of the rich in the big cities, the sumptuous girls who casually hold out a gold card to pay for a plate of sushi that costs what a teacher makes in a year, and the arrogant young men who, surrounded by an army of bodyguards with earphones, fly in private jets to Courchevel, where they fill their Jacuzzis with Veuve Cliquot. The "loans for shares" holdup worked beyond their wildest hopes: Khodorkovsky, for example, paid $168 million for the oil company Yukos, which brings in three *billion* a year. The oligarchs now have absolutely everything: immense fortunes that are based on raw materials and not on technology, fortunes that create no public wealth and disappear into an opaque network of offshore businesses, in Liechtenstein or the Cayman Islands. You can be shocked, or you can say, as my mother does: "Of course they're gangsters. But this is just the first generation of capitalism in Russia. Things were the same in America at first. The oligarchs aren't honest, but they're sending their children to the good schools in Switzerland so that they can have the luxury of being honest. Wait a generation; you'll see."

Politics was also privatized. The book that my courageous cousin Paul Klebnikov wrote on the basis of his research is called *Godfather of the Kremlin*, and that sums it up perfectly. Berezovsky isn't exactly discreet about his triumphs. He never misses a chance to remind people that when you say power in Russia it's him you're talking about, that the old czar owes him for being allowed to keep his throne—and in turn does just what he says. The opposition is in tatters, the people are catatonic, and Eduard, well, he's furious at not being able to use all his pent-up energy. The romantic thrashing he suffered didn't calm him down in the least. He's replaced Natasha with Liza, a ravishing, long-limbed punk who's twenty-two, looks like Anne Parillaud in Luc Besson's *Nikita*, and is crazy about him. But neither this new love, nor the underground newspaper, nor literature, fulfills the idea he has of his own destiny. "If an artist," he writes, "doesn't understand soon enough that he must focus on something higher than himself, like a party or a religion, then what awaits him is a pathetic fate made up of nothing more than drinking binges, talk shows, idle gossip, petty rivalries, and, to finish things off, a heart attack or prostate cancer." As far as religion goes, he'll keep that for later. But he does have a party. He doesn't quite know what to do with it, but in any event it's something, a force, and to take stock of just how big a force this is he decides to hold a convention.

They came, they're all there. No, not all of them—there are seven thousand total in Russia—but several hundred came in from all over, as if for a rock festival. The most impatient delegates arrived a couple of days early and settled in at the bunker. Sleeping arrangements for the others were made at a workers' hostel. That wasn't easy, and it wasn't easy to find a meeting place either. Each time a venue agreed to host, the owner would come back the next day to say that after thinking it over, sorry but no. The police must have explained to him in the meantime that it wasn't a good idea. The worst is feared right up to the end: a bomb scare, police harassment, or a ban, pure and simple. But the worst doesn't happen. The convention opens, Eduard stands on the podium, and he's beaming. For the last three years he and a handful of others have been busting their asses hauling copies of their paper to the stations where the trains leave for the sticks, and today they see the result: real people, brothers.

They're not the Siegfried types that Dugin dreamed of, but morose, pimply adolescents from the provinces, with pale, blotchy skin who trundle down the street in groups, and if by chance they happen to end up in a café, they count their money in embarrassment, look at their big boots, and split a drink in four. Poor customers, the *nazbols*. Afraid to look ridiculous, they bare their teeth so they won't be made fun of. Without Eduard they'd be alcoholics or delinquents. He gave their lives a meaning, a style, an ideal, and for that they're ready to die for him. He's proud of them, proud that now there are girls as well, who, as Zakhar Prilepin observed, are either very pretty or very ugly, no middle ground, but even the ugly ones are welcome, and the prettiest of all is his own, this long Liza with her shaved head who looks at him with love in her eyes while he talks and talks, bathed in the *nazbols'* adoration.

He tells them that Russia is governed by old, fat, corrupt politicians, and that they are its future. The usual refrain. But he tells them something else too, something he's thought about a lot: the political situation isn't yet ripe. A great man, as he repeated in vain to that half-wit General Rutskoy during the siege of the White House, senses when the time is ripe, and now it isn't. Better to let the stupid coalitions with Orthodox anti-Semites or Stalin's grandsons drop. The *nazbols* are not about to take power in Russia. One day, yes, but not now. But they're not just going to sit in a corner, read *Limonka*, and strum away on their guitars either. There's something they can do. Not in the country itself but on the periphery, in the former Soviet republics abandoned by that traitor Gorbachev, because when he abandoned them, he also abandoned 25 million Russians. These Russians ran these territories on behalf of the Soviet Union, and now that the Soviet Union no longer exists, they're nothing at all. They brought civilization to these boonies, now they're surrounded by Islam, or the new democratic ideology, which is no better. Once, they dominated, now they're victimized, ostracized, or at best tolerated in countries that owe them everything, countries that they irrigated with their blood, just like the Serbs in the former Yugoslavia. The traitor Yeltsin didn't want to go to the rescue of the Serbs, and he's not going to do any more to help the 900,000 Russians in Latvia, the 11 million Russians in Ukraine, or the 5 million Russians in Kazakhstan. So the new battle will be to fan insurgency in these territories, and to foster the creation of separatist republics. There are two targets: the Baltic countries and Central Asia. The party is already well established in the Baltic states, there are a good hundred or so *nazbols* in Riga. As for Central Asia, Eduard announces that he's going on a canvassing tour there. He'll be leaving soon and is counting on ten or so brave volunteers to join him. All candidates are welcome.

A hundred hands go up. Thunderous applause, a wave of enthusiasm. A new frontier is opening up to the boldest *nazbols*. It's a historic moment: just like, Eduard thinks, when Gabriele D'Annunzio raised a battalion of heroes to join him in retaking Fiume. Liza blows him kisses from the wings.

The National Bolsheviks' tour through Kazakhstan, Turkmenistan, Tajikistan, and Uzbekistan lasted two months. Eight of them accompanied the boss, eight paramilitary-type guys that a series of photos, reproduced in *Anatomy of a Hero*, show in front of tanks beside some Russian troops stationed there. These photos were the source of much laughter from a friend I showed them to when we were getting drunk one night. "Come off it," he said, "they're just a bunch of homos who went all that way just to get into one another's pants." I laughed as well; that hadn't occurred to me. Honestly I don't believe it, but who knows?

What is certain is that Liza and the wives and girlfriends of the others, if they had any, waited patiently at home. Eduard's real regret, however, seems not to have been the absence of his girlfriend but that of the French mercenary Bob Denard; Eduard had met Denard in Paris and had tried to get him to come along. This professional organizer of putsches and other half-baked coups in Africa would have been a precious resource for detecting possibilities for destabilization. Unfortunately, Bob Denard had bigger fish to fry. What is also certain is that even if he failed to destabilize much of anything, Eduard discovered countries after his own heart. He adored Central Asia. Not so much, in fact, the Russians in Central Asia, who were the reason he'd gone there in the first place, as the Uzbeks, Kazakhs, Tajiks, and Turkmens, about whom he reels off clichés that are, I think, perfectly true: proud, easily offended, poor, hospitable peoples, with traditions full of violence and vendettas with which he wholly sympathizes. Filled with thoughts of Gabriele D'Annunzio when he left, he comes back inspired by Lawrence of Arabia and now sees himself as the liberator not of Russian boors, but of Uzbek and Kazakh mountain dwellers, who after all have their own reasons for resenting the local dictators. After being so dead set against Islam under the influence of his Serbian friends, by the time he comes back he's swearing by nothing but Muslims, extending this newfound infatuation to include the Chechens, whose frugality, brilliant guerrilla tactics, and elegant cruelty he now extols. You've got to say one thing for this fascist: he only likes, and has only ever liked, the underdogs. The skinny against the fat, the poor against the rich, the self-confessed assholes—who are rare—against the legion of the virtuous. And no matter how erratic his trajectory might seem, it's coherent in that he has always, absolutely always, been on their side.

5

WITH YELTSIN'S SECOND term coming to an end, the oligarchs look around for a successor who's just as cooperative, and the slyest of them, Berezovsky, has an idea: a Chekist who's completely unknown to the public, Vladimir Putin. A former intelligence officer in East Germany, he went through some rough times after the fall of the Berlin Wall before finding a new niche for himself at the FSB, which he's quietly headed for the last year. Wherever he's served he's demonstrated unfailing loyalty to his superiors, and it's precisely this quality that Berezovsky sells to his fellows: "He's no genius, but he'll eat out of our hands." Given the go-ahead by the gang, Berezovsky takes his private jet and lands in the airfield in Biarritz, where Putin is on vacation with his wife and kids at a midpriced hotel. When the oligarch offers him the job, he says modestly that he's not sure he's got what it takes.

"Let's have none of that, now, Vladimir Vladimirovich, where there's a will there's a way. And don't worry, we'll be there to help you."

To jump ahead: Berezovsky, so proud of his Machiavellian maneuver, has just made the worst decision of his career. As in a film by Joseph Mankiewicz, the bland, obsequious officer will turn out to be a

remorseless powermonger and will take down, one by one, all those
who made him king. Three years after the meeting in Biarritz, Berezovsky and Gusinsky will be forced into exile, Khodorkovsky, the
only one to try to turn over a new leaf by making the management of
his oil empire more ethical, will be arrested and, after a rigged trial,
sent to Siberia just like back in the good old days. The others watch
their step; they've understood who's the boss.

But that comes later. Now the modest and unsullied Vladimir
Vladimirovich is presented to the populace by Yeltsin, who, six months
before the presidential elections, designates him as his heir apparent.
The election now seems like no more than a formality, but to make
sure that the new arrival will be seen as a savior, there's nothing like
a good little war. And the pretext for this good little war, once again
in Chechnya, is a series of bombings on buildings in the suburbs of
Moscow in the fall of 1999, which claim more than three hundred
civilian lives. According to one theory that makes the rounds, these
attacks, blamed on Chechen terrorists without a shred of proof, were
in fact committed by the FSB. The theory was publicly expressed by
General Lebed, the journalist Artyom Borovik, the former FSB officer Alexander Litvinenko, and my cousin Paul Klebnikov. All four
died violent deaths: Lebed and Borovik in suspicious accidents, Litvinenko poisoned with polonium, Paul gunned down with a Kalashnikov. Both paranoid and not entirely implausible, this theory about
the 1999 attacks remains quite widespread among the Russian population; the strangest thing is that people aren't particularly bothered
by the idea and vote overwhelmingly in Putin's favor several times—
all the while believing that he's guilty, or at least capable, of such
a crime.

In any event, just a few months after his promotion Putin is no
longer modest or unsullied in the least. He proclaims his intention to
"waste the terrorists in their shithouses," and this sets the tone for his
presidency. This catchphrase immediately becomes a kind of inside
joke with the *nazbols*: "Hey, pass the vodka or I'll waste you in your
shithouse." Like Berezovsky, Limonov and his cohorts have no idea
what awaits them.

Things happen fast, very fast. Even before the presidential election, the Ministry of Justice passes a law banning extremism and fascism— which it reserves the right to define—and lets the National Bolshevik Party know that the decree concerns it directly. Eduard requests a meeting with the minister in person, obtains it, puts on his suit and tie, and pleads his case. Extremist? Him? Fascist? Not on your life. The minister listens, tells him how much he respects his talent, seems very open. But three months later, after the deadline for granting authorizations has passed, the ax falls: the answer is no. The National Bolshevik Party no longer has the right to exist. Stunned, Eduard once more requests and, to his great surprise, is granted an audience, puts his suit and tie back on, and this time he doesn't beat around the bush. One hundred and thirty political parties are recognized and registered in Russia, he says to the minister, including many phantom parties, without members. That's not the case with his own, which has seven thousand adherents. The situation is simple: if it's not authorized, the National Bolshevik Party will be obliged to organize itself in secret, and he, Limonov, won't be able to do a thing if young people who care about the future of their country are pushed toward extremism and terrorism.

The minister raises his eyebrows: "You're telling me that if your party's not authorized you're going to start setting off bombs?"

"What I'm telling you," Eduard responds, "is that if you stop us from going the legal route, we'll take another."

Not long afterward, Eduard is summoned to the Lubyanka by an officer who tells him flat out that he's in charge of the dossier on him and his party. This officer doesn't play at being a friend to the literary arts, but he's not unpleasant, which confirms Eduard's conviction that the Chekists are better than the civil servants. "What's this grenade supposed to mean?" he asks, pointing to the logo of *Limonka*. "An incitement to murder?" Eduard answers that the model is one manufactured in a Russian weapons factory and that as far as he knows reproducing images of it isn't banned by law. The officer laughs affably and gives him his cell phone number, inviting him to call if he notices any of the young people in his entourage being tempted by terrorism. "Will do," Eduard says politely.

As far as terrorism goes, it seems that in all of its history, legal and illegal, the National Bolshevik Party has never distinguished itself through anything other than peaceful demonstrations. It's not just the *nazbols* and Eduard who say that, but the very authorities who have prosecuted and imprisoned them for such minor offenses as bellowing "Stalin! Beria! Gulag!" at a speech given by ex-prime minister Gaidar, slapping Gorbachev with a bouquet of flowers—without thorns, Limonov points out—or distributing a leaflet entitled "Our Friend the Torturer" at the end of the official premiere of Nikita Mikhalkov's film *The Barber of Siberia*. The torturer in question was the president of Kazakhstan, Nursultan Nazarbayev, the film's patron, and the leaflet denouncing the unenviable fate of the opposition in his country was more a humanitarian than a fascist tract—except that humanitarian organizations would have prudently avoided running afoul of such a powerful and popular figure as Mikhalkov, who was now to Russian cinema what Putin was to power: the *khozyain*, or in other words, the boss. The response to this protest wasn't long in coming: a Molotov cocktail in the bunker, then OMON riot police muscle in, confiscate, beat up, and imprison any *nazbols* who happen to be there at the time—all, Limonov is certain, at Mikhalkov's bidding. At another screening, two *nazbols* retaliate by throwing rotten eggs in the filmmaker's face, and both are immediately arrested and slapped with six-month prison sentences.

Six months seems quite a lot for rotten eggs. But it's not much if you compare it to the sentences meted out in the Baltic countries—which, let's recall, Eduard singled out as a region for priority action. The Latvian operation involves a tangled knot of post-Communist paradoxes, all well worth telling. Latvia, an ex-satellite of the USSR, had become an independent and democratic state. The country's judiciary condemns and imprisons an old Soviet partisan, hero of the Great

Patriotic War, and, until the Wall came down, a Chekist well known for his savagery. From a foreign perspective, this is sound historical therapy: society is exercising its duty of remembrance and calling the torturers to account. From the *nazbols'* perspective, it's a humiliation, an insult to the twenty million who died in the war and the hundreds of millions who believed in communism. For these young romantics, the old KGB crocodile becomes a hero, a martyr. To show their support, three of them burst into the Cathedral of Saint Peter in Riga, throw a fake grenade to clear out the tourists, barricade themselves in the bell tower, and shower the ground with leaflets. In so doing, they know perfectly well what to expect: battalions of cops with megaphones who call on them to give themselves up, negotiations, demands that will never be met (that the old Chekist be liberated, that Latvia renounce its plans to join NATO), followed by others that are more realistic (that the Russian ambassador be present when they come down). Finally they surrender; the ambassador is there but doesn't do a thing to protect them, they're manhandled as badly as if they'd opened fire on the crowd, tried not for hooliganism but for nothing less than terrorism, and sentenced to fifteen years in prison, with the Russian government's blessing.

That's right: fifteen years. What makes things even more convoluted is that the Russian authorities against whom the *nazbols* are rebelling have, at the moment, just as little patience as the *nazbols* do for insults to the glorious past: Putin practically declares war on the Estonians when they want to get rid of a monument to the Red Army. In substance the *nazbols* and he agree—though the *nazbols* would rather commit mass suicide than admit it, of course. But when it comes to "fighting terrorism"—as benign as this terrorism might be—the Russian Chekists work hand in hand with the Latvian police and hunt down the romantic defenders of their persecuted old colleagues without the slightest qualm.

All this is complicated, I know, and it's to untangle conundrums like these that I'm writing this book. Even Eduard, who, God knows, isn't afraid to swim in troubled waters, starts to get fed up and dream of fresh air and wide open spaces. Moscow's a grim place, and he tells himself he'd feel better in Central Asia. He decides to combine a new field trip to explore the possibility of destabilizing Kazakhstan with a Rambo-type survival course in the Altai Mountains. That's the definition of a good vacation for this man who never takes any, and it reminds me of the pictures I've seen of Stalin's holidays in Abkhazia: you only ever see him in army boots and a tunic, surrounded by guys with mustaches dressed just like him who, if they'd prefer to be lying in beach chairs, taking the occasional dip, are doing a good job of hiding it.

Take a look at the map: you'll see that the Altai region, which is right next to Kazakhstan (mind you, these territories are five times bigger than France), is the most landlocked location in the world, equidistant—and very far—from the Atlantic, Pacific, Indian, and Arctic oceans. Like Mongolia, where Baron von Ungern-Sternberg founded his order of Buddhist legionnaires, it's a region famed for its breathtaking landscapes—high plateaus, tall grass blown flat by the wind—and low population density. Vast expanses, the sky, and no one under it: it's into this elemental, almost abstract universe that Eduard ventures in the summer of 2000, squeezed into a jeep with four of his men, bumping up and down on potholed, rutted roads. Their guide, a taciturn and expressionless guy named Zolotarev, has located, in the moutains to the south, a spot that seems to correspond to what they're looking for: a sort of remote and isolated retreat that could serve as a training camp. The training camp is a myth in the party. Many *nazbols* are absolutely certain that Eduard has already set up several ultrasecret ones, modeled on those of the jihadists in Pakistan. He does nothing to dispel the rumors, but there's no truth to them: for the moment there are no camps.

At the end of a road, six miles from the nearest village—and it takes almost an hour to cover these six miles—the travelers arrive at a log cabin with a roof that's half caved in and plastic-covered windows. Two rooms, four beds, a stove that seems to work. They get out their gear, sleeping bags and provisions, and settle in. At night they picnic under the stars. The magic begins.

Pantheist lyricism isn't my strong suit: although I like hiking in alpine landscapes, I'm not altogether in my element describing campfires, rivers, the thousand varieties of grass, mushrooms, and animal tracks, so I'll pass quickly over the Robinson Crusoe stuff. Eduard spends three weeks there, during which time the men devote themselves, apart from hunting and gathering, to firing practice and close combat. No one bothers them. A child of the concrete, Eduard discovers a whole new world. And now that he's in his element, their guide Zolotarev turns out to be a fascinating character. In the city he'd struck Eduard as a sort of old provincial hippie with dirty hair and a bandanna, who only broke his silence to mumble vague new-age bunk full of words like *energy* and *karma*. Leaving the cabin on the first morning, Eduard found him meditating in the lotus position facing the rising sun. At first that made him smile, but in less than three days he finds he really can feel the calm and positive vibrations emanating from the guide. Zolotarev takes him fishing in the mountain streams, teaches him to gut and cook the catch, and choose the herbs and berries to go with them. He knows the natural world like no one else. But more than just knowing it, he's part of it, he's completely at ease. Eduard is almost intimidated: in his presence he feels like the all-too-civilized traveler before the Mongol trapper Dersu Uzala in the adventure novel of the same name that's read by every Russian schoolkid and that inspired Kurosawa's famous film. Zolotarev has the trapper's small build, his slanted eyes, his sparing way with words. At first glance you don't notice either his force or his mischievousness, but once you've caught a glimpse of them that's all you see, and you understand that you almost missed out on an extraordinary person. A sort of master, in his own way.

Flanking the cabin there's a *banya*, one of those rudimentary saunas that serve as baths in the Russian countryside. Between four walls made of moss-covered logs, you sweat in the steam rising from coals and sizzling stones onto which you ladle cold water from time to time. Ordinarily the *banya* isn't really Eduard's thing. He can stay in for a long time because he's got a robust constitution, and if there's snow on the ground he's not afraid of going outside and rolling naked in it between two good sweats, but he gets bored quickly sitting there doing nothing; he feels like he's wasting his time. For Zolotarev, on the other hand, the *banya* is almost a religious ritual, and he manages to initiate the impatient Eduard. In the evening, after their long treks through the mountains, drunk on fatigue and wind, they spend an hour or so drinking vodka in the cloud of steam, letting their muscles relax, remaining silent, peaceful, and confident, and every now and then when Zolotarev pronounces, oraclelike, a sibylline sentence by his favorite author, Lao-tzu, Eduard doesn't see anything ridiculous about it anymore; he agrees. "He who knows does not speak. He who speaks does not know." The old hippie speaks little but he knows; he's in harmonious contact with something bigger than himself, something Eduard also feels connected to in his company. He's calm, he feels good.

At the beginning of September it starts to turn cold. Icy fogs rise from the valley at dawn. They cut and stack wood for the winter. Because right from the start the idea was that three of the *nazbols* would spend the winter there, cut off from the world as soon as the snow makes the road impassable. It will be hard but exhilarating, Eduard thinks. He envies them: if he didn't have a party to take care of back in Moscow, he'd love to stay with them. The plan is that he'll come to relieve them in April, when the thaw arrives. They make sure they've got enough of the few indispensable things you can't find in nature: sugar, candles, nails . . . In a Jules Verne novel they'd make up one of those three-page lists that my hero and I read with racing hearts when we were little. They give one another manly hugs, and Eduard and the two others set off down the road back to Barnaul, the capital of the Altai region, where Zolotarev lives. Saying their emotional goodbyes, Eduard admits to the trapper that he didn't think much of him at first, but that he's got to know him better and is proud to be his friend. Zolotarev's face remains wooden, his slanted eyes don't blink. "I was watching you," he says to Eduard. "You have a soul. And I'm not in politics, but I like your men as well."

"If you like I'll bring you a party membership card when I come back," Eduard says. "It'd be a pleasure."

6

ALL WINTER, FROM October to April, Eduard dreams of the Altai. It's a terrible winter in Moscow. The atmosphere in the bunker is completely poisoned by the conviction of the Latvian commando. A handful of Moscow *nazbols*—real kamikazes, considering what they're risking—want to leave for Riga but are arrested at the train station in possession of drugs, the police claim, and end up in prison as well. Their parents think that it's Eduard's fault they've gone astray: they come to the bunker and berate him, threaten to take legal action. One of the very first *nazbols*, among the eight who did the grand tour of Central Asia, is beaten to death on the outskirts of Moscow. The inquiry concludes it was a drunken fight and maybe that's the truth, maybe not. Taras Rabko, the most loyal of the loyal, the historic third member of the party, comes to see Eduard one day and announces in tears that he's leaving. He held out as long as he could, but his family, his career in the judiciary . . . he just can't anymore. That's the fate of a party by and for the young: as soon as they start making something of their lives, they leave. Liza, the girl who looks like Anne Parillaud in *Nikita*, left Eduard as well, to get married and have kids with a computer programmer her age. He replaced her with an even younger girl named Nastia: in fact she's underage, which boosts his ego on the one hand and is yet another motive for paranoia on the other.

Nastia ran away from home to move in with him. Coming back late one night they see a light in their window. Taking the stairs four at a time, they open the door and find that the light's out. Everything seems in order, which is even more worrying: Eduard is less afraid of robbers who take things than visitors who leave things behind. They search the place; the apartment is so small that if anyone had hidden weapons they'd find them, but a gram of heroin is small too. To cover himself, Eduard decides to inform his case officer at the FSB, the one who gave him his cell phone number. The officer doesn't set up a meeting in his office at the Lubyanka, though Eduard's been there twice already, but on the platform of a subway station, as if they were con-spirators. As I've said, Eduard doesn't dislike the guy and levels with him: about the nighttime visit to his place, the anonymous calls he receives, the impression he has that a noose is tightening around his neck. The officer nods with a look of concern, both as if he were in the know and as if it didn't all depend on him but on another department with which he was at loggerheads. "Honestly," Eduard goes so far as to say, "what do you think about this Riga thing? Do you think it's normal for Russia to leave its citizens in the lurch?"

The officer sighs: "I agree with you, but that's not for us to decide. It's a matter of state."

"The truth," Eduard goes on, "is that we do the work that your people should be doing. Instead of persecuting us, you should be using us. Letting us do the work you're not allowed to."

He's sincere when he says it: he's got nothing against the organs; on the contrary. And he's got no problem seeing himself and his party working hand in hand with them, as Bob Denard and his squad of mercenaries did with French policy makers in Africa. But the officer is noncommittal, looks at his watch, takes his leave.

7

HE HAD HOPED he'd be able to breath in the Altai. But he can't. During the entire trip—three days by train from Moscow to Novo-sibirsk, plus one day from Novosibirsk to Barnaul, in third class as usual—he felt as if he was being watched, under surveillance. Don't get paranoid, he kept repeating to himself like a mantra. But don't forget that you're often *right* to be paranoid. Difficult, in this situation, to follow the "middle path" recommended by Lao-tzu, who, thanks to Zolotarev's influence, has become his bedside reading. Things will be better when I'm there, he thinks. He looks forward to meeting up with the trapper in Barnaul and hitting the road with him. He thought of him often over the course of this dreadful winter, and the thought soothed him, as reading Lao-tzu did: a calm, silent vibration, the promise of contemplation even in the midst of the waves, of the world's sound and fury.

When he arrives at Zolotarev's place, he's told the trapper was buried the previous day. A woman who'd gone out to walk her dog in the early hours of the morning had found him lying dead, at the foot of his building. A fourth-floor window in his apartment was open. Suicide? Accident? Murder? The *nazbols* with whom he'd spent his last evening claim he wasn't depressed or drunk when he left them.

Eduard nervously fingers the National Bolshevik Party membership card he'd brought the trapper as a gift. He feels unsteady on his legs.

Something strange happens the next night. As previously planned, he's headed off with two *nazbols*, silent like him, all devastated by what's just happened. Absorbed by dark thoughts, he doesn't pay the least attention to the things that had so amazed him on his last trip: the infinite sky and the landscapes under it reduced to their most elemental expression; the caravansary where they stop to drink tea; the ascetic, noble faces of the mountain dwellers who offer them hospitality. They stop for the night at the same place where they stayed last time. Calling it a village would be saying too much: a couple of yurts and a log cabin where he goes to lie down almost as soon as they arrive, without dinner, without a word. As luck would have it the *nazbols* have brought their tent: he's alone.

Lying on his cot he thinks of the dead. Of the people he's known in his life who are now dead. There are starting to be quite a few of them. He thinks that if he counted, the dead would outnumber the living, but he can't bring himself to count. He doesn't feel like sleeping either, just lying there without moving. He thinks that he's also going to die, and strangely, it's as if he's never thought about it until this very night. He's often dreamed of the kind of death he'd like: in combat, or shot by a firing squad, executed on the order of a tyrant and defiant to his last breath. But these fantasies, he now sees, have nothing to do with the certainty that is right then taking hold of him: he's going to die.

He thinks about his life, about the journey that's taken him from his childhood in Saltov to this log cabin in the Altai where he's lying this evening, almost sixty years old. A long journey, full of obstacles to overcome, but he hasn't given in. He wanted to live like a hero—he did live like a hero—and he never balked at paying the price.

He thinks of something the trapper said to him last fall: according to Buddhist tradition, this is the center of the world, the place where the world of the dead communicates with the world of the living. It's the place Baron von Ungern-Sternberg was looking for, and he's here.

Looking out the window he sees the moon shining over the dark hills. It's full. And he starts to hear music, at first far off and then closer. Gongs, horns, sepulchral chants. You'd think it was the soundtrack to *Bardo Thodol*, the *Tibetan Book of the Dead*, that Dugin introduced him to a while ago. That asshole Dugin, he thinks fondly. In spite of everything, he knows he'll be happy to meet him again in the warriors' paradise—that is, if they'll take that chickenshit . . .

He wonders if he's falling asleep or dying. He thinks a ceremony's taking place very nearby, maybe a shamanic rite of initiation. Normally he'd like nothing better than to go out and take a look, but now, in part because he wants to give his hosts their privacy, but mostly because he doesn't want to move, he remains stretched out on his cot, nestled in this music from the hereafter that blends with the sounds of his body: the blood beating in his temples, pumped by his heart, flowing through his veins. He doesn't sleep, he doesn't move. It's as if he is dead, as if he has gained access to another form of life.

The next morning he asks the *nazbols* if they were at the ceremony. What ceremony? There was nothing of the sort: neither a party, nor a concert, nor a shamanic ritual, nothing. Everyone went to bed after dinner. If you're looking for nightlife, they laugh, you're in the wrong place.

Eduard doesn't press the issue. He remains in a reflective mood for the rest of the trip, but he's not as distraught as he was the day before.

He thinks that this celestial music, this experience of the hereafter, was a gift from the trapper and that it was announcing something. Perhaps his accession to the Eurasian throne, which he'll conquer with a handful of *nazbols* from their retreat in the mountains, succeeding where Baron von Ungern-Sternberg failed. Perhaps his imminent entry into Valhalla—that is, death. But he's not afraid of dying, he'll never be afraid of that again. He's on the other side of fear.

The three *nazbols* up at the camp aren't unhappy to see them arrive. They look good: tanned, ascetic, like honest to goodness monk-soldiers. From their voices and their bearing, you can tell they've matured. That evening, shadowed by Zolotarev's death, they're both grave and lighthearted, marvelously relaxed. The guys tell stories about the winter: the times when they were down in the dumps, their moments of elation, the day one of them met a bear. They grill shashliks, those lamb shish kebabs they serve in the Caucasus and Central Asia, on long wooden skewers. They drink wine, brought in from Barnaul in the back of the jeep, but they don't get drunk. Everything is tender, friendly. They feel good, the seven of them, under the kerosene lamp. Eduard, who's so little given to sentimentality, wants to tell these guys who could be his sons that they're the most noble and courageous beings in the world. He feels very distant and yet very close to them. He's never been so sentimental. In hindsight, he thinks the Last Supper must have been something like that.

He's woken by barking at the crack of dawn. They don't have a dog, but he doesn't have time to be surprised. Everything happens very fast: the special forces men burst into the cabin, pull the sleepers from their bags, and force them to kneel outside in the snow that still lingers in the morning at these heights. There are a good thirty of them, with balaclavas and machine guns at their hips, holding back German shepherds that are barking like hell. Eduard has lost his glasses and feels his way around. He's in his wool underwear, barefoot: as the leader he's the first one allowed to get dressed. The soldier charged with leading him into the cabin takes the opportunity to tell him that he just loves his books and that he's proud to be arresting him. The soldier's not kidding; he really does seem proud and happy; he's all but asking Eduard for an autograph.

Now, to get down to business: "Where are the weapons?"

"What weapons?"

"Don't play dumb."

The search is meticulous—dogs, metal detectors—but apart from the two hunting rifles they don't turn up any weapons—and I must admit that amazes me: it would have been so easy to plant some there. You've got to give the FSB credit for having such prim legal scruples.

The six *nazbols* are loaded roughly into an army truck with their hands on their heads. Eduard shares a comfortable sedan with Colonel Kuznetsov, a colossus with mirrored Ray-Bans who takes some vodka and zakuski from a little fridge in the car as soon as the raided camp has disappeared from view. They can sit back and relax; it's an eight-hour drive to the FSB base at Gorno-Altaysk, where a special plane is waiting for the prisoners. "VIP treatment," the colonel comments. Delighted at the success of the operation, he knocks back shot after shot, and insists that Eduard join him—which he does, though not as enthusiastically. Cracking open the second bottle, Kuznetsov goes so far as to say that the *nazbols* are almost like family for him, after all the time he's spent on their dossier. Eduard's surprised: he thought he knew the officer in charge. "Oh, no," the colonel says. "That guy's a wimp, he was taken off the case two years ago. When the whole thing with Mikhalkov was taking place." He, Kuznetsov, was the one who cracked down on them at the filmmaker's request. And he was also the one who locked up the *nazbols* leaving for Riga two months ago.

"That was a setup," Eduard says. "They didn't have any drugs on them."

The colonel lets out a knowing laugh: "No, you're right, they didn't. What a joke!"

This pisses Eduard off, and when he gets pissed off his voice becomes increasingly dry and staccato. "Didn't it bother you," he says, "to set a trap for kids who were fighting to get one of your own men out of prison? Felix Dzerzhinsky, your founder, would turn over in his grave if he saw you. He was a great man, and you, you know what you are? Assholes! You don't deserve to call yourselves Chekists!"

Insulted, the colonel could use his position to his advantage, but he turns sheepish all of a sudden. You'd think he was going to burst into tears.

"Why don't you like us, Venyaminovich?" he sighs. "Why isn't someone like you on our side? We could do great things together . . ."

"You hiring me?"

The colonel holds out his hand. He's drunk, but he seems sincere. Eduard shrugs.

"Go fuck yourself."

IX

Lefortovo, Saratov, Engels,

2001–2003

✺

I

EDUARD HAS BEEN dreaming of it his whole life. When he read *The Count of Monte Cristo* as a kid. When he heard his prison guard father tell his mother one night the story about that courageous young condemned man, so calm, so in control of himself, who became the hero of his adolescence. For a man who sees himself as the hero of a novel, prison is one chapter that can't be missed, and I'm sure that, far from being devastated, he took pleasure in every moment—I almost said every shot—of those scenes you've watched in films a hundred times: the arrival; the few possessions—clothing, keys, watch, wallet— handed over; the pajamalike uniform that's issued in return; the medical exam that includes a cavity search; the walk through the labyrinth of corridors, sandwiched between two guards; the succession of fences and gates; finally the heavy metal door that opens and closes behind you, and there you are: these are the ninety square feet where you'll spend the next months or years and, as in war, it's here that you'll show your true mettle.

He wasn't treated like a small fry: he's at Lefortovo, where they put the worst enemies of the state. Every big-time political prisoner or high-level terrorist first the Soviet Union and then Russia had to offer spent time there. Even today this KGB fortress, situated near Moscow, isn't shown on any maps, and it's shrouded in so much secrecy that at first Eduard doesn't know what he and his companions are accused of. He hasn't seen a lawyer, isn't allowed to receive visitors. Nor does he know when the trial will start, what people on the outside are saying about his arrest, if anyone's even talking about it, or if those closest to him know he's in there at all.

Unlike most prisons in Russia, Lefortovo isn't dirty, it's not overcrowded, and you won't get raped or beaten up. On the other hand you're subjected to strict isolation. Not only do you not have to work, you can't even if you want to. Private, white, sterile, the cells are all equipped with a television that the inmates are free to watch morning to night, and this fuzzy-headed addiction plunges them for shorter or longer periods into apathy and then depression. Daily exercise takes place up on the prison roof in the very early morning, but each prisoner is allocated just a couple of square yards, entirely fenced off, and, to prevent any conversation between cubicles, loudspeakers play music so deafening that you can shout as loud as you want and you still won't be able to hear the sound of your own voice. This unappealing exercise isn't obligatory either, and many of the prisoners end up not bothering to take part: they stay in bed, turn their faces to the wall, and never breathe the outside air. In winter, when it's still dark and horribly cold, no one goes out at all, and the guards, who've gotten used to coming back and sipping their tea in peace once the wake-up call has sounded, are astonished when the prisoner Savenko demands the right to this exercise to which he's entitled by the prison regulations. "But it's minus twenty-five out there," he's told. No matter. The whole time he's in Lefortovo, Eduard won't let a day go by without going out onto the roof for half an hour and running like mad on his square of concrete, doing push-ups and sit-ups and boxing the icy air. The guards are somewhat irritated at having to leave their well-heated locker room for just one customer, but they're impressed too. Add to that the fact that he's polite and even-tempered, that you can see he's educated: soon they're calling him "Professor."

If there's one thing in the world that Eduard hates, it's wasting his time. And prison, particularly one like Lefortovo, where the inmates are left to their own devices, is the kingdom of wasted time, of time that drags on without form or direction. While the others sleep in, he gets up at five in the morning and gets the most out of every moment until he goes to bed. He makes it a rule to watch nothing but the news on television: no films or variety shows, which he considers the beginning of moral decay. In the library, likewise, he spurns easy novels with which you "kill time," as they say, and borrows, one after another, the dry volumes of Lenin's correspondence, which he reads sitting upright at his table, jotting down ideas in his notebook. These are the only favors he requests: a table, a bright lamp, and a notebook, which the guards, filled with growing admiration, willingly provide. At this pace he writes four books in one year, including a political autobiography and an unclassifiable text, in my mind his best since the memorable *Diary of a Loser: The Book of Water.*

The previous summer, before going to the Altai, desperate for cash, he pushed himself to finish off his *Book of the Dead*, from which I've drawn a great deal, in just one month. In sketching portraits of people both famous and unknown whose paths he crossed and who have since died, he wrote down his own memories, as they came to him, and, despite being forced to write over twenty pages a day to meet the deadline, he enjoyed the exercise so much that he wanted to do something similar in prison. Like Georges Perec, he could have drawn up a list of all the beds he's slept in; like Don Juan he could have cataloged all the women he's made love to; he could have even, like a good dandy, told the story of his clothes. But he chose the waters: seas, oceans, rivers, lakes, ponds, and swimming pools. Not necessarily waters he's swum in—even if, as soon as he learned to swim, he promised himself that he would do it at every possible opportunity, and knowing him as we do, there's no reason to imagine he ever let himself be thwarted by the cold, the dirt, the height of the waves, the treachery of the currents. The book follows no set course, neither chronological nor geographical; it moves on a whim from a beach on the Côte d'Azur, where he watches Natasha swimming, to a dip in the Kuban River with Zhirinovsky. He remembers his walks along the Seine when he lived in Paris; the foghorns of the boats he watched passing one another on the East River from his window at the millionaire Steven's place; a fountain in New York where he bathed when he was drunk and lost his contact lenses; the coast of Brittany with Jean-Edern Hallier and the beach at Ostia, near Rome, where he went with Tanya a couple of months before Pasolini was murdered

there; the Black Sea during the Transnistria war, the torrents of the
Altai where the trapper Zolotarev taught him to fish; and the large
basin of the Luxembourg Gardens where, newly arrived in Paris and
starving, he decided he was going to try to catch the carp. There are
around forty short chapters, precise and lucid, telescoping locations
and periods, but which despite their apparent disorder are organized
around the women of his life.

Anna, Tanya, and Natasha we know already. He's told at length of
the love he bore all three, how he left the one and how the two others
left him, how they drove him mad with grief and how they both
missed him bitterly because he was their chance to lead an extraordinary life—at least so he says. By contrast, we've only gotten a glimpse
of Liza, and then of Nastia. I know how violently our era condemns
an older man's fondness for young flesh. But what can you do, that's
how it is, and *The Book of Water* is a hymn to little Nastia, who was
sixteen when he met her and looked twelve. He bought her ice cream,
helped her with her homework. When they walked hand in hand
on the banks of the Neva in St. Petersburg or the Yenisey in Krasnoyarsk, no one was shocked because they thought they were father
and daughter. Nastia wasn't a spectacular beauty like Tanya, Natasha,
or Liza, but a petite punk, just five feet two inches tall, timid, intro-
verted, almost autistic, who'd placed the scandalous writer Limonov
on her altar of transgressive demigods between the provocative rocker
Marilyn Manson and the serial killer Andrei Chikatilo—the Ukrainian Hannibal Lecter. She worshipped him, and, from prison, he
started worshipping her as well. In his book, he sets the memories of
their two years together like so many jewels. Now she's nineteen, and
he wonders in apprehension what's becoming of her out there, if she's
forgotten him, if she's sleeping around. In principle he prides himself
on being a clearheaded, realistic man. While he believes that he himself is able to be faithful, he doesn't nurse any illusions as far as other
people go. Tanya, Natasha, Liza: he doesn't think for an instant that
they'd wait for him in a similar situation. But with Nastia it's different.
He hopes she's waiting for him, he believes she's waiting for him, it
would drive him crazy to find out that she isn't.

But for how long? He entered prison a man of fifty-eight who didn't weigh an ounce more than he did when he was twenty, a man at the height of his powers, supremely seductive—but no one knows when he'll get out and whether, despite his willpower and his resilience, he won't by then have become, like the overwhelming majority of ex-convicts, a broken man.

The prisoners at Lefortovo aren't forced to shave or cut their hair, and he lets his grow, defiantly. It swishes across the table as he writes. If this continues it'll end up touching the floor. Then he'll look less like Edmond Dantès in *The Count of Monte Cristo* and more like his old prison companion in the Château d'If, Abbé Faria.

2

HE STAYS IN Lefortovo for fifteen months, subject to this regime of strict isolation. Then, in a government Antonov aircraft, accompanied by a police escort so impressive it's as if he were Carlos the Jackal or maybe the entire Baader-Meinhof Gang rolled into one, he's transferred to Saratov, on the Volga, where he's to be tried. Why Saratov? Because it's the Russian jurisdiction closest to Kazakhstan, where he's supposed to have committed the crimes he's accused of. What crimes, exactly? It's impossible to be ignorant of your crimes at Saratov, where on every possible occasion you not only have to state your last name, first name, and patronymic but also the articles of the criminal code that you're imprisoned for having violated. As soon as he arrives, Eduard learns to reel off in quick succession the mantra that even today springs to his lips when he's woken up with a start: "Savenko, Eduard Venyaminovich, Articles 205, 208, 222 paragraph 3, 280!"

To explain: 205 is terrorism; 208, organization of an illegal armed group or participation in one; 222 paragraph 3, illicit acquisition, transport, sale, or storage of firearms; and 280, incitement to extremist activities.

When the investigating judge cites the charges and the heavy sentences they bear during the first hearing, Eduard is torn between pride at being accused of such serious stuff and the vital interest he has in exonerating himself. On the one hand, it's not easy for him to admit that half a dozen muddlers roughing it in a log cabin in the Altai sixty miles from the Kazakh border, with no arms other than a couple of hunting rifles, had as little chance of destabilizing Kazakhstan as they did of sparking a nuclear war. On the other, if he doesn't want to get locked away for twenty years as a terrorist, he has no choice but to pass himself off as a bungling fool. The judge, however, seems ill-disposed to listen to his arguments and holds to the version presented by the FSB, according to which he and his six accomplices constitute a serious menace to the country's security.

To top it all off, the FSB's version is graphically illustrated by a TV film aired by Channel One Russia just as he arrives at Saratov. While he was in prison, 9/11 happened, and you can sense it: the film presents the National Bolshevik Party as a branch of Al-Qaeda, the hut in the Altai as a secret camp training hundreds of fanatic fighters—which was in fact his dream and which, as he knows, is a far cry from reality. Everyone in the prison has seen *The Ghost Hunt* (the name of the film), everyone knows that Eduard's the hero, and everyone starts calling him "bin Laden"—which is of course flattering, but also dangerous.

Saratov is the opposite of Lefortovo: there the risk isn't isolation but overcrowding. Although the cells are built for four, often seven or eight inmates are crammed into them. When Eduard enters his for the first time, all the beds are occupied. Without protesting, he rolls out his mattress on the ground; it seems right that the last to arrive should be the most uncomfortable. This humility is surprising, and it works to his advantage. He was preceded by his reputation as an intellectual, a political prisoner, and a celebrity, three reasons for his fellow inmates to consider him a pretentious pain in the ass; three reasons things might not work out for him. But he shows right away that he's a simple, straightforward guy who wants nothing more than to *sidet spokoino*, that is, to wait things out without making waves, without shooting his mouth off and without getting himself or anyone else into trouble. And everyone appreciates the wisdom of an experienced prisoner; at the same time, everyone senses that he's a tough nut under his placid air. He's not the kind of guy who stupidly asks, "Can I help?" when he sees someone cooking or repairing something; instead, he figures out what has to be done and does it. He avoids useless words and gestures, doesn't shirk chores, shares with everyone when he gets a package, and respects the unwritten rules that govern life in the prison without them having to be explained. Which isn't to say he takes courtesy to extremes either; he imposes his own way of seeing and doing things with a calm authority. Initially, the other inmates are a bit surprised when he refuses to play cards or chess because he thinks they're a waste of time, and instead spends this time reading or writing on his cot. But they quickly see it's got nothing to do with snobbery: that's just the way he is, and it doesn't stop him from readily lending a hand when someone needs help writing a letter to his girlfriend or even completing a crossword puzzle. It only takes a week for everyone to reach the same conclusion: he's a good guy.

While writing this book there were times when I hated Limonov, and others when I was afraid that in telling his life I was completely on the wrong track. Finding myself in San Francisco during one of these periods, I went to my friend, the film producer Tom Luddy, to talk through what I was doing. Tom's the most talented person in the world at putting people together (no matter what question's on your mind, he's always got a suggestion about where you should go or someone you really have to meet), and he responded immediately. "Limonov? A friend of mine knows him very well. We can have dinner with her tomorrow if you want." That's how I met Olga Matitch, a White Russian in her sixties who teaches Russian literature at Berkeley and who knew Eduard when he was living in the States. When *It's Me, Eddie* came out, the people who were interested in Slavic literature, whether they were French or American, scratched their heads and wondered just what they should think of its author; then, very quickly, they chose as one to hate him. Olga's the exception; she was always on good terms with him, she teaches classes on his work, goes to see him when she's in Moscow. She's liked and admired him for the past thirty years, and she's all the more significant an exception in that she impressed me as being not only intelligent and civilized but also a profoundly good woman. I know, that's just an impression, but as with Zakhar Prilepin, I trust it.

And this is what she said: "God knows I've met writers, and above all Russian writers. I've met them all. And the only really good man among them is Limonov. Really, he's one of the most decent men I've met in my life."

On her lips, the word *decent* had the sense George Orwell gave it when he spoke of "common decency": that high virtue, a composite of honesty and common sense, mistrust for big words and a respect for one's own word, a realistic appreciation of reality, and attention to others—more widespread among commoners than among the upper classes and extremely rare among intellectuals. That said: no matter how much I trust Olga, I have a bit of a hard time seeing this halo adorning Eduard's head when he shoots in the direction of Sarajevo or plots with sinister shitheads like Colonel Alksnis (and, reassuringly, so does Olga). Nevertheless, there are moments when I see what she means, and Eduard's time in prison is one of them. This was perhaps the high point of his life, the moment he came the closest to being what, with bravery and childlike doggedness, he always did his best to be: a hero, a truly great man.

His cellmates are ordinary criminals, condemned to long sentences for serious crimes. Most of them have been charged under Article 105, paragraph 2: murder with aggravating circumstances—and, having always respected gangsters, he's proud now to have commanded their respect. Proud that they consider his party not a pack of young idealists but a gang ("You've got seven thousand men? Holy shit!"); proud that they call him—if not bin Laden—"Limon the boss"; and proud above all that a godfather asked him one day, discreetly, the way you'd let a man know that there's nothing stopping him from becoming a member of the Académie française, if he'd like to be welcomed into the brotherhood of the *vory v zakone*, the thieves in law, that aristocracy of the underworld that had been the source of so many of his adolescent dreams. All this impresses me without surprising me: it's Eduard through and through. What surprises me more, and proves Olga right, is that in the three books on his time in prison he writes far less about himself than about the others. Eduard, the narcissist, the egotist, forgets himself, forgets to pose, becomes sincerely interested in how his cellmates ended up where they did.

Some say to him, "You're a writer, you should write my story." And he does, without having to be asked twice; the result is dozens of micronovels. For example, there's the saga of the Engels gang: eight mafia types who systematically bled an industrial city in the region dry, liberally gunned down rivals and cops, and received in return sentences ranging from twenty-two years to life. There's the terribly sad story of the inmate who's just about to get out and has been going on and on for weeks about every step he'll take on the path that will lead him back to his bride-to-be. But then, the day before his release, he receives a letter from her admitting that she's moved in with another guy. While he does what he can to comfort the poor boy, Eduard is thinking, of course, of Nastia. There's the horrible story of the two cousins who raped and killed an eleven-year-old girl. He spent quite a while with these two provincial adolescents, one of whom is mentally retarded, and sensed about them the aura of misery and shame that surrounds sex offenders. Fascinated, he sketches the tale of "how two lonely, very young men managed to break a delicate and graceful doll because they had no idea how to handle her." And when, before he leaves Saratov, one of these boys who's going to spend the rest of his life getting bullied in an extremely harsh prison camp says to him, "Good luck, Edik," he's troubled, overwhelmed even. He's got nothing but respect for a sendoff like that.

"I've met a lot of them, the strong, mean men who've killed and are now tortured by the state," he writes. "I'm their brother, a little muzhik like them, buffeted by the bad winds of prison. You asked me to, guys, so I'm writing for you, the dungeon dwellers. I don't judge you. I'm one of you."

It's true, he doesn't judge. He's got no illusions, no compassion, but he's attentive, curious, even helpful at times. With his feet on the ground. Right there. It makes me think of my friend, the judge Étienne Rigal, who appears in my novel *Lives Other Than My Own*: the biggest compliment he can pay someone is to say *they know where they are*. If there's one person in the world about whom it would never have occurred to me to say that, it's Limonov, who for all his courage and vital energy seems to me most of the time to be way out in left field. But not in prison. In prison he's not way out in left field. He knows where he is.

Another quote I like a lot: "I'm one of those who is never lost, wherever he is. I approach other people, other people approach me. Things fall naturally into place."

One of the prisoners he gets along with best is a guy named Pasha Rybkin. At thirty, this colossus with a shaved head has already spent ten years in prison, and, as Eduard charmingly sums it up, he "is surrounded by crimes the way forest dwellers are surrounded by trees." That doesn't prevent him from being a peaceful man, always in a good mood, half Russian holy fool, half Asian ascetic. Summer and winter, even when the temperature in his cell drops below zero, he walks around in shorts and flip-flops, he doesn't eat meat, he drinks hot water (not tea), and he does impressive yoga poses. It's not a very well known fact, but a huge number of people from all walks of life do yoga in Russia, even more than in California. Pasha very quickly recognizes a wise man in "Eduard Venyaminovich." "They don't make people like you anymore," he assures him. "At least I've never met any." And he teaches him to meditate.

People make a big thing of it if they've never tried it, but it's extremely simple. In fact you can teach yourself in five minutes. You sit down cross-legged, as straight as possible, stretch your spine from the tailbone to the back of the head, close your eyes, and concentrate on your breathing. Inhale, exhale. That's all. The difficult thing is precisely that that's all there is to it. The difficult thing is to do nothing else. When you start out you overdo it and try to chase the thoughts away. Very quickly you see that that doesn't chase them away, but if you watch your thoughts on their carousel as it turns, bit by bit you're carried along with it less and less. Your breathing slows. The idea is to observe it without modifying it, and that too is extremely difficult, almost impossible, but with practice you progress a little, and a little is enormous. You catch a glimpse of a calm zone. If you're not calm for one reason or another, if your mind is racing, no problem: you observe your agitation, or your boredom, or your desire to move, and as you observe them you put them at a distance, you're a little less held hostage by them. I've been doing this exercise for years. I don't talk about it because I feel uncomfortable with its new-age valence, let's be Zen and all that stuff, but it's so effective and it does you so much good that I have a hard time understanding why everyone doesn't do it. Recently a friend of mine joked to me about the filmmaker David Lynch, saying he'd gone totally gaga because he no longer talked about anything but meditation and wanted to persuade the government to require it in schools, starting in first grade. I didn't say anything, but it seemed clear to me that my friend was the one who was gaga, and that Lynch couldn't be more right.

In any event, as soon as the good, wise gangster Pasha Rybkin explained to him how it worked, Eduard, with his customary pragmatism, immediately saw its utility and fit spells of meditation into his rigorous schedule. At first he sits in the lotus position on his cot, with his eyes closed, but once he's gotten the hang of it he discovers you can do it anywhere, discreetly, without having to adopt this somewhat showy posture that advertising campaigns—whether for mineral water or for insurance policies—have abused so badly. Through the various double doors, metal cages, and paddy wagons that punctuate the prisoner's journey from his cell to the office of the investigating judge, amid the barking of the police dogs, the suffocating odor of piss, and the morning curses of the security guards, he learns to retreat within himself and reach a zone where he's calm, beyond reach. Again, if there's one person I'd never have imagined giving himself up to this practice, it's Eduard. But I think it has a lot to do with the remarkable equanimity he demonstrated while in prison. I also think that meeting Zolotarev and the strange experience he had in the Altai after learning of his death prepared him for this gift, and you wouldn't have to twist my arm too far for me to say it's the trapper who sent it to him, from wherever he is.

3

ON THE EVENING of October 23, 2002, his cellmates are watching one of the crime films they're so fond of despite Eduard's attempts to make them see how insulting they are: the cops are depicted as heroes, the criminals as monsters, they know perfectly well that's not how it is—but who cares, they can't get enough. Suddenly the program is interrupted, and over dramatic music it's announced that the actors and audience at a Moscow theater have been taken hostage by a commando troop of Chechen terrorists. The others couldn't care less—reality interests them less than their idiotic movies and they want to turn it off—but Eduard objects. Over the next fifty-seven hours, he watches news story after news story; he doesn't miss a thing, right up to the gas attack launched at dawn on the twenty-sixth against the eight hundred people in the theater, terrorists and hostages alike.

He's extremely caught up by the affair, in part because of course he himself is charged with terrorism, his trial is approaching, and the paranoia sweeping the country isn't going to do anything to help his case. But it's also because his cellmates' crimes pale before the mountain of corpses gassed by the special forces, and forever after he'll continue to return to the contrast between crimes committed in an instant of passion or drunkenness for which the perpetrators will pay for the rest of their lives, and crimes of the state whose perpetrators will be decorated. But the most striking thing about the notes he jotted down day by day during the Dubrovka tragedy is that his spontaneous analysis, gleaned only from the information broadcast on television, tallied exactly with that of a woman he doesn't know, and probably wouldn't even like if he did, who was in a position to follow events at much closer hand: Anna Politkovskaya. Like her, he fears a bloodbath right from the start. And when this bloodbath occurs, like her, he guesses (though from his cell in Saratov) that the officials are lying, that there are many more victims than they admit and that nothing was done to save them. When Putin declares with a macho air, "understand this: we will not let ourselves be intimidated by the terrorist menace, regardless of the losses!," like her he remembers the persistent rumors that the terrible attacks of 1999 were committed not by Chechens but by the FSB with the president's endorsement, a president he now, like Politkovskaya, calls a "fascist." As far as I know, it's the first time he's used the word negatively.

Little Nastia comes from Moscow for a visit: half an hour, separated by a pane of glass. She's twenty, and cute as anything with her Chinese jacket and her long black braid. She tells him about the journalism program where she's enrolled as a freshman, and the odd jobs she does to pay for school: selling ice cream, taking care of the dogs in a kennel. She asks if it's all right with him if she brings home a pit bull. He agrees, laughing: "I'd rather you come home with a dog than with a guy."

Does he have the right to say that? His doubts on the subject torment him. Sometimes he thinks it would be both wise and noble to say to her: "Don't wait for me. Keep your distance. You've got your own life to live and you're not going to live it with me. There are forty years between us and God knows how long it'll be till I get out of here. Find a boy your age, think of me from time to time, I give you my blessing." But he can't bring himself to say it. Not only because he needs her—no inmate in any prison in the world will ever reject the love of a woman—but also and above all (at least that's what he says) because saying these words would be an insult to her. That would be treating this courageous girl like an ordinary person, subject to ordinary laws, whereas with every bone in her body she wants to be an exceptional person, a heroine, the only woman worthy of the hero he is, the only one to hold firm in the face of adversity and stay true when all the others would have betrayed him.

"You know," she says, "the youngest wife of the Prophet Mohammed was still playing with dolls when she met him."

"With dolls? Really? But tell me something. Are you planning on waiting for me for a long time?"

She looks at him, naive, astonished. No one's ever looked at him like that. No one's ever loved him like that.

"I'll wait for you forever."

On January 31, 2003, the representative of the General Prosecutor's Office of the Russian Federation, a guy named Verbin, who, according to Eduard, looks like a chainsaw on legs, demands for the accused Savenko a prison sentence of ten years under Article 205, four years under Article 208, eight years under Article 222, paragraph 3, and three years under Article 280: twenty-five years total. In a show of great leniency, the prosecutor proposes reducing them to fourteen. The accused Savenko, who has pleaded not guilty from the first, forces himself to listen to the indictment without batting an eye; but inwardly he collapses. He hasn't even served two years; if the judge agrees with the prosecutor he'll be seventy-five when he gets out. Courage and willpower notwithstanding, he knows what you are when you get out of prison at seventy-five in Russia: a zombie.

Three days later, a second blow. On the news, the station NTV announces the death of Natasha Medvedeva, ex-wife of Eduard Limonov and figure in the alternative rock scene; a kind of Russian Nico, per the journalist's description. They don't state flat out that she died of an overdose, but everything points in that direction. Once, a long time ago, when they were still living together, she and Eduard compared the different ways of committing suicide and concluded that heroin is the best: the big flash of ecstasy and then, finally, peace. After Anna, Natasha . . . Is he someone who falls in love with women destined for a tragic end, or did their lives end tragically because they met him, loved him, and lost him? He believes that Natasha, like

Anna and even Tanya, Spanish marquess or not, never stopped loving him; maybe it was even when she heard about the prosecutor's nightmarish sentence that Natasha decided to end it all. He remembers her body, her open legs, their savage, almost incestuous way of making love. He thinks that he may never make love again. Lying motionless on his cot, not in the lotus but in the fetal position, he soothes his distress by singing, very softly, this little ballad he's just made up:

Somewhere my Natashenka
under a soft, warm rain
is now walking barefoot.
Up there, on a cloud,
the good Lord plays with a cutlass
casting reflections on her face.
Ba-da-da-da! Boom-boom-boom-boom!
sings Natasha, naked.
She puckers her thick lips,
she moves her big dead hands,
she spreads her long dead legs,
she rushes up to paradise,
her body naked and dripping.

4

WITH ITS BRIGHTLY colored walls instead of wire fences, its rose-bushes, and its pseudo Philippe Starck sinks, Penal Colony 13 at Engels is the work camp I wrote about at the beginning of this book, the one that's shown to human rights advocates to convince them that prison conditions are improving in Russia. Just like in 1932, when, at the height of a famine that was so bad that the peasants resorted to killing their own children, H. G. Wells concluded from the excellent meal he was served in Kiev that my God, they ate well in Ukraine. In fact, Engels has such a bad reputation among Russian prisoners that some have inflicted injuries on themselves in the hopes of not ending up there. Nevertheless, Eduard feels he's been lucky, and you've got to admit that he's dodged quite the bullet: two months after the prosecutor Verbin called for a sentence of fourteen years, the judge condemned him to four, half of which he's already served. Just two more years to wait when he was preparing for twelve is a miracle, and he's more determined than ever to watch his step and not provoke any officers or screws who might be irked by his fame. He knows that at any moment and under any pretext someone in a bad mood can turn around and slap you with a week in solitary, or worse. Among the dreadful stories that make the rounds at Engels there's the one about the inmate who, the day before he was due to be released, was unlucky enough to cross paths with a drunken junior officer. The officer found him poorly shaved, and on a whim, to show him who was boss, prolonged his sentence by a year. Just like that, completely arbitrarily. And sure, you can always appeal to a judge, but before he can reverse the decision, you might have already picked up an extra ten years. That's why at Engels Eduard works to make himself invisible, and as his great talent in life lies in taking advantage of everything that happens to him, he's not long in finding an interesting angle even here.

Lefortovo and Saratov have made him an expert on prison, but camp life is new to him and what he discovers is that the condition of the *zek* has hardly changed since Solzhenitsyn described it. Like that of Ivan Denisovich, Eduard Venyaminovich's day starts at 5:30, when a siren sounds the wake-up call. In fact it starts a bit earlier, because he wakes up on his own at five o'clock. While everyone else in the barracks is still snoring, he alone, lying under his blanket like a tombstone effigy, observes his breathing. This moment belongs to him, he loves it, he takes pleasure in it. He doesn't have a watch, but he doesn't need one to know right down to the minute how much time he still has before pandemonium breaks out. As it approaches he feels like a motor waiting for the key to turn in the ignition. And bingo, the siren wails, the wardens shout and swear, the occupants of the top bunks tumble down onto those below, everyone yells, and we're off.

First thing, all the inmates rush out into the courtyard for a cigarette before heading for the toilets. As he's one of the rare nonsmokers, Eduard takes advantage of the break to be among the first to go take a shit. And though his bowel movements are of an exemplary regularity, he's noticed that his shit smells stronger than it did outside, and even than it did in prison. He's also noticed that though the *zeks'* shit stinks, their garbage cans don't smell at all. That's because apart from cigarette butts they don't contain any organic material, as everything that's organic is edible and everything that's edible is eaten: camp law.

At 6:30 it's the first roll call, in the central yard. Last name, first name, patronymic, articles you're sentenced under. There are three roll calls a day, and since there are eight hundred prisoners, each one lasts a solid hour. In the summer it's all right, you tan—in the winter it's harder. Eduard considers himself lucky to have arrived at Engels in May, that way he can get used to things bit by bit. After the roll call is the *zariadka*, half an hour of collective gymnastics, and then— finally!—breakfast. Eight hundred *zeks* with shaved heads file in batches into the immense mess hall. The clatter of spoons, the sound of slurping, quarrels that die down immediately, and in the background indefinable music, somewhere between hard rock and a symphonic medley whose martial accents, Eduard thinks, should incite the prisoners to revolt, to smash everything, to mount heads on spikes, but no: with hunched backs, sheltering their tin bowls with their arms as if fearing their neighbors will try to swipe their meager grub, the *zeks* chow down in silence on kasha and thin soup, with a bit of black bread. This food without vitamins gives them a gray pallor, gives their shit the noxious odor that Eduard has noticed, and, without starving them to death, saps them of their energy. That's no doubt on purpose.

Unlike the other prisons he's been in, Engels is a work camp, even a rehabilitation through work camp: after breakfast it's time to get cracking. As a rule what distinguishes this work is that it serves no purpose. Just after Eduard arrived there were torrential rains that permanently flooded the buildings. The administration decreed that the ground had to be dry for each of the three daily roll calls, other-wise no television. Personally Eduard couldn't care less, but for the others that'd be a tragedy. The result could be a scene straight from a slapstick comedy: line after line of inmates using water glasses to empty the puddles that fill right back up again, from morning till night. At first Eduard thought it'd be more rational to improve the drainage system with some masonry work. He even considered saying something about it, but luckily he didn't, understanding in time that if the prison administration doesn't behave like a rational employer, it's because this Sisyphean labor is an old camp tradition: nothing is more depressing, all the veterans of the Gulag have observed, than busting your ass at a futile and absurd task: digging one hole, for ex-ample, then a second for the dirt from the first, and so on. A good *zek* is an exhausted, demoralized *zek*: that's also on purpose.

At sixty, Eduard is considered a senior citizen and as such ex-empted from forced labor, but that doesn't mean he's allowed to write, read, or meditate as he could at Lefortovo or Saratov. He's prohibited from going back to his barracks, his books, and his notepads until evening, so he has to devote himself to cleaning tasks that are no less absurd than the other jobs. Scrubbing down a row of toilets until they're absolutely spic and span takes an hour at most. He's given four to do it. Fine, he'll take four hours. He does the entire job four times over, no toilet bowl in the world will shine more brightly, and he doesn't daydream, even for a minute.

This fervor isn't just outward. Inwardly he's not idle either. Te-dious and repetitive occupations are conducive to daydreaming, and Saint Pasha Rybkin, the Saratov yogi, warned him: daydreaming is the exact opposite of meditation. A little mental white noise that most people don't even notice, even though it's the worst waste of time and energy. To elude it either he counts his inhalations, prolonging them, concentrating on the path taken by the air from his nostrils to his lower abdomen and back, or he recites poems he knows by heart, pay-ing close attention to each verse, or—most often—he writes. In his head, of course, as Solzhenitsyn did fifty years before: composing sen-tence by sentence, paragraph by paragraph, chapter by chapter, memorizing as he goes along, and in this way improving, day by day, the memory of an already impressive hard drive.

In theory the camp rules don't forbid writing, but, first, he doesn't have much time to record his day's work—at most an hour in the evening—and second, the screws wonder what he's doing, and this curiosity isn't as respectful as it was in the other prisons. Once one of these dense, suspicious wardens wanted to see his notebook, flipped through it in a menacing silence, and finally asked, "You talk about me in here?" After that close call, Eduard just jots down notes that have been diplomatically softened, counting on his memory to help him flesh them out when he's released.

And it's a good thing. Right before he gets out his notebooks mysteriously vanish, and he's got to rewrite the book he composed in Engels from start to finish without them. It's all the better for it, he thinks.

5

HOW TO TELL what I have to tell now? You can't. There are no words to describe it. If you haven't experienced it you don't have the first idea, and I haven't experienced it. Apart from Eduard I only know one other person who has. That's my best friend, Hervé Clerc. He recounts the experience in a book that's also an essay on Buddhism, called *Les choses comme elles sont* (Things as They Are). I prefer his words to Eduard's, but it's Eduard's experience that I've got to write about here. Let's give it a go.

He remembers very well the moment that preceded it. An ordinary moment, like the ones that make up ordinary time. He's busy cleaning the aquarium in the office of a senior official. All the offices of senior prison officials have aquariums in them. Do they all like fish? And if they don't, could they ask to have the aquarium removed? Most likely they don't think about it. As far as he's concerned, Eduard likes cleaning aquariums; it's more fun than cleaning toilets, and not as dirty. He's transferred the fish to a bucket with a net, removed the water pail by pail, and now the tank is empty and he's scrubbing the sides with a sponge. As he gives himself over to this task, he's focused on his breathing. He's calm, concentrated, attentive to what he's doing and feeling. He's not expecting anything in particular.

And then without warning everything stops: time, space—but it's not death. Nothing around him has changed in any way—not the aquarium, not the fish in their bucket, not the office, not the sky outside the window—but it's as if all of that was just a dream and only now has it suddenly became absolutely real. Raised to the second power, revealed, and at the same time erased. He's sucked into a void that is fuller than all that is full in this world, filled by an absence that is more present than everything that fills the world with its presence. He's no longer anywhere and he's *totally there*. He no longer exists and he's never been as alive as he is now. There's nothing, there's everything.

You could call it a trance, a rapture, a mystical experience. My friend Hervé says it's an abduction.

I'd like to go on longer about this, in more detail and more convincingly, but I see that all I can do is string together oxymorons. A dark brightness, a full emptiness, a still vibration, I could prattle on for a while without either the reader or myself getting any farther along. What I can say, bringing together their experiences and their words, is that Eduard and Hervé know with absolute certainty that they have, the one in his Parisian apartment thirty years ago, the other at Penal Colony 13 in Engels, in the office of a prison official whose aquarium he was cleaning, attained what the Buddhists call nirvana. Pure, unfiltered reality. Sure, from the outside we can always object: okay, but what proves to you that it wasn't a hallucination? An illusion? A sham? Nothing, apart from the most essential thing: namely that when you've been there you know it's for real, that that darkness and that light can't be imitated.

They say something else too: that when you're taken, carried away, lifted to that place, you feel, to the extent that there's still someone there to feel, something like immense relief. Gone is the desire, the anxiety that are at the basis of human life. They'll return, of course, because unless you're one of the illuminated—and according to the Hindus there's only one every century—you can't remain in this state. But you've had a taste of what life is like without them, you know firsthand what it means to be *in the clear.*

Then you come back down. In a flash you've experienced the entire duration of the world and its abolition, and then you fall back into time. You return to the old yoke of desire and anxiety. You wonder, What am I doing here? After that you can spend, like Hervé, the next thirty years thoughtfully digesting this incomparable experience. Or, like Eduard, you can go back to your barracks, lie down on your bunk, and write in your notebook: "I was expecting that of myself. No punishment can reach me; I'll know how to transform it into bliss. Someone like me can even find pleasure in death. I'll never return to the emotions of ordinary men."

I wrote this tricky passage at Hervé's chalet in Switzerland, where we meet twice a year to go walking in the mountains of the Valais region. And in the bookshelf there I came across a collection of articles on Julius Evola. Evola was, in a few words, an Italian fascist and also an impressive intellectual, both a Nietzschean and a Buddhist, a hero to cultivated fascists like Dugin. Along with a hodgepodge of traditional scholarship, the collection also includes a beautiful text by Marguerite Yourcenar. I jotted down the following, which struck me and brought Eduard vividly to mind:

> Any tendency toward greed, pride, or the will to power does not annul the benefits of mental discipline, but will bring them back into a world where every action enslaves and every excessive use of force boomerangs back at the one who exerts it . . . Clearly Baron Julius Evola, who ignored nothing of the grand Tantric tradition, never thought to arm himself with the secret weapon of the Tibetan lamas: the dagger-to-kill-the-ego.

6

EDUARD IS SUMMONED to the director's office. For a *zek* such a conference is a priori a bad sign. He's only seen the director once, the day he arrived, and he'd like it to stay that way. This time, the man who's known for his coldness welcomes him politely and announces the visit of another one of those delegations periodically shown around the colony. One of its members, the presidential adviser on human rights Pristavkin, has said he'd like to meet the prisoner Savenko. Does the prisoner Savenko consent?

The prisoner Savenko can't believe his ears. First, that he's being asked his opinion—because a *zek* doesn't consent or not, he just toes the line—and second, that Pristavkin is interested in him at all. He's a cultural apparatchik, a dyed-in-the-wool Gorbachevian; they once clashed during a debate on the crimes of communism. They got into a huge fight, Eduard called Pristavkin a traitor and a sellout, and forever after Pristavkin always took the opportunity lash out at Limonov the fascist; he even wrote in the *Literaturnaya gazeta*, "Let him rot in prison, that's the best place for him."

So Eduard is suspicious, both of the man and of what negative signals this invitation might send to those around him. But he accepts, and, when the day comes, he finds himself in a waiting room next to the director's office with ten or so well-shaven, squeaky-clean inmates, clearly hand-picked to make a good impression on the delegation. They wait in silence, without daring to look at one another, embarrassed to be there. Finally the delegates arrive, and you can tell by their flushed faces that they've just come from a lunch where there was no shortage of drinks. They spend half an hour asking the inmates how they are, if they're well treated—which makes Eduard snicker inwardly: are they dumb enough to think that a *zek*, in the presence of the director and knowing full well what awaits him as soon as the visitors have turned their backs, will have the courage to say that no, things aren't good, that he's poorly treated? Out of the corner of his eye he watches Pristavkin, who's watching him out of the corner of his. He's lost some hair since the last time they saw each other, he's put on a few pounds and has a few blotches on his skin: an adventurer's life keeps you in better shape than that of an apparatchik, the lanky Eduard thinks. Finally Pristavkin says to the director, but in a voice that's loud enough for everyone to hear, that he'd like to have a word in private with the prisoner Limonov.

"Savenko," Eduard corrects him.

"Of course, of course," the director agrees. "Please, go into my office."

The two men retire to the office as the others look on in amazement. A moment of hesitation: Where to sit? If it had been up to Eduard he'd remain standing while the visitor sat in the director's chair— that's the reality of their situation, and if he were asked if he wanted to switch places he'd say no. But Pristavkin takes him by the arm and they sit side by side on a sofa behind a coffee table, like old friends.

"Cigar?" Pristavkin asks. Eduard says he doesn't smoke. "Look here," Pristavkin continues, his breath smelling of cognac, "this little joke has gone on long enough. You're a great Russian writer, Eduard Venyaminovich. Your *Book of Water* is a masterpiece. Yes, yes, I insist: a masterpiece. And in fact, all the connoisseurs agree. Have you seen that you've been shortlisted for the Russian Booker Prize? The PEN Club is worried about you and, of course, even if the organs will never admit it officially, these terrorism charges don't hold water. Times change, you've got to be sure not to aim at the wrong target. These days the real crime is economic: someone like Mikhail Khodorkovsky, who embezzles billions of dollars—now that's a criminal, and the worst kind. They were right a thousand times over to lock him away. But an artist like you, Eduard Venyaminovich, a master of Russian prose . . . Your place isn't among killers."

"Some of them are great guys," Eduard says.

"Oh really? You think killers are great guys?" Pristavkin lets out a jovial laugh. "That's writers for you. Dostoyevsky said the same thing . . . Anyway, you've been dealt with too harshly. But don't worry, Eduard Venyaminovich, we'll take care of that."

"I'm not going to say no," Eduard ventures.

"Well! Who would? Now, it'd make things a whole lot easier if you admitted your guilt. Don't look at me like that, I know you refused to at your trial, but hear me out: it'd be purely formal, just to keep our friends at the FSB from losing face, you know how touchy they are. If push comes to shove, no one even needs to know about it. It'll be buried in your file and that's that. You fess up and you're out of here in a month, two at the most."

Eduard looks at him, trying to tell from his face if it's a trap. Then he shakes his head: more than his freedom he holds to his reputation as a tough guy who refuses to fold.

"Think about it," Pristavkin says.

After this visit his fate hangs in the balance, and the fact that it's being decided in the upper echelons of power gives him a bizarre status: respect and jealousy blend with the idea that it's probably better to stay away from him. When asked about the incident he plays it down: Pristavkin must have been drunk, nothing'll come of it.

He's wrong, as his lawyer confirms when he visits him from Moscow. Public opinion has turned in his favor. He's no longer considered a terrorist but a sort of Dostoyevsky, writing great books from the house of the dead, and the opportunist Pristavkin must have thought it was a perfect occasion to play the liberal. Eduard, however, continues to refuse the offer as it's been put to him. He feels his honor is at stake. The lawyer proposes a sophistical solution: the question of guilt is avoided, but stress is placed on the fact that he never contested the verdict.

Put like that, fine, Eduard consents.

After that things happen very fast. Too fast, even. He'd settled into the rhythm of a long prison sentence, he'd adjusted his thoughts, his projects, and even his metabolism to the term, and now he's told that in ten days, eight, three, it's over, the set will be struck, the extras dismissed, time for the next film. The director doesn't summon him, he *invites* him to come to his office and now treats him like a VIP—as if what came before was all a joke, a role play that you can talk about in polite company now that it's over. He asks him to sign his copy of *The Book of Water*, and voices concern about the memories the prestigious ex-inmate will have of his establishment. "I won't hesitate to recommend it to my friends," Eduard answers, and the director is enchanted: "You'll recommend it to your friends! Ha ha! What a joker you are, Eduard Venyaminovich!"

Early releases are rare at Engels, and his smells so much of string pulling that he's embarrassed around his cellmates. After having done everything, in all honesty, to show them that he's a little muzhik like them, buffeted by the bad prison winds, he's not far from seeing himself, in their eyes, as one of those journalists who play at being homeless or a convict for as long as it takes to get a story, and then say to their buddies when the safari's over, "Ciao guys, it was great, I'll think about you and send you foie gras for Christmas"—a promise they usually forget. Eduard would have nothing but disgust for someone like that, and he's both relieved and surprised to see that no one at Engels holds it against him; his prestige even soars. It seems they're all happy to know an important guy whose affairs get sorted out through shady deals at the highest level, and to be able to tell people they knew him. In the end he's even a little disgusted by so much candor.

The day before his release he's authorized to pick up his suitcase from storage. This suitcase is one of his prized possessions. He swiped it from Steven when he left New York for Paris and it's been everywhere with him: to war, in the Altai, in one prison after the next. It contains two shirts, one black and one white. That night there's a farewell party in the bunkhouse, with goodbye hugs and slaps on the back, and a long discussion about which of the two shirts he should wear for his release. The question is especially important because the event's going to be filmed: a TV station made the request, Eduard hesitated but the camp director insisted, and the inmates are as excited as children who have been promised a trip to the circus.

"You've got to wear the white one, it's more stylish," says Anton, a nice boy sentenced to thirty years for torturing and then murdering someone.

"But Anton," Eduard objects, "I'm leaving prison, not a nightclub."
"Still, you've got to be stylish. You're a famous writer."

"There are no famous writers here, just a bunch of *zeks*," Eduard
replies, and even before finishing the sentence he's embarrassed at
how false and hollow it sounds. Of course he's a famous writer. Of
course his fate has nothing to do with Anton's.

Since the crack of dawn the camp's been turned upside down because
of the television crew. There are half a dozen of them: a journalist, the
director, the cameraman, the soundman, and several assistants, including three girls. Young girls, wearing short skirts and tight tank
tops in the summer heat, girls that smell of perfume, and under that
perfume there's the smell of women: armpits, pussy—these girls drive
the *zeks* completely mad as they line them up in the central yard for
the morning roll call. In fact the roll call took place ages ago, the team
didn't get there early enough to film the real one, and in any event the
director has his own idea about what the real one should be like. The
prison director expected the most presentable inmates to be put out in
front, just as he himself demands when a delegation comes to visit,
but as the filming proceeds it becomes increasingly clear that the idea
of the documentary isn't to accentuate the charm of the prison or the
healthy glow of its inmates, but on the contrary, to show that the adventurous writer Limonov is returning from hell. Ignoring the prison
director's protests, the pretty assistants are gathering the most hideous
faces, the cameraman is filming cutaways of lizards, mud puddles,
piles of garbage—not an easy task in a camp that's all in all extremely
tidy. I'm not blaming them: I did exactly the same thing when I shot
part of my documentary at the penal colony for minors in Kotelnich.
I'd hoped for something out of Dante's *Inferno* and had a hard time
resigning myself to the fact that it wasn't like that at all.

In the middle of all this commotion, Eduard conscientiously does
what he's told to do. He plays himself. In the roll call scene, with ideally sinister-looking extras on either side, he belts out his last name,
first name, patronymic, and the articles he was sentenced under. It's
the last time he'll do it, but he's got to do three takes because the di-

rector isn't happy with the first two. Then in the mess hall he pours sauce on his dish while continuing to talk "naturally" with the others. "Just pretend we're not here, guys," the director says, "pretend it's like any other day."

Most of the inmates are having a ball, vying with one another for the honor of getting into the frame beside the hero. "Can you see me here? Can you see me?" they ask, digging in their elbows. And Eduard—while keeping up this falsely natural, falsely ordinary conversation, of which all that will remain are his lines, because he's the only one with a microphone under his collar—thinks that he was an idiot to agree to this television thing. He thinks it's too bad to be leaving like this. Maybe he's even thinking it's too bad to be leaving at all. Of course he's dying to regain his freedom, to see little Nastia and the guys in the party. But he'll never again be the man he was here. You can say work camps are hell, but through the force of his mind alone he was able to make it a paradise. It became as hospitable to him as a monastery is to a monk. The three daily roll calls were his services, the meditation was his prayer, and once the sky opened up for him. Each night, surrounded by the snoring in the bunkhouse, he became secretly intoxicated by his own power, by the caliber of his superhuman soul, in which a mysterious process that started in the Altai in the company of the trapper Zolotarev was nearing completion: a true, eternal liberation; and he worries all of a sudden that being freed from prison might deprive him of this truer freedom. He's always thought that his vocation was to dive as deeply as he could into reality, and reality was here. Now it's over. The best chapter of his life is behind him.

Moscow, December 2009

ও

I

HERE WE ARE, back at the beginning of the book. When I began
my reporting on Limonov he'd been out of prison for four years. I had
no idea about any of what I've just told, and it took me almost four
more years to gather all the information—nevertheless, I had the
confused feeling that something was wrong. It was as if he still had
a microphone under his collar, as if he were still playing himself in a
reality show. In his country he'd become the star he dreamed of being: an idolized writer, an urbane freedom fighter, good copy for the
"Society" pages. As soon as he was out of prison he dumped the courageous little Nastia for one of those grade-A women he's never been
able to resist: the beautiful actress who'd risen to fame in a soap called
The KGB in a Tuxedo. His spell in prison made him a teen idol, his al-
liance with Kasparov a socially acceptable politician, and I can't rule
out the possibility that he *really* thought he'd be swept to power by a
Velvet Revolution, like Václav Havel before him.

Finally, as readers will perhaps remember, everything happened in
the 2008 elections just as the British journalist I'd met at the Limonov-
Kasparov press conference said it would. Putin respected the constitution and didn't run for a third term, but set up an ingenious arrangement
instead, reminiscent of those driving-school cars with two driver's
seats: the new president, Medvedev, sits in the learner's seat, while
Putin, the prime minister, takes that of the teacher. He lets the learner
drive; he's got to get the hang of it sooner or later. He congratulates
him with a paternal nod when he handles himself well, and it's reassuring to know that if anything goes wrong there's an experienced
man around. But two questions are on everyone's lips. Will Putin retake the wheel in 2012 as the constitution allows him to, forbidding as
it does only three *consecutive* terms? Or will the docile Medvedev,

having got a taste for power, confront his mentor and perhaps even crush him, as Putin himself crushed those who made him king? (Looking back as this translation goes to press, I see of course that the 2012 elections answered the first question with a clear yes and the second with just as clear a no. It seems that all of Russia has resigned itself to eight more years under Putin.)

I think a lot about Putin as I come to the end of this book. And the more I do, the more I think that Eduard's tragedy is that he believed he was rid of the Captain Levitins that poisoned his youth, and it was only later, when he believed the coast was clear, that a super–Captain Levitin rose up before him: Lieutenant Colonel Vladimir Vladimirovich.

During the 2000 elections, a book of interviews with Putin came out titled *In the First Person*—a title coined no doubt by some PR guy, but good nonetheless. It could apply to Limonov's entire body of work, and part of my own. As far as Putin goes, it's fairly representative. They say he waffles when he talks: it's not true. He does what he says, he says what he does, and when he lies it's with such audacity that no one could fall for it. Looking at his life, one gets the troubling impression of being confronted with Eduard's double. He was born ten years after Eduard in the same sort of family: the father a junior officer, the mother a factory worker, everyone together in a single room in a *kommunalka*. A puny, timid little boy, he was raised in the cult of the fatherland, of the Great Patriotic War, of the KGB and the fear it inspires in the wimps of the West. As an adolescent he was, in his own words, a small-time hoodlum. What prevented him from becoming a thug was judo, to which he devoted himself with such intensity that his friends still remember the ferocious shrieks that came from the gym where he trained alone on Sundays. He joined the organs out of a kind of romanticism, because they were composed of elite men who defended their homeland, men with whom he was proud to be associated. He was suspicious of perestroika, he hated it when masochists or CIA agents made a big deal about the Gulag and Stalin's crimes, and not only did he experience the fall of the empire as the biggest catastrophe of the twentieth century, but he'll repeat the sentiment today in no uncertain terms. In the chaos of the first years of the nineties he was one of the losers, the swindled, reduced to driving a cab. Like Eduard, once in power, he enjoyed having himself photographed bare-chested, muscular, wearing combat pants, a commando knife at his belt. Like Eduard he's cold and cunning; he knows that men are wolves; he only believes in the right of the strongest and that values are relative; he prefers to make people afraid rather than to be afraid himself. Like Eduard he despises whiners who think human life is sacred. The crew of the submarine *Kursk* can die over the course of eight days at the bottom of the Barents Sea, the Russian special forces can gas 150 hostages at Dubrovka Theater, and 350 children can be massacred at the school in Beslan: Vladimir Vladimirovich gives the people news of his dog and her newborn puppies. The litter is doing fine, drinking their mother's milk: you've got to look on the bright side.

The difference between him and Eduard is that he succeeded. He's the boss. He can order school textbooks to stop teaching bad things about Stalin, and bring the NGOs and the noble souls of the liberal opposition into line. He bows perfunctorily at Sakharov's tomb but keeps a bust of Dzerzhinsky on his desk for all to see. When Europe provokes him by recognizing the independence of Kosovo, he says, "Go ahead, but then South Ossetia and Abkhazia will be independent as well, we'll send our tanks to Georgia, and if you're not polite when you talk to us we'll cut off your gas."

If he were being sincere, Eduard would admit he's impressed by these virile airs. Instead, like Anna Politkovskaya, he writes pamphlets explaining that Putin is not only a tyrant but a bland and mediocre one at that, who's in a hand-me-down suit that's too big for him. This opinion strikes me as glaringly wrong. I think that, say what you like, Putin is in his own way a great statesman, and if he's popular, it's not just because people are dumbed down by the media he controls. There's something else. Putin repeats at every turn something the Russians absolutely need to hear, which can be summed up like so: "You have no right to say to 150 million people that seventy years of their lives, of the lives of their parents and grandparents, that what they believed in, what they fought and gave their lives for, the very air they breathed, was nothing but shit. Atrocious things were done under communism, okay, but it wasn't the same as Nazism. This comparison that Western intellectuals now take for granted is a disgrace. Communism was something grand, heroic, beautiful, something that was confident and that bestowed confidence. It had an innocence to it, and, in the merciless world that succeeded it, everyone confusedly associates it with their childhood and with the kinds of things that make you cry when childhood memories come back to you in a flash."

I'm certain that Putin was perfectly sincere when he spoke the sentences I quoted as the epigraph of this book. I'm certain that it came from the bottom of his heart—after all, everyone has one. And it spoke straight to the hearts of everyone in Russia, starting with Limonov, who would certainly say and do everything Putin says and does, or even worse, if he were in his place. But he's not in his place, and the only place left to him—an incongruous one—is that of the virtuous opposition figure, the defender of values he doesn't believe in (democracy, human rights, all that crap), alongside honest people who embody everything he's always despised. Not quite checkmate, but still, in such circumstances it's difficult to know where you are.

2

THE PROTOCOL HASN'T changed, except that now it's not two but just a single *nazbol* who takes me to see his boss, and he no longer picks me up in a car but fixes a meeting at a subway station. I remember this *nazbol*: Mitya. I met him two years before, he remembers me as well, and we talk about this and that on the fifteen-minute walk to Eduard's new apartment. He's not very young, around thirty, and like all the party members I've met, he strikes me as being a nice guy: open, intelligent, friendly. He's wearing black, but the jeans and the bomber jacket are gone: his stylish coat and herringbone jacket make you think he's doing all right in life. He's married, he tells me, he's got a little daughter, he works in one of those occupations linked to the Internet whose details elude me but which allow you to earn a more than respectable living. I have the impression that for him spending a couple of hours a week protecting Eduard Limonov is a way of staying true to the ideals of his youth, the way others keep on playing in an amateur rock band they know full well will never make it big, because it's fun to get together with their buddies. When I ask him how things are going with the party and all that, he smiles and answers, "*Normalno*," the way the manager of a busy restaurant might say, "Right now things are calm."

Since the elevator's broken, we take the stairs to the ninth floor of a modest apartment building. With the usual precautions, Mitya lets me into the small one-bedroom apartment where Eduard is waiting for me, still in black jeans and a black sweater, still slim, still sporting a goatee. I look for a place to put my coat; the only objects in the room are a table, a chair, and a single bed. For having said in an interview that the judges in Moscow are at Mayor Luzhkov's beck and call, which is common knowledge, he was fined 500,000 rubles, he tells me. They seized everything that could be seized, which hardly covered a tenth of the fine: he still owes the rest.

Leaving Mitya to read the paper on the only chair in the bedroom, we go into the other room, the kitchen, where there are two more. Eduard makes coffee, I open my notebook. I've told him by mail about my project to write not just a story about him, but a whole book. His answer was neutral: neither enthusiastic nor displeased; he's at my disposal if I need him. My research is already quite far along. I've even got a sort of first draft, and I think we should take the time to do a long interview, several hours, why not several days? But I'm not sure, and to be on the safe side I haven't asked him yet.

"So, what's happened in the last two years?"

What happened first was that his wife, the pretty actress, left him. He doesn't really understand why. It doesn't cross his mind that the thirty-year age gap may have played a role, or not being able to set foot outside without two guys with shaved heads at your side: at first that must be romantic, but soon it becomes a burden. He suffered for a couple of months, he says, then thought that she was a cold, lying, unloving woman: she disappointed him. But not to worry, he assures me that he's got several mistresses, all very young; he doesn't always sleep in the single bed in the next room. He continues to see his children, that's the most important thing. His *children*, yes: he's also got a little girl, Alexandra. The boy's called Bogdan, in honor of his Serbian years. I think that Bogdan got off lightly: he could have been called Radovan or Ratko. End of the chapter on his private life.

Now, his public life. He doesn't say it outright, but it's clear that he's completely had it. The historic occasion, assuming he really had one, has passed. Harassed in a thousand different ways, Kasparov didn't even try to run, and after what can't even be called its failure in the presidential elections, the movement Drugaya Rossiya no longer exists. Eduard, however, hasn't thrown in the towel. He's created a new movement called Strategy 31, in reference to Article 31 of the constitution, which guarantees the right to demonstrate. To make use of this right they gather on Triumfalnaya Square on the thirty-first of every month with thirty-one days. In general there are a hundred or so demonstrators and five times as many police officers, the latter arresting a few dozen of the former. So Eduard regularly spends a couple of days in prison. The foreign correspondents file their reports, but it's just a formality. Apart from that, he's trying to set up and preside over a "national assembly of opposition forces," a project supported by a few old democrats and human rights activists, which Kasparov does his best to preempt by launching his own platform. The two men are rivals now, but even their rivalry strikes me as somewhat tame. Eduard is happy that his website gets more hits than Kasparov's.

What else? His literary output. He's published three books since we last met: poems, a collection of articles, memories of his Serbian wars. But writing is no longer really his thing. It doesn't pay enough nowadays, the print runs are around five or six thousand copies at the most, no reprints: he prefers to earn his living by freelancing for magazines, Russian editions of *Playboy* or *GQ*.

That's it, all the topics have been covered. It's four in the afternoon, night has fallen, you can hear the hum of the refrigerator. He looks at his rings, strokes his musketeer's goatee: it's no longer Dumas's *Twenty Years After* but *The Vicomte of Bragelonne: Ten Years Later*. I've asked all my questions and it doesn't occur to him to ask me any: How do I live, am I married, do I have children? Do I prefer a warm climate or a cold one? Stendhal or Flaubert? Plain or fruit yogurt? What type of books do I write, since I'm a writer? He says it's part of his mission in life to show an interest in other people, and no doubt he'd be interested in me if he met me in prison, guilty of a beautiful, bloody crime, but that's not how it is. The fact is that I'm his biographer: I ask him questions, he answers, and when he's finished answering he says nothing, looks at his rings, waits for the next question. I think to myself that there's no way I can spend several hours on an interview like this, I'll get along fine with what I've got. I get up and thank him for the coffee and his time. It's right on the doorstep that he finally does ask me a question: "It's strange, you know. Why do you want to write a book about me?"

I'm taken aback but I answer, sincerely. Because he's living—or he lived, I don't remember what tense I used—a fascinating life. A romantic, dangerous life, a life that dared to engage directly with history.

And then he says something that cuts me to the quick. With his dry little laugh, without looking at me: "Yeah, a shitty life."

3

I DON'T LIKE this ending, and I don't think he'd like it either. I also think that anyone who risks a judgment about anyone else's karma, or even about his own, is certain to be wrong. One evening I expressed these doubts to my eldest son, Gabriel. He's a film editor, we'd just written two television screenplays together, and I like talking with him screenwriter to screenwriter: this scene I buy, this one I don't.

"Basically what bothers you," he says, "is painting him as a loser."
I agree.

"Why? Because you don't want to hurt him?"

"Not really. Well, a bit. But mostly because I think it's not a satisfying ending. That it's disappointing for the reader."

"That's something else," Gabriel says, and he cites a whole slew of great books and films whose heroes finish as failures. *Raging Bull*, for instance. In the last scene you see the boxer played by De Niro on his last legs, a complete washout. He's got nothing anymore, no wife, no friends, no house, he's let himself go, he's fat, he earns his living doing a stand-up act in a dingy nightclub. Sitting in front of the mirror in his dressing room, he waits for the call to go on. Then it comes. He pulls himself heavily from his chair. Just before leaving the frame he looks at himself in the mirror, bounces from foot to foot, mimes a couple of boxing moves, and you can hear him murmur, not very loud, just to himself: "I'm the boss. I'm the boss. I'm the boss."

It's pathetic; it's magnificent.

"It's a thousand times better than seeing him victorious on some podium," Gabriel says. "No, really, after all these adventures, ending with Limonov counting on Facebook to see if he's got more friends than Kasparov, that could be great."

It's true. Still, something keeps nagging at me.

"Okay, let's turn it around then. What would the perfect ending be for you? I mean, if you could choose? For him to take power?"

I shake my head: too unlikely. But there's one thing in life he hasn't done, and that's start a religion. To do that he'd have to quit politics—where, let's face it, things seem hopeless—go back to the Altai and become either the guru of a community of fanatics like Baron von Ungern-Sternberg, or, even better, a true wise man. A sort of saint, even.

Now it's Gabriel's turn to look skeptical.

"I think I know the kind of ending that'd make you happy," he says. "For him to get shot and killed. That'd fit perfectly with the rest of his life: it's heroic, it prevents him from dying of prostate cancer like any normal Joe. That way your book'll sell ten times more copies.

And if he dies of polonium poisoning like Litvinenko, instead of ten times it'll sell a hundred times more, all over the world. You should tell your mother to go talk to Putin about it."

And Limonov, what does he think?

One day in September 2007, we went out into the country together. I thought it was for a meeting, but in fact it was to have a look at a dacha situated a couple of hours outside Moscow that his wife at the time, the pretty actress, had just bought. Actually it was much more than a dacha: what's called an *usadba*, a veritable manor. There was a pond, meadows, a birch forest. Abandoned and vandalized, the old wooden house was immense. It must have been magnificent once, and if it were renovated it would be magnificent once more, and that's why he'd come. As soon as he arrived he started talking with a local crafts-man, the way someone who's done manual labor himself knows how to talk to a contractor and not get ripped off. I wandered away while they were talking, strolling through the gardens overgrown with tall weeds, and when, coming to the end of a bridle path, I saw his little black silhouette from a distance, gesticulating in a pool of sunshine, his goatee unkempt, I thought: he's sixty-five, he's got an adorable wife, an eight-month-old child. Maybe he's had enough of war, of biv-ouacs, of the knife in his boot, of police breaking down his door at dawn, of prison bunks. Maybe he finally wants to put his suitcase down. To come and settle here, in the countryside, in this beautiful house, like the landed gentry of the old regime. That's what I'd have wanted, in his place. That's what I *do* want. It's exactly the old age that I wish for Hélène and myself. There would be big bookshelves, deep couches, the shouts of our grandchildren outside, berry jam, long conversations in chaise longues. The shadows grow longer, death approaches softly. Life was good because we loved each other. Maybe that's not how it's going to end, but if it were up to me that's how it would.

Coming back, I ask him: "You see yourself getting old in this house, Eduard? Ending your days like one of Turgenev's heroes?"

That makes him laugh, but not with his dry little laugh this time: heartily. No, that's not how he sees things. Really. Retirement, a life of calm, that's not for him. He's got another idea for his old age.

"You know Central Asia?"

No, I don't know it, I've never been there. But I saw photos of it when I was very young, taken by my mother when she went on that long trip during which my father looked after me with an awkward tenderness—in those days fathers weren't used to taking care of little kids. Those photos weighed on me, and made me dream. For me they represented the remotest places on earth.

It's in Central Asia, Eduard goes on, that he feels the best. In cities like Samarkand or Bukhara. Cities parched by the sun; dusty, slow, violent. In the shadow of the mosques, over there, under the high crenellated walls, there are beggars. Whole groups of beggars, gaunt, tanned old men without teeth, often without eyes. They wear tunics and turbans that are black with dirt; they place a scrap of velvet before them and wait for someone to throw down a few small coins, and if someone does they don't even say thank you. You don't know what their lives were like before; you know they'll end up in a communal grave. They're ageless, they don't have possessions any longer—assuming they ever did—they hardly even have names. They're castoffs. They're wrecks. They're kings.

That, okay, he'd be fine with that.